DATE DUE

WITHDRAWN

GAYLORD | | | PRINTED IN U.S.A.

THE DESTRUCTIVE
POWER OF RELIGION

**Recent Titles in
Contemporary Psychology**

Resilience for Today: Gaining Strength from Adversity
Edith Henderson Grotberg, editor

THE DESTRUCTIVE POWER OF RELIGION

Violence in Judaism, Christianity, and Islam

Volume 4
Contemporary Views on Spirituality and Violence

J. Harold Ellens, Editor

Foreword by Martin E. Marty
Ad Testimonium by Archbishop Desmond Tutu

Contemporary Psychology
Chris E. Stout, Series Editor

Westport, Connecticut
London

Library of Congress Cataloging-in-Publication Data

The destructive power of religion : violence in Judaism, Christianity, and Islam / edited by J. Harold Ellens; foreword by Martin E. Marty.
    p. cm.—(Contemporary psychology, ISSN 1546–668X)
  Includes bibliographical references and index.
  ISBN 0–275–97958–X (alk. paper)
    1. Violence—Religious aspects. I. Ellens, J. Harold, 1932– II. Contemporary psychology (Praeger Publishers)
BL65.V55D47 2004
291.1'78—dc21   2003051061

British Library Cataloguing in Publication Data is available.

Library of Congress Catalog Card Number: 2003051061
ISBN: 0–275–97958–X (set)
         0–275–97972–5 (vol. I)
         0–275–97973–3 (vol. II)
         0–275–97974–1 (vol. III)
         0–275–98146–0 (vol. IV)
ISSN: 1546–668X

First published in 2004

Praeger Publishers, 88 Post Road West, Westport, CT 06881
An imprint of Greenwood Publishing Group, Inc.
www.praeger.com

Printed in the United States of America

The paper used in this book complies with the Permanent Paper Standard issued by the National Information Standards Organization (Z39.48–1984).

10 9 8 7 6 5 4 3 2 1

For Brett Alexander, faithful, hopeful, and full of love!

CONTENTS

FOREWORD

"Too bad this set of books is so relevant." That phrase is not a dismissal of, but an advertisement for, this work that will inform and provide perspective for people anywhere who are trying to make sense of the outburst of religiously based violence around the world.

That phrase also echoes the title and theme of the talk, "Too bad we're still relevant!" that I gave at the annual meeting of the American Academy of Arts and Sciences (AARS) in 1996, while closing the books on a six-year, twelve-conference, hundred(s)-scholar, five-volume work, *The Fundamentalism Project*, that the AARS had sponsored between 1988 and 1994.

For more than six years, my associate R. Scott Appleby and I labored with that anxiety, "What if we are irrelevant by the time this is finished?" while we directed the project. My talk included a reminder to the academy that in 1988 they could have chartered all kinds of relevant studies (e.g., U.S.-Soviet Relations in the Twenty-First Century, or Exporting Apartheid from South Africa) that would have been irrelevant by 1996. Since he and I had not asked for the work but had been chosen by the academy, we armed ourselves with yellow highlighters and daily marked the newspaper references that dealt with our subject. We went through many yellow markers, and found the number of references to such hard-line religion increasing.

That report foresaw frustrations and rages of religion-rooted conflict in the new millennium and mentioned that even terrorism would be an instrument of the religiously violent. Still, there were some reasons to hope for a measure of decreased religious conflict, even if it was only to be replaced by other kinds, such as territorial or ethnic conflict, as in Kurdish areas of Turkey or in Rwanda or the former Yugoslavia. Yet all of these conflicts are eclipsed by religious furies and violence.

It is in that context that I help J. Harold Ellens turn this subject over to you who, in libraries, at desks, in classrooms, or at home, are working your way through bafflement over the explosion of violence that grows out of the dark side of religion. "Too bad it's relevant."

Twenty years ago I was blithely teaching American religious history, remarking on the relative tolerance to which we citizens had worn each other down in values and practice. On days off from history, as a former pastor and a theologian-at-the-margins I also found many ways to affirm the healing side of religion. As peers in my generation face the debilitation and death that come with our advanced years, we find ourselves consoling each other with stories about the promises of God the healer. At the same time, many of us have joined forces, professionally, to measure and encourage efforts at employing spiritual means to address issues of health and healing.

We see religion represented through churches, synagogues, and mosques, located cozily next to each other in the alphabets of the Yellow Pages. There are few dead bodies in America as a result of religious conflict. Of course, there were always tensions, bloodless schisms, arguments, and contentions, but the violence related to each has been reasonably held in check.

Then *The Fundamentalism Project* forced me and people with whom I worked to "go global," where we got a very different perspective. Domestically, as we listened to the voice of people who had been victimized or oppressed in the name of religion, we noted how many other words ending in *–press* matched "oppress": repressed, suppressed, and so on, suggesting the negative and destructive roles of religion. We had begun to explore an underside of the presence and power of this force in life and history.

Two days after 9/11 I was scheduled to lecture at the University of Illinois on a theme chosen a year before: "Religion: The Healer that Kills; the Killer that Heals." When the terrorists struck in the name of God in New York, they ensured good crowds for talks like that and gave new impetus for scholars to explore the themes gathered so conveniently in these four books on *The Destructive Power of Religion, Violence in Judaism, Christianity, and Islam.*

I am no newcomer to this field, and I know that most of the authors in these volumes, from biblical scholars to psychoanalysts, have long been at their inquiries. Many of them include just enough autobiography for us to learn that they themselves were often among those who experienced the destructive side of religion. They tell us how they countered it, and some testify to its lasting effects. As I read those chapters, however, I noticed also how often they "kept the faith," pursued the spirit, or stayed with religion, however one wishes to put it, even as they wanted to rein in the destructive forces that issue from it. Professor Ellens himself slips in a word that he thinks characterizes the dimensions of religion that one can affirm: *grace*.

How does one square the study of destruction and the affirmation of construction in this one area of life, religion, as many of the authors undertake to do on these pages? Rousseau once said that readers could expect his thoughts to be consistent with each other, but they could not expect him to express them all at the same time. So here, too, one pictures that when assigned another topic, when placed in the role of the therapist, healer, or pastor, these authors could write essays of note about the constructive side.

But if there is anything consistent in these essays, or, rather, because there is much that is consistent in these essays, it is this coherence that the authors bring to their theme, namely, "it is futile to experience grace or healing so long as":

- People think that all would be peaceful if the whole world turned godless, secular, free of religion.
- Humans live with delusion or illusion about the really destructive aspects of faith and faiths.
- We believe that the dark side of religion is all in the mind, heart, and company of "the other," those people who have the wrong God, the wrong books, the wrong nation in which to live.
- People fail to explore their own scriptures, traditions, and experiences, as they have inherited them from ancestors (e.g., when Christians see *jihad* as the main mark of Islam or when Muslims think *crusades* against infidels are what Christians are all about).
- Humans do not engage in psychological probing of themselves and others, to unearth the tangle of themes and motifs that are destructive when faith or God enters the scene.

The authors of these books are helpful to all who want to effect change in the destructive power of religion. For example, the biblical scholars among them bring to light many destructive stories in scriptures that adherents want to overlook. More and more we learn from these volumes the complex, nether-side of the animating stories of the strangers' faiths. We are compelled here to look at their traditions and sacred scriptures: Qur'an, Torah, New Testament, and more. Too often we read them only in ways that portray an ugliness associated with the other person or company.

Since most writers of these volumes stand in biblical traditions, they take on the stories most would like to overlook: Abraham and Isaac, Jephthah and his daughter, some aspects of God the Father and Jesus the Son relations. They see no way around such texts, and do not offer trivializing pap to give them easy interpretations; but they give us instead tools for interpreting those narratives. These can make us aware and can be liberating.

Psychology plays a very big role in these volumes, in keeping with their auspices and intentions. During the six years of *The Fundamentalism Project*, Dr. Appleby and I, with our board of advisers, jokingly said that we would not let the psychologists in until the third or fourth year. Then we did, and they were very helpful. What we were trying to show the academy and readers around the globe was the fact that there were some irreducibly religious elements in Fundamentalisms.

Of course, religious Fundamentalists think they are *purely* religious; but many scholars in the social sciences "reduced" them: their hard-line views were considered by such scholars to be "nothing but" a reflection of their social class (Marx), or of their relations to their fathers (Freud), or a reflection of their descent from particularly vicious simian strands (Darwin).

In our project we were not able to disprove all that the reducers claimed, and had no motive to do so. *The Fundamentalism Project*, like this one, was to issue new understanding, not new evasion or new apologetic sleights of hand. We simply wanted readers of those books to see, as readers of *The Destructive Power of Religion* should see, the psychological dynamics that are present at the center of all human faith commitments and explanations. One sees much of such connection and illumination in these essays. The introduction of insights from the humanities balances those of social scientists. The religiously committed authors, and those who, at least in their essays, are noncommittal, together with numerous other aspects of these important volumes, help produce a balanced depiction.

What I took away from the chapters, especially, is a sense of the pervasiveness of violence across the spectrum of religions. Not many years ago, celebrated students of myth, or romantic advocates of anything-but-our historic religious traditions, won large enthusiastic audiences for their romantic pictures. *If only* we could get away from Abraham's God, Jesus' Father, and Mother Church's Mary; if only we could move far from Puritan Protestantism with its angry God; if only we left behind Judaism with its Warrior God; if only. . . .

There was great confidence in and propaganda for the notion that we could find refuge in any number of alternatives: gentle, syncretic Hinduism; goddess-rule; mysticism; transcendentalism; animism; Native American thought. However, closer scrutiny showed that only relative distance and the intriguing exoticism of nonconformist alternatives made these other models seem tolerant and gentle. The closer and informed view found violent stories of Hindu-Muslim warfare, tyrannies by what were proposed as the "gentle" human sacrifice, and tribal warfare everywhere. All this is not designed to violate what we are not supposed to violate after reading *The Destructive Power of Religion*, namely, the principle that we are to be self-critical and not irrationally attacking the "other" with finger-pointing. Of course, the "others" *are* in some degree also victims and often perpetrators of the violent and destructive sides of faith.

What goes on, however, as these chapters show, is that there is a dark underside, a nether, shadowed side to every enduring and profound system of symbols and myths, hence to every religion. That may result from deep psychic forces discerned by many of the scholars authoring these volumes. It may result from the realization that the grand myths and stories deal with the wildest and deepest ranges of human aspiration and degradation.

Most of these authors are anything but fatalistic. While there are no utopians here, no idealists who think all will always be well, most of them have a constructive purpose that becomes manifest along the way.

We historians learned from some nineteenth-century giants that we overcome history with history. That is, there is no escape from the world of events and stories and constructions; but we are not doomed to be confined among only violent actions. So with these essays, they make it plain that we are to overcome analysis with analysis, analysis of destruction, which gives insight that can lead to construction. These essays are not preachy: the authors set forth their cases and let readers determine what to do with whatever emerges. I picture a good deal of self-discovery following the discovery of this important work. One hopes that here will be found some glint of discernment that is an expression of—yes, grace!

Martin E. Marty

**Fairfax M. Cone Distinguished Service Professor Emeritus
University of Chicago Divinity School**

Lent 2003

AD TESTIMONIUM

The Destructive Power of Religion is a work of profound research and engaging writing. It is a groundbreaking work with tremendous insight, a set of books that will inform and give perspective to people anywhere trying to make sense of religiously based violence. Professor Ellens has assembled a brilliant stable of insightful and concerned authors to produce four volumes of readable, thoughtful analysis of our present world situation. This contribution will have permanent value for all future research on the crucial matter of religion's destructive power, which has been exercised throughout history, and continues today to give rise to violence in shocking and potentially genocidal dimensions. Future work on this matter will need to begin with this publication. This will become a classic.

Professor Ellens and his team have not produced this important work merely out of theoretical reflection or as viewed from a distant ivory tower. I first met Professor Ellens while he was heavily engaged in psycho-social research in the Republic of South Africa in the 1970s and 1980s, when my country was struggling with some of the worst oppression wreaked upon much of its citizenry by the religiously driven, destructive policies of Apartheid. His comparative studies of educational, health care, and psycho-spiritual resources provided for the black South Africans and the black citizens of the United States were important contributions at a critical time. His orientation is always from the operational perspective, down on the ground where real people live and move and have their being.

In consequence, this massive work is a challenge to those in the professional worlds of psychology, sociology, religion, anthropology, pastoral care, philosophy, biblical studies, and theology. At the same time, it is so highly readable that it will be accessible and downright informative to the layperson or general reader who finds these volumes at the local library. These books are helpful to all who want to effect change in the destructive process in our world, a process too often created or fostered by religious fervor.

It must be noted with equal enthusiasm that the four volumes of *The Destructive Power of Religion* are as urgent in their emphasis upon the positive power—religion's power for healing and redemption of personal and worldwide suffering and perplexity—as they are in boldly setting forth the destructive side. Particularly, the numerous chapters by Professor Ellens, as well as those by Professors Capps, Aden, Wink, Sloat, and others, constantly move us toward the healing perceptions of grace and forgiveness.

Professor Ellens has repeatedly, here and in other works on his long list of publications, called attention to the role redemptive religious power played in the formulation and operation of the Truth and Reconciliation Commission in my country at a time of extreme crisis, thus making possible a thoroughgoing sociopolitical revolution with virtually no bloodshed. He claims, quite correctly, I think, that if it had not been for the pervasive presence of biblical concern and religious fervor in the black, white, and colored populations of our republic at that time, there would have been no way through that sociopolitical thicket without a much greater denigration of the quality of life in our society, and an enormous loss of life itself. I am grateful to him for his insight and his articulation of it for the larger world community. That is typical of the practical approach evident in his work and that of his entire team, which has provided us with this very wise work, *The Destructive Power of Religion*. I commend them unreservedly. I am honored that I have been asked to provide this testimony to the profound importance of these volumes for the worldwide community of those who care.

Archbishop Desmond Tutu
Pentecost 2003

PREFACE

While deeply occupied with the preparation of these volumes, during the Christmas season of 2002, I fell rather inadvertently into a conversation with a young and thoughtful woman, Mollie, who has, consequently, become a genuine friend. Pain prompted our connection; hers, which was more than anyone so young and vital should have to bear, reawakening mine, long, old, deep, soaked in my earliest memories from when I was less than five. Mollie was injured at a tender age and in a manner that made her feel betrayed by God and humankind. My particular personal perplexity started with my mother's frequent illness and absence in my infancy, and was fixed forever in my character and consciousness by the death of my dearest friend on August 3, 1937. Her name was Esther Van Houten, we were both five years old, and we were madly in love. We talked all that summer of starting school together in the fall. We were infinitely joyful. We were gracefully oblivious of the Great Depression in which both our families were caught, and of the lowering clouds of war which would soon take away my older brother and five of hers.

August 3 of that year was a brilliantly sunny day on our remote farmstead southwest of McBain, Michigan. I was standing by the well outside the kitchen window of our farmhouse, vaguely conscious of my mother's image in the window as she prepared my father's mid-morning "lunch." I was thinking of Esther and expected any moment to run across the country road and up the driveway to her yard to while away the morning with her. I heard the screen door of her home slam shut.

My heart leaped, and I looked up anticipating seeing her with her long blond hair and bright blue eyes—like my mother's eyes. There she stood, at the top of the driveway, completely on fire, and she burned to death right there. I helplessly called for my mother, but there was nothing one could do out in that remote place on August 3, in 1937. A sheet of darkness came down on me and did not begin to rise again until I was seven. During those two years, my brother Gordon died, my sister, my dear grandfather, and two neighbor children. Death seemed everywhere. The darkness has never completely gone away.

What connected me with Mollie is our common "case regarding God." It is our common case in that we discovered that we hold it in common and that is how we found each other; but it is also a common case because the longer I live and the more I learn the clearer it is that this is the case every thinking and feeling person has regarding God. It is common among humans to live with this perplexity. The ancient Israelites who gave us their Bible, and with it the heritage Jews, Christians, and Muslims hold in common, formulated the perplexity in the question, "How is God in history, particularly our usually troubled and often wretched history of wickedness, destruction, and death?" How can God promise so much prosperity and security through the prophets and deliver so little safety for faithful, vulnerable, hopeful humans? How can God entice a fourteen-year-old girl into the quest for faith and in that very context fail to protect her from injury and betrayal? God seems perfectly capable of engineering a majestic creation and strategizing its evolution through eons of productive time, but he cannot keep a five-year-old girl from death by fire? I spent my entire life, from age seven on, devoted to a single course toward, into, and in the ministry of theology and psychology, confidently trying to recover the trust that God, in a prosperous providence, would embrace my children and carefully shepherd them into health, wisdom, safety, and success; in the faith, in fruitful marriages, in joyful parenting, and in the fulfillments of love. I entrusted my children to God's care while I was busy "doing the work of God's Kingdom." I did my side of the "bargain" very well. God did not do as well on his side of the equation.

All this has caused me to work very hard to rethink my entire notion of God, and especially my theology of sacred scriptures. I do not see how any honest and honorable person can get through an entire lifetime without being forced to do this very same thing, forced by what has always been the ordinary horror and daily trauma of life, personal and universal. Unless one is able to see the unsacred in sacred scriptures, what can the sacred mean? Unless one has a comprehensive way to come to terms with the horror of life, how can celebration of the gracious be anything but psycho-spiritual denial? There can be no question that the God of the Hebrew Bible, and the God who is reported to have killed Jesus because, after getting ticked off at the human race, he could not get his head screwed on right again unless he killed us or somebody else, is abusive in the extreme. To salvage a God of grace out of that requires some reworking of the traditional Judaic, Christian, and Muslim theologies of sacred scripture. The difficulty that prevents us from writing God off completely and permanently is the fact that both the Old Testament and the New Testament, as well as the Qur'an, have woven through the center of their literary stream a more central message as well. The notion, unique in all human religions, that Abraham seems to have discovered, which is so redemptive in these sacred scriptures, is the claim that the real God is a God of unconditional grace—the only thing that works in life, for God or for humans. The human heartache is universal. The perplexity pervades everything in life. The question is, "Is there any warrant that the claims for grace do too?"

I do not feel like the Lone Ranger in this matter. Of course, there is Mollie's case, but everyone who has been around for a while knows a long list of the Mollies in this world. I have sat in my psychotherapist and pastoral counselor chairs for 40 years and have noticed that this is the "case regarding God" that perplexes most thoughtful and informed people; and most have been afraid to say it aloud, or have had no good opportunity to do so. Mollie said it aloud to me and immediately I recognized the sound of it. It is our common human story. It has ever been so, since reflective humans first opened wondering eyes upon this planet. Many years ago Barbara Mertz wrote a telling book about ancient Egypt. She called it, *Red Land, Black Land.*[1] She noted that we cannot speak of those mysterious days and people of so long ago without being awed by their way of dying and their funerals. They recorded them grandly in their even grander tombs. It is a simple story, the same as ours; a story in Mertz's sensitive words, "of our common human terror and our common hope."

The Destructive Power of Religion, Violence in Judaism, Christianity, and Islam, is a work in four volumes about our common human terror and our common hope. I hope you will find it stirring, disturbing, and hopeful.

J. Harold Ellens
Epiphany 2003

Note

1. New York: Dell Publishing, 1966, 367.

ACKNOWLEDGMENTS

Dr. Chris Stout invited me to write a chapter in his earlier, remarkably important four-volume set, *The Psychology of Terrorism*. I was pleased to do so, and we published my chapter there under the title "Psychological Legitimization of Violence by Religious Archetypes." Debbie Carvalko, acquisitions editor at Greenwood Press, found the chapter valuable and asked me to expand it by editing a work, which I have titled *The Destructive Power of Religion*. Thus, these four volumes were thoughtfully conceived and wisely midwifed. The birth is timely, since it seems everywhere evident that the world needs these reflections just now, more than ever. I wish, therefore, to acknowledge with honor and gratitude, Debbie's kind proficiency and Chris' professional esteem. I wish, as well, to thank the 30 authors who joined me in creating this work. I wish to express my gratitude to Beverley Adams for her meticulous work in reading the proofs of these volumes, while I was too ill to do so.

CHAPTER 1

INTRODUCTION: SPIRALS OF VIOLENCE

J. Harold Ellens

Introduction

Jesus acted violently on a number of occasions in his life. This comes as a surprise to most Christians, who have been led to think of him as passive, or at most assertive, but hardly aggressive, certainly not violent. It is clear, however, to those who are willing to see it that Jesus was violent in "cleansing the temple," in the style of chastising his mother at the wedding in Cana, in both his method and content when reprimanding Peter in Mark 8, and in exploiting the blind man in John 9.[1] Numerous other narratives might be cited in which Jesus was violent in the sense of behaving aggressively, or more often, in violating other persons' prerogatives.

Such stories from the life of Jesus are troubling to some Christians. Nearly two decades ago Richard A. Horsley addressed this problem in his important book *Jesus and the Spiral of Violence,* and his *Jesus and Empire: The Kingdom of God and the New World Disorder* (2003) relates the issues of Jesus' violence with the crises of the violent international disorder of our present moment.[2]

These books focus upon the problem of the violence or nonviolence in the master story of Christianity, and hence in the core metaphors that shape Western thought, culture, history, and politics; indeed, that have shaped it for 20 centuries. I wish here to review these important works of Horsley and so prompt a dialogue between the master story of our lives and the perplexities of violence in our modern world. In this way, I should like to introduce this fourth volume in *The Destructive Power of Religion*, titled *Contemporary Views on Spirituality and Violence*. Nine brilliant scholars have joined me in presenting this study, which ranges from the anti-Semitism of the medieval Christian crusades to the challenges of modern spirituality, from reflections on biblical reports of God's violence to current concerns regarding cultural abusiveness, from just war theory to pacifism, and from redemptive violence to redemptive love.

Exposition

Horsley's general argument is that the standard picture of Jesus as the advocate of nonviolence is not historically credible. Jesus lived in a society of structured violence, shaped by the dominance of the Roman Empire, and he advocated assertive resistance rather than nonviolence. If we want to understand the real Jesus of the gospel narratives we must give up our long tradition of glorifying his passivity and look at his behavior as the person he is reported to have been in his own moment in time. The picture often painted, Horsley claims, is that of a "sober prophet of nonviolence" who operated in Galilee and Judea with the violent Zealots as a foil for his own clear objectives and smooth style. That picture assumes that the Zealots were a prominent and fanatical force in Judea in Jesus' day, with a special zeal for the Torah and a militant expectation of the restoration of the golden age of David's kingdom, by then a memory 1,000 years old, but nonetheless a glorified and cherished memory in Jewish society in the first century C.E.

This standard portrait of that age represents the Zealots as advocating a violent messianic holy war against the Roman oppressors. Jesus is represented in this glorified Christian tradition as the politically neutral teacher of righteousness and truth, who calls his followers to the nonresisting and nonaggressive loving of their enemies and turning the other cheek. After all, did he not disagree with the Zealots in their refusal to pay the Roman tax when he commanded, "Render to Caesar the things that are Caesar's, and to God the things that are God's"? Surely this meant that Jesus believed one could cultivate genuine piety and serve the God of Israel authentically, indeed, be the true Israel, while also complying with the formal regulations of the socially pacifying imperialists of Rome.

Of course, the knotty problem that arises in this scenario is that Jesus was killed as a traitor and insurrectionist. He was crucified for capital crimes, namely, he was understood by the chief priests of the Jews and the Roman authority, Pilate, to have set himself upon a course that challenged the legitimacy of Caesar. He made himself out to be a king. He was crucified as the King of the Jews. This has been explained in Christian tradition, of course, by the claim that he was falsely accused, that he did not promote the notion that he was the King of the Jews. It was all based upon a misunderstanding. When Jesus was interrogated he said he was the Son of Man. When Caiaphas suggested that this meant that Jesus thought he was the "Son of the Blessed," namely, the Messiah, Jesus had not denied it. Jesus' notion of the Messiah was the model of the Son of Man from Ezekiel, Daniel, and 1 Enoch, a heavenly figure called to proclaim the kingdom of God on the earth and ultimately bring history to its divinely destined end. The Jerusalem idea of the Messiah, obviously present in Caiaphas' mind, was that of the Son of David, a human king, who would restore the fortunes of Israel and throw out the Romans.

Thus when Jesus was brought to trial before Pilate, and then later before Herod, the accusation against him was that he claimed to be the King of the Jews. When Pilate asked him about this, Jesus did not directly deny it. Instead he said that his kingdom was not an earthly kingdom but one that reigned within people. Well, that was quite a lot to expect an old politician like Pilate to understand, so he killed Jesus as an insurrectionist or revolutionary. But the Christian scenario emphasizes that he was innocent of the charges of being a revolutionary, and the cleansing of the temple was just a call to authentic spirituality, not a violent act.

This understanding of the scenario by Christian apologists trying to preserve the nonviolent reputation of Jesus was nearly correct. It was also beside the point of the question of his nonviolence versus his aggressive resistance of evil. Indeed, Horsley insists in *Jesus and the Spiral of Violence* that when the scene is painted like that, nearly all of the components are historically invalid or inaccurate, because they are given the wrong cast. He declares that the elements of the story are false, "as they stand in most of the scholarly and popular literature, and the foil (the Zealots) on which the whole picture depends is now known to be without historical basis. Thus it is necessary to reexamine these along with many other aspects of Jesus' ministry, in order to understand how Jesus dealt with the reality of violence" (150).

Horsley paints a picture of first-century Galilee and Judea, in which Jesus had to work. It is worth our reviewing, as we set the

Christ Before Pilate, an engraving in Currier & Ives, 1847. Library of Congress.

stage for the contemporary views on spirituality and violence that fill
this volume. To understand Jesus, in his day and ours, we must distance ourselves from the long-standing notion that his "love command" was a general and absolute principle, unrelated to the setting
in which he worked. That setting was the dominance of all of life by
Roman imperial power and coercion. This included the spiritual, psychological, emotional, material, political, economic, and cultural life
of the subjugated populations. Coercion, and the violence inevitably
attendant upon it, was structural and pervasive in the society: "In
order to understand the concrete situation in which first-century
Palestinian Jews, including Jesus, were placed historically, the issue of
Jesus and violence clearly requires a more complex and comprehensive approach than we have previously pursued" (ix).

For Jews in Palestine in Jesus' day, religious, social, economic, and
political life were all parts of each other. A great variety of Judaisms
was prevalent in the society, ranging from almost neurotic hysteric
apocalypticism to the settled but mystical Essenes and on to the
rather rational religious communities of the Pharisees, Sadducees,
and Scribes. Culturally Palestine, and particularly Galilee, where
Jesus grew up and carried out much of his ministry, had been heavily
influenced by Greek culture as a result of the conquests of Alexander
the Great in the late fourth century B.C.E. This influence persisted
under the Romans, creating a situation of immense cultural variety
and ferment in Jesus' world, constantly regulated or oppressed by
Roman intervention. In summary, Jesus' world was one in which the
experience of being dominated was universal. The psychological and
spiritual, cultural and political state of affairs was that of domination
by one empire after another for centuries. The antagonism and conflicts that prolonged subjugation produces in a spirited people were
an important part of Jesus' world.

The Jews saw themselves in a constant state of crisis and rose frequently to violent revolution. In 168–167 B.C.E. the Judeans rebelled
successfully under the leadership of the Maccabees and established
the Hasmonean quasi-independent state, under the Seleucids of Syria.
In 66–70 C.E. another revolt brought a vicious Roman response in
which the city and temple of Jerusalem were destroyed. In 132–135
C.E. the Bar Kochba revolt was wide-ranging and resulted again in a
massive slaughter and repression of Jews as well as their culture, religion, and political ambitions. Suspended in this kind of violent culture, between the Hasmoneans and Bar Kochba, arose the Jesus
Movement and the beginnings of early Christianity. Many subjugated

Roman provinces saw resistance and rebellion, from northern Europe to northern Africa, but none were so intense and volatile as those in Jewry. Nonetheless, " . . . these frequent armed rebellions were only the most violent manifestations. Underlying these highly visible rebellions were the continuing tensions and conflicts in which the more violent outbursts were rooted. It thus seems obvious that we should consider the principal aspects of the imperial situation in which the Judean people lived during the second Temple period" (5) if we are to understand the dynamics that prevailed in the life and ministry of Jesus.

To be relevant to his setting Jesus had to deal with the processes of imperial pacification, domination, and development of a subject country and "enslaved" society, always trying to work out an accommodation with the dominators or attempting to blow them up with rebellion. The modern world is not ignorant of what this means, the demise of Western colonialism being a fresh memory in the minds of everyone over 50 years of age, and a near-time historical knowledge for everyone else. Moreover, the Liberation Theologians of Latin America have not permitted us to forget what their experience of Jesus and of oppressive domination is, in the context and aftermath of South American colonialism.

At some level we all know very well that Horsley has put his finger on a key issue. Dominating imperialism is always predatory and exploitive. The most obscene example of the wretched and subhuman character of some forms of colonialism was seen in that of French predatory and abusive dominance in Algeria, central Africa, and what used to be called "French Indo-China." It is impossible to imagine that such a nation with a long Catholic Christian tradition could have become so depraved in its exploitation of other humans and cultures. It can only be explained by the fact that, whereas the American Revolutionary War really was about liberty and the establishment of democratic institutions, the French Revolution, as was seen already by many of the scholars and national leaders of that day, was about killing royalty and overturning traditional structures. When the mob ran out of royalty, they were so addicted to killing that they continued until they had killed 300,000 of their own rabble. That chaotic character persisted in their colonialism and afterward. Let it not be forgotten in this day of French attempts to reimpose their dominance upon the world order that their fickle contrarianism is a persistent quality. We should remember that nearly all of France caved in to Hitler and went over to a French Fascism know as Vichy France.

Our interest here, however, is the desire to understand the real model of resistance to violence that was championed by Jesus and that is, supposedly, the true ethic of biblical Christianity, one of the elements at the root of the Western world and American life. What went wrong with it in France and almost all the time in Western history? Why do we have a theological ethic of nonviolent love and a political practice of violence? What was Jesus' style and what should we have taken from him? How should we handle overt physical abuse and destruction, and equally urgently, how should we stand against the violation of any person's space, prerogatives, feelings, and personhood? Desecration of any of these is overt and unacceptable violence. Moreover, permitting such desecration or failing to prevent it makes us complicitous with it, and therefore ourselves guilty of the violence.

Horsley describes a virtually inevitable spiral of violence that arises when the oppression of domination and the desecration of a person or a people take place. The spiral is made up of a number of stages. First, there is the structural violence introduced into a society by the injustice and inherent violation of personhood and social order imposed by dominating forces who also, incidentally, are exploitive and predatory. Second, this structural violence will inevitably produce a reaction against the injustice, giving rise to protest and resistance. This is inevitable because the dominant power seldom seeks to exterminate the subjugated people since that would remove one of the major resources that make dominance profitable. The subjugated people are human beings with imagination, wisdom, and vigor. They will long for and eventually lunge for freedom from the oppression. Third, the protest and resistance will bring repression to the extent necessary for achieving an equilibrium of repressive tolerance on the part of the dominant power and tolerant dependence on the part of the subjugated people. Finally, the spiral completes its progression in violent and destructive revolt, destructive to both the oppressor and the oppressed.

It was in this setting of imperialistic institutionalized injustice and repression, on the one hand, and the search for constructive resistance, on the other, that Jesus came upon the scene and in which the metaphors and patterns later to become Christianity were forged. So our question comes back into focus in a new way. How should we view this fellow from Nazareth in Galilee, in his first-century setting; and what would he think of us in our violently turbulent twenty-first century? Since religion, politics, and social operations were all one and the same in the Jewish experience in Jesus' day, the sacred scriptures were the charter for Jewish operations and future vision. The mainstream metaphors in this charter were almost all centered in the celebration of a memory of the Exodus. This led many Jews to expect that God would momentarily inject into history a new intervention of deliverance and vindication. This seemed obvious because the Exodus tradition indicated that this was the sort of thing God does when his people are in conditions of extremity. When were things ever worse than right then, under Roman imperialistic injustice and abuse? The logic seemed obvious. God must act. God will act. God is acting, and we must get on board this cresting wave of divine intervention on our behalf. Horsley (38) cites Josephus to report that numerous guerrilla bands of brigands and bandits operated in Jewish society at that time, wreaking much havoc upon Romans and complicit Jews alike. The Romans successfully repressed most of them and crucified these insurrectionists by the hundreds, perhaps by the thousands. It was a common thing. It went on every day.

Our Proper View of Jesus

The Romans conquered and maintained control by massive acts of violence. In response the bandits sometimes were able to produce the fourth stage of the spiral of violence by arousing virtually the entire oppressed population to revolution. Most of the time, however, the Roman methods produced alternative responses. The Pharisees, frustrated in their desire to form a political society that conformed to the religious requirements of the Torah, resorted to a well-worked-out system for personal piety and the cultivation of a society of brotherhood and the love that justice ensures. Other Jews practiced more subtle forms of aggressive resistance, short of violence and revolt. Most of these approaches were existential and ad hoc responses to specific situations rather than taking the form of causes and movements (Horsley, 61). They tended to be responses of immense patience and discipline, but usually in a surprisingly forceful defensive-aggressive mode, and frequently producing an equilibrium of accommodation on the part of both the Romans and the Jews.

This seems to be where we can find the real Jesus. A number of relatively minor incidents in Jewish history illustrate actions by a few Jews, now and then, that would have been highly visible to the Romans but of little national or ultimate consequence except to prompt the Romans to be somewhat more careful in avoiding excesses. Two teachers and two of their students, for example, tore

Herod's eagle from the lintel of the entrance to the temple in Jerusalem. The Pharisees resisted as far as they could the repression of the observance of Torah. Visionaries such as John the Baptist cultivated an independent individualist perspective by concentrating attention upon inner spirituality rather than social reform. Jesus cleansed the temple. There was a correlation in all of this between the hope for resurrection after death and the willingness to risk martyrdom. This is clearly true in Jesus' case. His words make that plain. Moreover, there was a further correlation between the apocalyptic worldview held by many Jews in Jesus' day, and by Jesus himself, and belief in the resurrection.

Regardless of the particular method or worldview of any given Jew, there seemed to be a common psychology of zealousness for the integrity of Israelite life, religion, hope, and future. The conscious or unconscious model for this zeal was the biblical narrative of Phinehas, the then ancient priest, whose zeal for the Lord God and God's cause was an archetypal byword in Jewish consciousness in Jesus' day.[3] This zeal is evident in almost all of the leading characters in the Jesus Movement who are described at any length in the biblical literature. It is specifically cited with regard to Jesus' violence in the temple, and Paul frequently applies the term to his own sense of urgency in his mission work.

Jesus' sense of zeal for God and for the onset of God's kingdom in this world was set within his apocalyptic worldview, a notion that he was caught up in a cosmic conflict between God and the devil, good and evil. He saw this cosmic conflict as the story of all of history and for which the battlefield was the human heart. In terms of this stage set Jesus spoke and acted. Central to this drama was the conviction that "God was bringing an end to the demonic and political powers dominating his society so that a renewal of individual and social life would be possible" (Horsley, 157). "What would appear as the overall thrust or perspective of apocalyptic literature and the preaching of Jesus . . . if we read them . . . less literally but with greater appreciation of the distinctive function of apocalyptic imagery, . . . less doctrinally as a synthesis of theological ideas, . . . without imposing the modern separation between religion and social-political life?" (159).

The answer, Horsley persuasively leads us to believe, is that apocalyptic literature focused aggressively upon the judgment and defeat of the oppressive powers in history, who were the enemies of God's reign of grace and love. Since this also made the powers into the enemies of God's people, the latter would be vindicated and restored to righteousness and freedom within the divine kingdom on earth. "What earlier biblical scholarship labeled as expectations of 'cosmic catastrophe' typical of Jewish apocalypticism would be called, in ordinary contemporary language, eager hope for anti-imperial revolution to be effected by God" (160). "Jesus' proclamation and practice of the kingdom of God indeed belonged in the milieu of Jewish apocalypticism. But far from being an expectation of an imminent cosmic catastrophe, it was the conviction that God was now driving Satan from control over personal and historical life, making possible the renewal of the people Israel. The presence of the kingdom of God meant the termination of the old order" (160).

In response to Horsley's scenario it can be said that a reflective modern psychological assessment of this apocalyptic vision in Jesus would see it as intensely aggressive, though a highly rationalized, transcendental expectation. Its surface-level passivity is merely the patient, disciplined form of the deeper, potentially world-changing, passive aggression. This makes his arrest and execution as a political agitator and criminal understandable. Moreover, Jesus had threatened the temple and had taken at least symbolic violent action to make that threat real and highly noticeable. In connection with this act he predicted the destruction of the temple. So Horsley seems justified in his summary. We must face the fact that the gospels " . . . present a Jesus whose actions as well as perspective appear to have been revolutionary. Apparently he did not simply protest against or resist the oppressive features of the established order in Jewish Palestine; he articulated and acted upon his anticipation that God was now bringing an end to that order with the coming of the kingdom" (164).

We must conclude that Jesus perceived all of life and history to be a religious phenomenon in which God was actively present. This divine dynamic was oriented toward the sociopolitical enhancement of the quality of life of human beings. The outcome would be the extermination of the unrighteous and the vindication of the righteous in a new world order, by the advent of the Son of Man. Jesus clearly expected that this divine intervention of judgment and vindication was arriving in his generation. He said so. Rome's hegemony was in the process of overt divine destruction. Jesus' dogmatic assertions of the nature and will of God for his moment, as well as his healings and exorcism, were expressions of the presence of the divine rule already breaking in upon his moment in time. The demonic forces were being defeated. This was part of the aggressive action that would undo the demonic Roman oppressors as well.

Jesus clearly took Isaiah 61 as his charter. There the prophet describes the messianic figure, who is empowered by the spirit of God, as the one who would bring good news to those who are poor and oppressed, bind up the brokenhearted and bereaved, set free those captured by the authorities, give sight to the blind, comfort the mourning, and declare that The Day of the Lord had arrived, a day of vengeance and vindication. The prophet also promised that the nation of Israel would be rebuilt, the devastated areas renewed, the ruined cities repaired, and that instead of being oppressed, demeaned, shamed, and dishonored, Israel would be exalted. The nations of the earth would be dragged kicking and screaming into servitude to Israel, which would become rich from their revenues.

In the Synoptic Gospels Jesus' citation of this passage as his charter caused the people to be amazed at his vision. It is interesting that only in the very late gospel of John, the audience was furious with Jesus and wanted to kill him, apparently for overlooking the last half of that promise. They claimed that he was talking like a Samaritan, namely, focusing only on Israel's deliverance from oppression but overlooking the nations being cast into servitude to Israel. The audience wanted the other half of the prophet's promise in which the oppressors get the divine vengeance they deserve. The positive response in the Synoptics suggests that Jesus had adopted the entire chapter, with all its anti-oppressor vision, as his charter.

The question remains: Was Jesus just a passive-aggressive talker, or did he act out his aggression in some useful or definitive way? Were his actions, whatever they were, merely paradigmatic and symbolic, or did he make a difference in his moment? Was it his style to act, or did he simply expect God to act in history? Horsley is sure there is no evidence that Jesus was an advocate of nonviolence. Neither is there evidence that he advocated violence. In his own behavior he perpetrated moderate violence on a number of occasions, one of which was against temple property and personnel (318–319).

> The socio-historical situation in which Jesus lived was permeated with violence. We can thus take a step toward a more adequate understanding of Jesus and violence by noting that Jesus, while not necessarily a pacifist, actively opposed violence, both oppressive and repressive, both

political-economic and spiritual. He consistently criticized and resisted the oppressive established political-economic-religious order of his own society. Moreover, he aggressively intervened to mitigate or undo the effects of institutionalized violence, whether in particular acts of forgiveness and exorcism or in the general opening of the kingdom of God to the poor. Jesus opposed violence, but not from a distance. He did not attempt to avoid violence in search of a peaceable existence. He rather entered actively into the situation of violence, and even exacerbated the conflict. Driving out the demons involved convulsions for the possessed, and the preaching and practice of the kingdom generally brought not "peace" but the "sword." (319)

So Jesus' preaching and practice were so situated in the spiral of violence that it is not surprising that he and his followers were "executed as rebels" (319). They gave no quarter and asked none. Loving enemies meant loving those next to you, not complicity with the international powers of oppression. The ethic was concrete and specific, not abstract and mythic; it required actions against the demonic sociopolitical and religious powers wherever they were to be found. The presence of Jesus and his followers in Jewish Palestine in the violent age of the first century C.E. constituted a serious revolt against the established order. This revolt, while not an armed aggression, ultimately changed the world order. Jesus had catalyzed a social revolution that he was sure would facilitate God's bringing in a political revolution. That is one way of describing what ultimately actually happened. Whether that proved to be good or ill, of course, remains to be seen twenty centuries later.

Jesus' View of Us

That brings us to Horsley's recent book, *Jesus and Empire: The Kingdom of God and the New World Disorder.* Desmond Tutu declares in a paragraph on the cover that this book is

[a] cogently argued critique of prevalent approaches to the historical Jesus that depict him as individualistic, depoliticized, and that ignore the real context in which he operated. Horsley makes a very good case for his relational-contextual approach, which makes . . . sense of the New Testament and other evidence available. But what I found quite exhilarating was his showing the crucial relevance of proper New Testament scholarship and theology in the amazing parallels he has shown to exist between the policies of the ancient Roman Empire and those of contemporary America. In the present highly charged atmosphere of international politics, this is a very important—indeed salu-

tary—book that should be read not just by New Testament scholars, but especially by politicians.

Horsley argues that the recent historical developments leaving America as the only superpower creates high ethical and political risks for the United States in that, like it or not, the nation is thrust into a position of a new Roman Empire. Moreover, having drawn its energies from biblical metaphors and constructed its constitution in the phrases of Republican Rome, the United States has a great deal of vulnerability in its inherent qualities and consciousness that makes it easy prey to notions of triumphalism and the arrogance of power. Her virtues can become her vulnerabilities, her power her weakness, her unchallenged strength her danger. Americans are inherently reluctant to be or to endorse an empire, but the role of empire has been thrust upon them, so to speak, by history and the creativity of American ingenuity, practicality, and hard work.

Is the apparent incongruity between America's role in the world and her historic grounding in biblical and/or republican principles as large or as real as it seems to many foreigners and some Americans? Is her imperial position in the new world disorder awkward for Americans who care about these things, in view of the fact that "Jesus of Nazareth carried out his mission precisely among an ancient Middle Eastern people who had been subjected by the Roman Empire" (5)? Unfortunately, the American separation of religion from politics and its emphasis upon a relatively radical individualistic and scientific approach to life castrate Jesus' power in these contemporary issues and render him irrelevant for many Americans. People addicted to that dualistic thinking would not understand the question about Jesus' view of us.

For those of us for whom the nature of the kingdom of God in the pragmatics of worldly existence is, however, a question of some urgency, at least intellectually, and also spiritually, the inquiry is worthwhile. In view of his posture in and reaction to the Roman Empire, what would be Jesus' view of America today? Or, to put it in a more customary way, what spiritual resources exist in the historic American tradition and the American soul that may set a course for this nation, reluctantly and accidentally to become an empire, that could help her transcend her vulnerability to adopting strategies of oppression and repression?

Rosemary Radford Ruether, in her cover comment on Horsley's book, says that the author pictures " . . . Jesus against empire in the context of the ambiguity of American identity as a people who see themselves as both liberated and liberating: the New Israel and the New Rome of global empire. He shows how these two identities are on a collision course post–September 11, 2001. Americans must ultimately choose between them." Walter Wink[4] says of Horsley's work that few authors have so well connected the biblical story with political reality: "The Roman empire becomes the foil that exposes the American Empire. The Kingdom of God reveals the hideousness of the new world disorder, and Jesus is discovered to be the purveyor of truths available nowhere else."

Let us suppose that Ruether is correct and America is standing in the valley of decision, caught between two potential destinies. What is the thing for her to do? Is it not possible for her to do both, to be a wise and humane empire, the ultimate republican experiment, and the ethical people of the divine reign of grace, justice, and love? Rome did not have the tradition of the Magna Carta. They were developing their experiment as they went. There were no adequate precedents or failed experiments from which to learn. Greece was a sort of democracy but not on the scale of a world empire, like Rome and modern America.

Is it necessary to take an apocalyptic view of America's destiny and imply, by the radical choices Ruether, Horsley, and Wink think she must make, that she is headed on a collision course of ideologies, expectations, and methods that will eventuate in cataclysm or a fall like that of Rome? There is no evidence to suggest that this is so. Rome's republic failed quickly and it resorted early to dictatorship. There is no smell of this in American history, current operations, or future destiny. Is not such an apocalyptic view the very thing that often, by its own inherent cynical character and depressive dynamics, becomes a self-fulfilling prophecy?

There have been, are, and will be inequities in American policy and practical operations, but the checks and balances are enormous in the system and the potential for popular political appeal is phenomenal, compared with any system that has ever before existed. America's presence in the world has been infinitely more beneficial, despite inadequate judgments and abusive actions, than that of any other entity in the history of the world. So what is the problem? Horsley says we ought to look at Jesus' alternative to the Roman imperial order. Then we will see the constructive alternatives to potential American imperial mistakes.

The Roman imperial order operated on the assumption that Rome's power authorized the use of subject peoples as resources for her empire. This was inherently exploitive, as was the British Empire in its day. This political subversion and economic exploitation disintegrated the natural coherence and internal adherence of the oppressed communities. Jesus' mission was to oppose this imperial process, declare the oppressing communities to be under divine judgment, and focus upon "healing the debilitating effects of imperial violence and on renewing the esprit de corps and cooperative spirit" in the oppressed communities (126). Jesus was interested in reempowering the cultural spirit and communal vitality of demeaned people. This led him to champion nonhierarchical social structures and family strength. It meant that for him love involved revolutionizing the structures of society as much as the interpersonal and intercommunity relationships of his world.

What has that to do with America? Surely Jesus' call is a shout in the world, echoing down the corridors of time, challenging any power that produces brutality, violence, or exploitation. These flaws in the American experiment appeared early, though they have not destroyed the system that still carries forward the torch of liberty and justice. Now this flawed human nation must face the inherent imperatives of its destiny as reluctant empire, to exercise power without oppressive and repressive methods. America must be committed to renovating the potentially destructive structures in her institutions and institutionalized methods and objectives, recognizing that every human institution stands under cosmic judgment regarding how it handles people—all people. The United States must continue to stand for the elimination of violence wherever it can be eliminated, in her world and in her own methods.

This implies, if we take Jesus' disposition toward Rome seriously, that all energy in the American enterprise must be oriented toward building of community and healing persons, worldwide. This can become a reality only if the American inclination to split off spiritual claims from political policy is terminated and in its place the inevitable intimacy between spiritual idealism, social development, ethical principles, and political policy and practice is recognized as essential to health and wholeness in a nation, as in persons. Horsley (2003) declares,

> ... [I]t is significant to note that it is in circumstances of relative powerlessness vis-à-vis the Roman imperial order that Jesus called for

the renewed commitment to covenantal economic and political values and behavior in . . . communities. But it was precisely in those circumstances of poverty and powerlessness that Jesus and his followers found it essential to struggle to practice those values and principles of justice, cooperation, and solidarity. The imperial order was still in place. But Jesus was calling people to take control of and rebuild their own community life in the confidence that the imperial order stood under God's judgment (128). . . . It should be possible . . . , with antennae attuned to imperial power relations, to discern more critically our own situation and roles in the current new world disorder established by the combination of American political power and the power of global capitalism. What implications Jesus and the Gospels might have for Americans who identify with this aspect of their cultural heritage, however, will become evident only through the collective deliberations and actions of communities located inside the society now at the apex of the new imperial disorder. (149)

Conclusion

This volume, *Contemporary Views on Spirituality and Violence*, teases out these vital issues in greater detail. In conclusion, this penetrating look at the rise of the Jesus Movement in the context of the first-century Roman Empire certainly alerts us in a graphic way to the fundamental incongruity between any expressions of brutality, exploitation, triumphalism, and the arrogance of power, on the one hand, and everything the United States of America intended to stand for from its outset and the people of America intend to stand for today. Thrust into the role of empire, however, the United States is also thrust into the dangers of all such human errors, misjudgments, and miscalculations. These were monstrous in Roman history. With modern-day technologies and the ranges of power possible in our world, the potential for horrid mayhem is infinitely greater. The difficulties for an empire to avoid these tragedies are also extraordinary because the potential for others in our world today to wreak havoc upon America and upon each other outside of America is also infinite. We have experienced firsthand that the tragic potential for violence in our world today is very far beyond our most cynical or terrified imaginations. Is Jesus' method relevant to our sophisticated world? Can you hear any other voice above the cacophony of history that sounds like a really good alternative?

We need a clear and certain trumpet to which we can march, or it is the spiral of violence all over again.

Notes

1. See volume 3, chapter 1, of this series, *The Destructive Power of Religion*, J. Harold Ellens, ed. The volume is titled *Models and Cases of Violence in Religion*, and the chapter is "Introduction: Toxic Texts," by J. Harold Ellens.

2. R. A. Horsley, *Jesus and the Spiral of Violence: Popular Jewish Resistance in Roman Palestine* (San Francisco: Harper & Row, 1987); and R. A. Horsley, *Jesus and Empire: The Kingdom of God and the New World Disorder* (Minneapolis: Fortress, 2003).

3. See John J. Collins, "The Zeal of Phinehas, the Bible, and the Legitimation of Violence," in *The Destructive Power of Religion*, J. Harold Ellens, ed., vol. I, *Sacred Scriptures, Ideology, and Violence*, chapter 2. See also Cheryl McGuire, "Judaism, Christianity, and Girard: The Violent Messiahs," in *The Destructive Power of Religion*, J. Harold Ellens, ed., vol. II, *Religion, Psychology, and Violence*, chapter 3.

4. See chapters 4 (Walter Wink) and 9 (Wayne G. Rollins) in this volume.

THE CRUSADE POGROMS: CHRISTIAN HOLY WAR ON THE HOME FRONT

Alfred J. Eppens

Introduction

In Cologne, Germany, a gang of youths vandalized a Jewish synagogue on the Eve of Christmas, 1959. Over the following days, the "Cologne Incident" was repeated in many German cities, then spread across Europe and beyond. Within three months, over 640 similar incidents had occurred just in the United States,[1] expanding to Jewish cemeteries, stores, and homes. Christian anti-Semitism: What are its origins, its foundations, its doctrinal or spiritual roots? How does it relate to the uses of Christian violence in general, and to conflict with that third major group of monotheists, the Muslims?

The historical base for widespread anti-Jewish violence is located in medieval Europe, in the late eleventh century, at the start of that dramatic and far-reaching phenomenon that we call the Crusades. Christianity had largely avoided widespread violence of this type for the first millennium of its existence. Nevertheless, doctrinal roots in support of such actions existed in the earliest Christian writings.

The eminent theologian Professor John J. Gager has lectured on the topic "Was the Apostle Paul the Father of Christian Anti-Judaism?"[2] Although Gager's answer to his own provocative question was a resounding no, he concedes that many of Paul's letters have been read to support such an anti-Jewish view; for example, Galatians 3:10–11, 6:15; Romans 3:20, 9:31, 11:28. But it is only within the context of the historical reality of early inter-Christian struggles that such writings can be accurately understood as referring not to unconverted Jews, but to newly converted Jewish Christians who attempted to mandate strict observance of Jewish law among all Christians. This context of historical reality was unrecognized by medieval Christians, who saw only a consistent, though low-key, support for discrimination against Jews in the writings of Paul and the early Church fathers, not license for widespread violence against them.

Exposition

Warfare and violence in general were problems for early Christians, although St. Augustine provided the outline of a "just war" as being legitimate for the defense of Christians and their homelands. The supplanting of the Western Roman Empire with barbarian monarchies made violence more acceptable for religious purposes, as evidenced by the "missionary and warlike" Charlemagne (probably a later construct), wherein the reign of Christ was expanded by the physical elimination or forced conversion of pagans. We are certainly dealing with mixed motives on the part of Christian monarchs, and the "holy war" involving forced conversion was rejected by all theologians and canonists. However, the "just war" doctrine revived after Charlemagne, due to the necessity of defending Europe against new invaders from both the North and the South.

This post-Carolingian 200-year (750–950 C.E.) defensive war had militarized Europe; an aristocracy of knights had formed their identity on violence, which became idealized and glorified. However, by the eleventh century, external threats had subsided, and the violent institutions of medieval society were turned inward, with internecine warfare proliferating. As a result of the frequent domestic carnage and devastation in Europe, the basic pacifistic values of Christianity were reasserted. A religious fervor arose, as people realized that eternal salvation would require the Christianisation of their personal and communal lives. This fervor manifested itself in two main forms.

The first was a revived monasticism, focusing on an increased separation from the world and a more demanding asceticism. New orders were formed, including the Cistercians, the Camaldoli, and the Carthusians. Monastic vocations became more frequent in noble society. Also, existing orders, particularly the Cluniacs, embarked on a reform movement that would culminate in the calling of the First Crusade. But in the beginning, Cluniac reform sought to Christianize, even monasticize, the people of Europe, rejecting the violent nature of society at that time. This seems ironic, since many of the images projected to common people involved spiritual warfare, a battle of good versus evil, Christians versus demons. Nonetheless, the Cluniacs encouraged the population of Europe to live in a Christ-like manner, through the attempted regulation of sexual relations and the sponsorship of penitential pilgrimages.

The second aspect of Christianisation was the peace movement imposed by the Church, various forms including the Truce of God and the Peace of God. Huge, emotionally charged councils were called, involving a broad range of society, both religious and secular. They proclaimed a peace that they called the Truce of God, defining a specific period during which all fighting was forbidden, enforced by groups of volunteer knights. These councils fed the preexisting religious fervor, engendering the opinion that war and violence were unchristian.

These manifestations of religious fervor were augmented by a famine of massive proportions in 1033. People began to believe that their sinfulness was causing God to destroy the world, as in the biblical flood narrative. The movements of peace and penitential pilgrimage took on a frantic character. Nevertheless, the church was able to reform neither the violent actions nor the violence-based structure of European society.

Ambivalent Anti-Semitism: Anti-Judaism and Anti-Islam

The prohibition of extreme force embodied in the Ten Commandments, and in the pacific model of the life of Jesus, was also applied to treatment of non-Christians, including the Jews, even as theologians sought to reconcile God's law with the necessities of human government and Christian expansion. The Byzantine Church required a penance of a soldier who had killed an enemy, and an imperial soldier on campaign was denied the sacraments. Similarly, the Penitential of Alan of Lille, in 1188, specified,

> He who has killed a pagan or a Jew ought to submit to a penance of forty days, because the person he killed is one of God's creatures and might have been led to salvation.[3]

Nonetheless, as time progressed, the focus of military action began to turn away from fellow Christians and toward those other non-Christians, the Muslims who had occupied the Iberian Peninsula and Sicily for three centuries. In 1085 Spanish Christians were able to retake Toledo from the Muslims, and in 1091 the Normans conquered Sicily. Although the Church was officially against warfare, these events showed that such aggression could be very useful indeed, if it could be channeled and made to serve a Christian purpose. Thus, Church leaders ended up sending a confusing or mixed message to Europeans, who were developing a new, sometimes aggressive self-help attitude and a new confidence in their own abilities.

Events in the East provided the circumstances for the revival of the older concept of Holy War. The emperor of the Byzantine Empire was Alexius Comnenus, who had assumed the throne in 1081, by which time almost all of Anatolia was in Muslim hands. Over the next decade, Alexius had begun to beat back the Islamic Seljuk Turks, succeeding both in battle and by diplomacy. Although Alexius had been excommunicated by Pope Gregory upon his ascension to the throne, there still was no official schism between the Eastern and Western Churches. Indeed, Gregory's successor, Urban II, had lifted the ban of excommunication against Alexius, and relations with the Eastern Church had improved.

Early in 1095, at the Council of Piacenza, envoys of the Emperor Alexius addressed the assembly, encouraging European help for the emperor's army, describing the suffering of the Christians in Muslim-conquered territories. They essentially made an appeal to the West that for the safety of all Christendom, their duty lay in assisting the Byzantine military offensive, an appeal to which Pope Urban was both sympathetic and receptive.

Later that same year, at the Council of Clermont, the Pope proclaimed the calling of the First Crusade. He appealed to the European tradition of pilgrimage, converting it into the ideal of a Holy War, a War of Liberation. Europeans would come to the aid of their fellow Christians in the East; the aggression of Europe would be directed outward, toward the Turks. Not only would they liberate Anatolia, but they would press on to liberate that most holy of cities, Jerusalem, "delivering the Holy Places from the Infidel Turk," as the Pope was purported to have cried. The expedition was to involve not only armed knights, but also people from all levels of society, in order to raise the numbers necessary for such an ambitious expedition.

From Urban's point of view, this grand plan would expand the influence of the Western Church enormously, while further improving relations between East and West. The council then passed a general decree granting freedom from temporal penalties for all who took part with pious intentions, and allowing those who par-

Illuminated manuscript depicting the capture of Antioch during the First Crusade. The Art Archive/Musée Condé Chantilly/Dagli Orti.

ticipated to place their property under the protection of the Church while they were absent. The response to Urban's call was immediate and enthusiastic, thoroughly unprecedented in European history. From all levels of society, from regions as disparate as Denmark, Scotland, and Iberia, masses of people stepped forward to sew the cross of red cloth to their shoulders and take the vow to reach Jerusalem.

Popular preachers began recruiting for the Crusade, and volunteers numbered in the thousands. Ultimately, the response was vastly larger than Urban had expected; its sheer size made it impossible to control. The message soon became garbled and distorted, and many of the people who responded had motives that were very different, indeed, from those of Pope Urban's call or of the official military leaders of the undertaking, motives that even today we are struggling to unravel, motives that define the very nature of Western civilization.

A case in point is the so-called People's Crusade. Led by the charismatic preacher Peter the Hermit in France, and Count Emlich of Leiningen in Germany, tens of thousands of knights, foot soldiers, and pilgrims set out immediately for the Holy Land. Only a small percentage actually reached Constantinople, the crossing point to the Asian continent, most having perished from the lack of provisions or having been forced to turn back by local armies along the way. The several thousand Crusaders who did arrive at Constantinople were a distressing sight to the emperor Alexius: ill-equipped and ill-prepared to function as the emperor had wished, as an adjunct force to the imperial army. Alexius transported these military pilgrims across the Bosphorus and into Anatolia. Discipline broke down, and within a short time all of the troops and pilgrims were massacred by Turkish armies.

This failed "People's Crusade" has been largely ignored or dismissed by chroniclers of the Crusades, partly because of the failure of its objective, and partly because of its unofficial status. Nonetheless, it illustrates several important points. First, the people of Europe possessed such an enthusiasm for the project that they were prepared to follow virtually any leader. Although Peter the Hermit was reportedly short, swarthy, ugly, stinking, barefoot, and filthy, his preaching was reportedly irresistible, due in large part to the particular readiness of the people of Europe to engage in such a grand enterprise. The idea of a Holy War had unlocked vast reserves of raw power and enthusiasm in the European masses, who responded to the call.

Second, Peter's message varied from that of Pope Urban and the bishops; his message had become clearly and strongly anti-Semitic. In the popular mind, the Crusade was the brainchild of Peter the Hermit and his message the official one. The extreme violence against Jews that Peter's message generated is another reason for the Church's disowning of the People's Crusade.[4]

Third, Peter's inability to maintain control of his enthusiastic masses is a microcosm of Urban's inability to direct or even to channel the raging passions ultimately unleashed by that call at Clermont. These passions were based on a spirituality and a set of social conditions that the Church, even the Cluniacs, could not estimate or understand, passions that in their expression would define and eventually handicap the West from that time forward.

In addition to uncontrollable spiritual fervor, lay-knights were inclined to interpret the call along the lines of their own patterns of loyalty obligations. Prominent in the behavior patterns of knights during this period was the concept of the vendetta. The interlocking and sometimes overlapping relationships that bound together European society at this time were made up of extended families and feudal groupings. Both of these imposed obligations on a knight to avenge a wrong done to a family member, lord, or vassal: the blood feud. The first sermons appealing for people to join the Crusade clearly expressed this vendetta mentality, and many European knights accepted that call on those specific terms.

Thus was the stage set for the spilling over of uncontrolled, unexpected, and unpredictable passions: the violence to be directed to the East could not even be contained pending its setting off to foreign soil. The gathering and departure of this first Crusade, as well as of subsequent Crusades, were to set in motion the "first holocaust" of European Jews. There were reports of violent anti-Semitism in Rouen, France, within months of the Council of Clermont. This attack may not actually have occurred, but French Jews wrote to communities in Germany, warning them to beware of the crusading movement. Initially, the German Jews did not take the warnings seriously, believing themselves to be extremely secure in their cities. Even after the initial pogroms in Lorraine, they wrote back:

> As for ourselves, there is no great cause for fear. We have not heard a word about such matters, nor has it been hinted that our lives are threatened by the sword.[5]

In Germany, rumors ran rampant that Duke Godfrey of Lorraine would begin his crusading journey by avenging the death of Christ with Jewish blood. The Jews of Mainz and Cologne paid large sums to the duke to guarantee their safety, actions that were ultimately to be proven fruitless.

The Shift toward Focus upon Jews: The Pogroms

Then, in connection with the departure of the first waves of Crusaders in the spring of 1096, violence broke out in Speyer. Emlich of Leiningen had gathered an army that attacked the Jewish community there without mercy. It appears that Emlich, a robber baron with a fierce reputation for lawlessness, was strongly influenced by the message of Peter the Hermit and encouraged by the successful extortion of Duke Godfrey. Emlich's attack is significant in that it ignored the special imperial decree of the Emperor Henry IV, granted at the request of Kalonymos, chief rabbi of Mainz, that the safety of the Jews on their lands be guaranteed. It was only the decisive action of the Bishop of Speyer that prevented widespread slaughter; 12 Jews were murdered by the Crusaders under Emlich, and one Jewish woman committed suicide.

By mid-May, the army had moved on to Worms. Again, rumors played a crucial role, this time involving the supposed poisoning of the wells by Jews using a rotted Christian corpse. This added the fury of the townspeople to that of Emlich's army, and all Jews whom they discovered were slain. As in Speyer, the bishop had tried to intervene by granting refuge to Jews in his residence, but the attackers broke down the gates, murdering any Jews they encountered. Overall, the dead numbered about five hundred, all Jews.

Soon, other armies joined the forces of Emlich, not only from Germany, but also from France, England, Lorraine, and Flanders. In late May, the combined armies approached the city gates of Mainz, which were closed against them. Nevertheless, after anti-Jewish riots occurred, friends of Emlich inside of Mainz opened the gates to him. In return for a large payment from the Jewish community, Emlich promised that he would spare them. Nevertheless, he attacked the next day, and the large Jewish community at Mainz was wiped out. Over a thousand Jews were slaughtered, and the headstones of the victims can still be found. Likewise at Cologne, Trier, Metz, Neuss, Wevelinghofen, Eller, and Xaten, Jews in the region were sought out and massacred, though on a smaller scale. At the same time, Peter the Hermit's army attacked the Jewish community at Regensburg, forcing them to undergo baptism; similar attacks occurred at Wesseli and Prague.

The reasons for these murderous attacks are manifold. First is the carrying out of the convention of vengeance as outlined earlier. This commonsense perspective is eloquently expressed by Karen Armstrong:

It seemed frankly illogical to most of the Crusaders to march thousands of miles to fight Muslims in the Middle East, about whom they knew very little, when the people who had actually killed Christ—or so they believed—were alive and well on their very doorsteps.[6]

The second reason for the attacks merged the vendetta into the extension of Christianity to the entire European community. Rabbi Eliezer bar Nathan, an eyewitness, relates the Crusaders' specific perspective:

Look now, we are going to seek out our profanity and to take vengeance on the Ishmaelites for our Messiah, when here are the Jews who murdered and crucified him. Let us first avenge ourselves on them and exterminate them from among the nations so that the name of Israel will no longer be remembered or let them adopt our faith.[7]

Certainly Pope Urban had not envisioned actions of this type when he called the First Crusade. Forcible conversion of non-Christians is prohibited in canon law, and some German bishops attempted in vain to prevent it. Yet we are presented with contradictory evidence on this point, since Hebrew accounts portray local bishops and townspeople as anxious for such conversions. The goal is crystal clear: eliminate European Jewry through conversion or slaughter.

The official Church leadership in Rome was generally appalled by this murderous persecution of the Jews. The Christian tradition was that the Jews were indeed a bad lot, so sinful as to have lost their position as God's chosen people, having failed to recognize Christ as the Son of God, and having crucified him as well. Christians were now God's chosen people, and the Jews were clearly inferior in spiritual, and thus societal, status. Nonetheless, their lives were to be spared, and some bishops did attempt to protect the lives of Jews under attack. This was a grossly inadequate response, and the Church was, in effect, powerless to stop the progress of the pogroms.

A third major reason for the widespread persecution of Jews was avarice. The despoiling of the Jewish communities provided some of the resources for the purchase of food and supplies for the Crusade journeys. The urban Jewish communities had much to yield to the attacking Crusaders. For centuries, Sephardic Jews had spread out from the Mediterranean basin, settling in many of the trading cities of Europe. They played a large part in international trade, providing a necessary link between Muslim and Christian countries. Christians in Europe could not lend money in an aboveboard way because of the Church's restriction on usury, so many of the money-lending houses were of necessity owned by Jews. Although they had no legal civic rights, the secular and Church leaders in the cities, including kings and archbishops, were eager to give such useful Jews certain protections. Indeed, except in Visigothic Iberia, Jewish communities had never been violently persecuted in the West. As trading expanded and the economy became increasingly based on coinage, people from all levels of society became indebted to the Jewish moneylenders; their high rates of interest bred resentment against them. Many Crusaders had to borrow money from the Jews to equip themselves for the journey, and the irony of becoming indebted to Jews in order to fight Muslims was not lost on the knights.

A fourth reason involved the effects of the separation of Jewish communities from the societies in which they lived. The Jews lived away from the center of urban life, in their own quarters, and had established a clearly defined alien identity. They were an outside group, an ethnic and religious minority, and the lack of contact with Christian townspeople fostered distrust and, ultimately, fear. A factor that exasperated this ignorance-based fear was the presence of the Kabalists within the Jewish communities. Kabalism was a system of occult theosophy or mystical interpretation of the Jewish scriptures by certain rabbis, handed down orally through chosen individuals. They believed that the writings were revealed as a means of penetrating into the divine mysteries. The Kabalists assume, for example, that every letter, word, number, and accent of scripture contains a hidden sense or meaning. This was a secret and mysterious aspect of Judaism that played into the fears of the supernatural, possessed by most medieval persons. It acted to increase the gulf between the Christian and Jewish communities within each city.

A fifth reason, involving the specific leadership of the German Emlich himself, involves his vision that he had an extraordinary apocalyptic destiny. He would become the mythical last emperor predicted by an ancient prophecy, would be crowned in Jerusalem, reign there for a thousand years, ushering in the second coming of Christ. But St. Paul had written that before the second coming, all of the Jews would be converted to Christianity. Emlich was determined to make that happen; the Jews would either convert or be slain. Most Jews chose death, or killed loved ones to prevent their conversion. Apart from any thoughts of vengeance, the elimination of the Jews was a necessity to fulfill Emlich's dream of conquest and empire.

All of these reasons, some of them specific to the historical context and persons involved in the First Crusade, some of them more general to the mind-set and religious beliefs of medieval Europe, point to important universal lessons. We see the medieval Church compromising its core beliefs and teachings for various reasons and setting into motion a series of events that it is unable to control. We see the underlying traditions of medieval society (i.e., the vendetta) transmuted in a new and alien context, resulting in an unprecedented scale of slaughter. Finally, we see the effects of the segregation of a minority group apart from mainstream society and the violent actions that result from the fear and distrust engendered thereby.

The Persisting Consequences

The specific long-term effects of these pogroms are vast. Karen Armstrong has described the Crusade-era events as the beginning of anti-Semitism as an incurable Western disease. Indeed, the Jewish communities were again attacked in the mid-fourteenth century, being blamed for the spread of the Black Death throughout Europe. The Church eventually supported anti-Jewish campaigns in the fifteenth century, all Jews being expelled from Spain in 1492. The Nazi Holocaust of the 1930s and 1940s increased the scale of annihilation to reach into the millions. Broadly speaking, the attacks against Jews in connection with the calling of the Crusades allowed for the legitimization of violence within European society and encouraged the identification of alien subgroups within that society, and beyond, as targets.

There are also international effects. Were it not for these first pogroms, the nation of Israel would not exist today, with the widespread international bloodshed associated with its creation and preservation. European colonialism might not have progressed as it did, and relations between the Muslim world and the West would be in a very different condition. This partial listing is only the beginning.

The application of religious doctrines, and the passionate beliefs they engender, to temporal events, in connection with an agenda of expansion, conquest, or control, leads inexorably to the snowballing of an unanticipated cascade of results. In this particular case, the results have been tragic beyond all description. This risk of unstoppable international calamity is history's greatest lesson from these distant horrifying events.

Notes

1. David Caplovitz and Candice Rogers, *Swastika 1960: The Epidemic of Anti-Semitic Vandalism in America* (New York: Anti-Defamation League of B'nai B'rith, 1960), 9.

2. John J. Gager, *Was the Apostle Paul the Father of Christian Anti-Judaism?* Lecture delivered at the University of Michigan on October 21, 2002, sponsored by the Michigan Center for Early Christian Studies and the International Institute for Secular Humanistic Judaism, along with various university departments.

3. Jean Richard, *The Crusades, c. 1071–c. 1291*, Jean Birrell, trans. (Cambridge: Cambridge University Press, 1999), 2.

4. Jonathon Riley-Smith, *The First Crusade and the Idea of Crusading* (London: Athlone; Philadelphia: University of Pennsylvania Press, 1986), 53–58.

5. "The Narrative of the Old Persecutions of Mainz, Anonymous" in Schlomo Eidelberg, translator and editor, *The Jews and the Crusaders: The Hebrew Chronicles of the First and Second Crusades* (Madison: University of Wisconsin Press, 1977), 100.

6. Karen Armstrong, *Holy War: The Crusades and Their Impact on Today's World* (New York: Random House, 2001), 72–73.

7. Eidelberg, 80.

CHAPTER 3

GENOCIDE OR JESUS: A GOD OF CONQUEST OR PACIFICISM?

Paul N. Anderson

Introduction

Of the many tensions rising from a careful reading of the Bible, none of them is as striking or problematic as God's commanding genocide in the conquest, indeed, extermination of the Canaanites; and Jesus' clearly teaching nonviolence and love for one's enemies. In fact, I consider this the greatest theological and hermeneutical problem in the Bible. It is theological in that Jesus claims to represent the will and reign of God, while at the same time God is portrayed starkly in the Hebrew Bible as the one commanding the lethal conquest. One cannot get around those facts. The question is what to do with them, and this is why the subject is such a pressing problem for interpretation, the hermeneutical issue.

If God is the one commanding either murder or nonviolence, such a presentation has moral implications for those seeking to follow the will of God. If indeed God commands both actions, God seems contradictory, or at least inconsistent, and the struggle then becomes how to decide which of those directives should be followed. What results from these considerations is that the Bible is often interpreted variously, and it ceases to speak with a clear and authoritative voice on a historically important matter, especially with relation to the Bible's role in supporting or resisting violence.

But how do we know that it is really *God* or *the divine will* that is represented by either of these directions? Were either or both of these presentations influenced by contextual factors that might help us understand better the content being conveyed? Did God change God's mind? Does the Author of life alone retain the right to grant and withdraw the gift of life, thereby requiring us not to question divine ordinances? Then again, how might one have known, either in biblical times or at other times, that a violent action is being commanded by God as opposed to being a projection of human psychological paranoia? How do we keep from simply applying parts of the Bible that seem most conducive to our prejudices and biases, thereby replacing the voice of authoritative sacred scripture with our own? How do we decide what sort of approach to take in addressing violent situations in the world today, when sticking to principle of any sort may lead to unfavorable outcomes? Or finally, must one simply choose one path only, either violence or nonviolence, siding with one portrait of God and rejecting the other? Is there a third alternative to be considered? These are the sorts of questions that emerge from this tension, and the approaches we take have profound implications. The focus of this chapter, however, will center on one point only: how do such scripture messages or stories reflect a unitive divine will? How can the same God be portrayed as commanding genocide and love of enemies in the same Bible?

Approaches to the Issue

Approaches to this conundrum have been numerous and varied. While the present discussion cannot cover them all, nor is there space to treat any of them extensively, a preliminary survey might be helpful. Consider these approaches. First, one might *appeal to the sovereignty of God:* "God commanded the conquest; who are we to question God? In the sovereignty of God's will, God alone gives life, so who are we to object if God decides to take a person's life away?" This may sound workable to some, but if God alone has the authority to end life, how dare we think that we know how to perceive the divine will to exterminate enemies? Moreover, why does the same God command through Jesus, as his presumed representative agent, the indiscriminate love of enemies? The sovereignty of God works well when respecting the sanctity of life; it fares more poorly when it comes to the taking of human life.

A second approach *infers a change of the divine will on the subject of killing:* "The God of the Old Testament formerly commanded killing, but he changed his mind with the New Covenant in which he now commands forgiveness and love. The God of the Old Testament was a God of judgment and punishment, but the God of the New Testament is a God of grace and mercy." Indeed, this was Marcion's opinion, and in the second century C.E. he and other Gnostic Christians were happy to marginalize the Old Testament God, replacing that being with the God revealed in Jesus and taught by Paul. The resulting crisis, however, threatened the authority of the larger canonical corpus, and the larger Christian movement was not willing to say that the Hebrew Scriptures were not inspired or canonical. Even if one retains the larger canon, however, many interpreters operate as "functional Marcionites" when it comes to taking seriously the God of the Old Testament conquest narratives. We might rather leave that presentation out of our authoritative collection of writings, but if we take the entire Bible as inspired in some way and authoritative at some level, we cannot escape this tension. We must find a way to deal with it.

An obverse problem is caused by *retaining a vindictive picture of God and marginalizing the ethical teachings of Jesus:* "I'm really an Old Testament Christian, and I believe people should get what's coming to them!" a fiery preacher might tout. "Even Jesus preached fire and brimstone according to Matthew's gospel, and despite presentations of God's love in the Bible, from Genesis to Revelation we have clear presentations of God's wrath!" This is one of the most damaging hermeneutical stances there can be. Some people really do envision a God full of judgment, and they seize upon the conquest narratives as sources of inspiration for pathological attitudes and behavior. For some reason they still call themselves Christians but refuse to take seriously the Sermon on the Mount, especially the Beatitudes! This stance is really hard to understand for those who claim to be followers of Jesus. Or, they might adopt an interim ethic and teach that only after the rapture and restoration of God's kingdom in the millennium would God's perfect moral will be done on earth as it is in heaven. Until then, the God of judgment supplants the God of grace.

A fourth approach *regards the commands to kill the Canaanites as a punishment for their sinfulness:* "God commanded the Israelites to kill the Canaanites because of their awful moral practices. When you consider the terrible things those people must have done, you can understand why God wanted to teach them a lesson." This kind of logic may seem to work until you start considering the specifics. Notice that not all wicked people in the Old Testament are punished, and even when Israel or Judah sins grievously against Yahweh, never are they wiped out by God. God forgives and is merciful, even in the original Covenant, and the commands for genocide have more to do with the Israeli foreign policy of clearing the land of its prior inhabitants than with teaching any individual or people a lesson.

A fifth approach *relativizes the damage, claiming it was a "necessary evil"* as the only path to a greater good: "God knew that the only way to bring a blessing to the whole world was to deliver Israel into the Promised Land, which unfortunately was inhabited by pagans. While God never rejoices in suffering, because the greater good justifies the initial cost, God's divine economy can be seen to be at work even in the killing of the Canaanites." Indeed, clearing the land was the primary rationale for the conquest narratives, but the God of Israel is portrayed as retaining sovereignty on other matters; why not on this one? Moreover, if one is going to argue that the end justifies the means on any ethical issue, one immediately sacrifices the option of standing up for any kind of objective principle of justice, decency, morality, or proportionality.

A sixth approach *supplants principle with realism:* "Jesus may have taught a doctrine of nonresistance, but that just doesn't work in the real world. This is a fallen world, as depicted in the Bible, and in a fallen world we must use fallen means—including violence, if necessary—to make the world a safer place." Part of the problem here is that the authority of scriptural teaching is minimized on the basis of imagined outcomes, and the principle itself is never given a full chance to work. Another way of putting it considers the call to principled faithfulness regardless of the results. In fact, results cannot be the motivation for faith or faithfulness; otherwise, it becomes a mere transaction, something less than faith and faithful living.

A seventh consideration takes the conquest narratives at face value, *seeing God as a violent and inhumane deity, worthy of being abandoned:* "If God indeed commanded genocide, and genocide is inhumane and morally reprehensible, God must be morally reprehensible and unworthy of a moral person's loyalty. The actions of the God of the Old Testament cannot but drive the moral individual away from these savage religious traditions." Many in the modern era might feel this way, especially given the fact that the biblical conquest narratives have been used historically to legitimate the resorting to violence by Jews, Christians, and Muslims. However, this approach fails to recognize that the God of the Bible is also one of the prime motivators toward conscientious and humane treatment of others, and rejecting the Judeo-Christian God because of the book of Joshua fails to account for the God revealed by Jesus in the gospels. This tension must be addressed to make any sort of judgment adequately.

A final consideration is the way some interpreters *infer from these scriptures a set of temporal "dispensations" wherein differing "rules" govern the human–divine relationship:* "There was a dispensation of law and conquest, followed by a dispensation of hope and deliverance, followed by a dispensation of the New Covenant, followed by a dispensation of the life of the Church, followed by the return of Christ, and so forth. In that former dispensation of OT life God permitted some forms of violence, but in later ones, they are forbidden." This is similar to the sovereignty-of-God approach, but it works more explicitly with punctuating epochs in eschatological history, seeking to itemize differing ethical and religious standards for each of these dispensations. A variant of this approach, though much more refined theologically, is process theology, which assumes that God's perfection may have involved growth and movement rather than static consistency, more of a Greek notion than a Hebrew one. Indeed, the basic Christian teaching is that Jesus fulfilled the Law without abolishing it, and the New Covenant does indeed do away with Jewish cultic observances but preserves the essence of the covenant of grace, making way for new approaches to God.

One of the greatest among the many problems with dispensational speculation is the tendency to apply arbitrarily differing sets of divine regulation over different epochs. The question of who makes those judgments, and by what standard they are made, reflects a couple of the major headaches with such an approach, but an even greater problem is that God ceases to be unitive and consistent. The more changes one adds between dispensations, the less God can be said to have a "changeless" character or even enduring ethical standards. Is God decent, consistent, fair, and just? Dispensational approaches are especially problematic when it comes to deciding moral standards of praxis.

For these and other reasons, the tension between the presentation of Jesus' teachings on the love of one's neighbors and one's enemies continues to be an enduring interpretive problem. As a way forward, we might consider first the teachings of Jesus. Perhaps he was getting at something else. We shall then consider the presentation of Yahweh's commands to kill in the Hebrew conquest narratives to see if we can learn anything by examining a theme in its context and moving from that point toward a meaningful interpretive approach.

Jesus' Teachings on Nonviolence and the Love of Enemies

Just what did Jesus teach about violence and peace? Some scholars may locate Jesus among the Galilean prophets mentioned by Josephus, claiming that Jesus' failed mission to overthrow the Romans was reformulated into a more inane presentation of Jesus as a teacher of nonviolence, but this approach is unconvincing.[1] Jesus is pervasively portrayed as distinguishing himself from the later Theudas, the Samaritan, and the Egyptian, and he seeks to flee attempts to rush him to a hasty coronation on the Galilean shore (John 6:14–15). Moreover, the Messianic Secret in Mark reveals a Jesus who is not interested in sensational publicity and who seeks to avoid creating a popularist stir. The fact that this presentation is more muted in Luke and Matthew suggests its origin was earlier and likely closer to Jesus than an image onto which later Christian notions might have been superimposed. A longer treatment may be found elsewhere,[2] but here are seven larger points regarding Jesus' teachings on peace within which smaller ones may be inferred.

First, Jesus commands his followers to love God with all of our hearts, souls, minds, and strength, and to *love our neighbors as ourselves* (Matt. 22:37–40; Mark 12:29–31; Luke 10:27). Jesus' followers will be known by the trademark of sacrificial love (John 13:34–35). The love of God and neighbor in Jesus' teaching reflects a radical understanding of the Decalogue. Jesus had apparently boiled down the Ten Commandments into their vertical and horizontal dimensions, effectively summarizing the Law of Moses within two basic commands. The love of neighbor, of course, gets applied in Luke to the unlikely Samaritans. Where the question "Who is my neighbor?" might be interpreted as an honest interest in identifying neighbors in order to do them good, Jesus picks up the real question and answers it wittily. Rather than narrowing down the categories of those to be loved, Jesus chooses the most unlikely of love objects, those detested Samaritans, and says *those* are the people to be loved as one's neighbor. This must have been a disappointing response to those hoping to find their provincialisms and prejudices protected in a religious guise.

A second motif takes things even further: Jesus calls his followers to *love even our enemies, and to pray for those who despitefully use us* (Matt. 5:43–48). Even the Gentiles and tax gatherers might return good for good, or evil for evil, but Jesus' teaching was really different. This teaching makes it especially difficult to consider Jesus as a political revolutionary who failed. The love of enemy would have been an unlikely development within such a movement, and it more likely represents another sort of revolution, seeking to overthrow not the Romans, but the myth of redemptive violence, replacing it with the domination-free order of God. To pray for one's adversary refuses to go along with worldly divisiveness. Rather, it embraces a transcendent value: the active reign and leadership of God, which cannot be furthered by going against its character. The way of the Kingdom involves love, forgiveness, and peace, and Jesus invites human involvement in its actualization by embodying those values unilaterally, regardless of the outcome.

A third motif casts fresh light on the truly subversive character of God's love: Jesus calls his followers to *renounce a spirit of vengeance and to embrace a spirit of exceeding generosity* (Matt. 5:38–42). When stricken with a backhanded slap, Jesus instructs his followers to stand with dignity and turn the other cheek. When one's cloak is required, give also the rest of one's clothing, and when asked to carry a soldier's pack for one mile, go twice as far out of love of God. These images have been misinterpreted by well-meaning Christians across the years to imply servile cowering and doormat passivity, when they are not meant to be taken as such. Indeed, they are highly activistic, in revolutionary ways.

In Walter Wink's profoundly creative analysis of this Matthean passage,[3] he argues several things that make a good deal of sense. Given that the right hand would have been used for striking (the left hand would not have been used for interpersonal exchange), to have been struck on the right cheek implies a backhanded slap, a gesture meant to *intimidate* rather than to injure. Likewise, a soldier might have "limited" the abuse of his Galilean subject by requiring "only" one mile as a means of feigning generosity, and a harsh creditor might have exacted one's cloak if that was the only thing between him and his land (the real goal of the creditor). For Jesus to advocate standing and welcoming the intimidating threat by saying in effect, "Go ahead, I'll take a forehand blow; I'm no less of a human being than you are!" would certainly have thrown the dominator off balance. What would have happened if a soldier's superiors heard that subjects were carrying the soldier's pack more than one mile? Would they really believe his claim that he did not coerce or demand such, or would he be punished *by his own Roman superiors?*

Wink invites us to imagine the ironic picture of a Roman soldier chasing a Galilean peasant beyond the mile marker, begging him to put down his pack! The third example was equally subversive. As the shame of the naked debtor would have fallen upon the observer, this would have drawn quick attention to the stern creditor and an unyielding system of leverage. In all these ways, Jesus' teachings and example subverted worldly systems of domination and provided an alternative to fight-or-flight dichotomies. Jesus intended to change the world with his nonviolent subversion of worldly domination, and he sought to teach others how to do so without falling prey to its devices.

A fourth motif regards *the character of the Kingdom*. Jesus' Kingdom is not of this world; if it were, his disciples would fight to defend it (John 18:36–37). Rather, we are exhorted to seek first the Kingdom of Heaven and its righteousness, and all we truly need will be given us (Matt. 6:33). Here Jesus orients his followers to another set of standards by which to measure one's success. Many mistaken views of Christianity rest upon the faulty foundations linking too closely the Kingdom of God with any human endeavor or organization. The active leadership of God transcends such ventures, and when the disciple remains focused on the advancing of truth, hope, and love, one's goals also become realigned by a new set of priorities. The *way of the Kingdom* is always counterconventional. Jesus' Kingdom turns things upside down: the first will be last, and the last will be first. The Gentiles lord it over their subjects, but not so among Jesus' followers. The one wishing to be first must be the servant of all (Matt. 18:4; Mark 9:35, 10:42–45; Luke 22:25–26), and only those willing to lose their lives will find them. The way of the Kingdom, therefore, is a paradoxical one, and this is why seeing it at all requires a revelation from above. It cannot otherwise be imagined.

A fifth motif presents itself in dramatic form: Jesus *commands his followers to put away their swords* (Matt. 26:52–53; Luke 22:49–51; John 18:11). He goes on to issue a wise warning that those wishing to live by the sword will die by it. This passage is extremely clear; Jesus commands his followers to refuse the path of violence lest they be ensnared in it. Of course, Luke adds a passage (Luke 22:36–38) in which Jesus tells his disciples that they will need a sword, and when they bring him two swords he exclaims, "Enough!" The interpretive question is whether the phrase in Greek (*ikanon estin*) means "That will do fine, thank you; two swords are enough," or whether it means "Enough of that! You haven't a clue about what this movement is really doing!" In the context of verses 49–51, the latter seems like the better rendering, and it is also doubtful that anyone would have been suggesting that two swords would have been sufficient to take on the Romans. No. Jesus commands his followers to put away their swords; his reign advances in other ways.

A sixth feature of the Kingdom is typified by Jesus' commanding his followers to *forgive even the undeserving* (Matt. 18:21–35). Despite Peter's being granted instrumental "Keys of the Kingdom," he is also required to be forgiving, even 70 times 7 times. But what if they aren't sorry? "Forgive," says Jesus. But what if they'll do it again? "Forgive," he says again. But what if they really do damage—blow down the World Trade Center towers and kill 3,500 people? Should we not hold it against them? According to Jesus, the answer is unequivocally "No!" The answer even then is "Forgive!" The way of the Kingdom overflows with abundant forgivness, and as we have received grace, so should we be willing to extend it. After all, this is the character of God's forgiveness, and it is also the kind to be emulated by Jesus' followers. Besides, nothing else works in life, and never has worked in history. Why is that so hard to notice and take seriously?

A seventh feature of the Kingdom is one in which Jesus calls for his followers to *embrace the cross* (Matt. 10:38–39; Mark 8:34–38; John 12:25–26). One who wishes to save one's life will lose it, but one who is willing to release one's life for the sake of Christ and his way will paradoxically find it. This is one of the hardest sayings in the Bible. It offers no guarantees when it comes to favorable outcomes; it simply invites believers to commit themselves to faithfulness whatever the result may be. This is not to be confused with seeking martyrdom in order to make a point. The issue here is faithfulness regardless of what the outcome might be, and this motif adds some realism to the mission. After all, following Jesus might *not* protect one from persecution; it may even provoke it (Matt. 5:10–12), and yet, therein lies the path of blessedness as the believer shares in the mission, and at times the sufferings, of the Lord. As James Parnell, that 19-year-old Quaker martyr, said, "Be willing that self shall suffer for truth, and not the truth for self."

Finally, Jesus says, *"Blessed are the peacemakers*, for they shall be called 'the children of the Most High'" (Matt. 5:9). Notice, however, that this passage does not spell out specifically what it means to be a peacemaker. On the other hand, James points out that the pursuit of peaceable goals by peaceable means distinguishes the workings of God from the methods of the world (James 3:18–4:4), and that may shed a bit of light on the Matthean insight. Jesus also promises his followers that he will bless them with peace, not as the world gives peace, bolstered by outward security, but inward peace, that which overcomes the strategies of this kind of world (John 14:25–27). In that sense, unworldly peace bears within itself great capacity to impact the world, and one gets the sense that in aspiring to such an ethic, the divine will is furthered.

The result of this brief survey is to outline some of the ways that Jesus' teachings really seem to be quite clear on the subject of peace and nonviolence. Some might object that the cleansing of the Temple was a violent act, or one in which Jesus lost his temper, but it is more suitably regarded as a prophetic sign designed to make a point in the name of God rather than an expression of violence. Also, there appears to have been intentionality behind the action. In the Gospel of Mark, Jesus arrived at the Temple site late in the day when the crowd may have dissipated, and he came back the next day, suggesting the action was intended to make a public demonstration rather than an uncontrolled fit of rage (Mark 11:11). Theologically, however, does Jesus purport to be representing the divine will when he calls for peaceable means to peaceable solutions? Pervasively, yes, and this is why the presentation of God's commanding violence and the use of lethal force in the Old Testament is *theologically* problematic.

Divine Commands for a Lethal Conquest

The voice of Yahweh in the Bible is an interesting phenomenon. It certainly plays a literary role, and that literary feature has theological implications. But what about the historical role of Yahweh's speaking? When we hear someone saying today "God told me . . . ," we might ask ourselves how this person is interpreting the divine voice. We might wonder if the person has had a flash of insight that is being crafted into a convention described as a divine address, or perhaps the person is alluding to being moved by a particular religious means. We would even think of the possibility that the person is suffering from psychotic delusions.

On the other hand, a Bible passage might have become especially meaningful; a priest or pastor might have offered some timely counsel, or perhaps a sunset has been especially beautiful and the person feels addressed by a voice within. I suppose we might imagine a sensory audition with one's ears, but most often we do not experience God "speaking" to us through our auditory senses. What, then, do we make of the Deuteronomistic convention "And Yahweh said . . . "?

It could be that people really did experience being addressed by God in the days described by the Hebrew Bible; certainly the calling of young Samuel is portrayed as his hearing the voice of God in a physical way (1 Sam. 3). But the theological question may be put this way: even if the divine address were experienced sensorily, how should we interpret the message *theologically*, as a factor of the transcendent, divine will for humanity? We must leave that question open for now, and the fact is that we must do so because we have no way of answering the question either way. Let me describe, however, some of the historical and literary layers we might have to peel back in searching for an answer.

Starting from the latest text tradition, we might work backward and see what happens. At the latest stages of the books of Joshua and Judges, material thought to have been finalized by the Deuteronomistic editors and theologians around 500 B.C.E., we have the material representing the importance of keeping the Law. Positive rewards for obedience and negative consequences for disobedience accompany at least one or two of the editorial versions. These were written about the time of the Babylonian exile of the Kingdom of Judah. Here the emphasis was placed on trusting Yahweh fully and keeping the Law of Moses. In these passages, the voice of Yahweh can be read as calling for faithfulness to the covenant with God, so that things might go well for the Israelites.

During the two or three centuries before that, these traditions probably came together as a way of explaining "how we got here in captivity in Babylon" and as a reminder of "what we need to be doing to get on well with God in the future." In captivity the Israelites seemed to get the clue to their big question: "How is God in our wretched history?" The answer was that the nations of the world had been sent to chastise them for their sin against God. Struggles faced from the tenth to sixth centuries B.C.E. included trying to sort out the meaning of the invasions by the Assyrians and the Babylonians; trying to figure out how it is that the Kingdom of Israel divided, sending both into a downward spiral toward trivialization and destruction; and finding out God's intentions with the rest of the land's inhabitants, Canaanites who did not seem to be part of God's original promise of grace and mercy.

Of course, the narrations of the conquest itself would have come down for two or three centuries before that, probably in oral form, and these stories would have included heroic tales from the past, together with a sense of God's provision and sustenance along the way. Moreover, we must remember that the records that we have are those told by the victors and from their point of view. A real conquest did happen; whether it was as expansive or as effective as portrayed in Joshua and Judges, we have no idea. At least some sort of warfare and Israelite occupation is more than plausible, and the point here is to consider historical origins of later, emergent narratives. This being the case, let us consider how some of those perceptions and theological constructs might have developed within Israel's conquest narratives.

A first level is a prehistoric, *anticipatory* one. Within this mythic phase, the hope for the future provides direction and sustenance for the present, and ideas formed early in Israel's history would have affected later perceptions and developments as well. The descendants of Abraham, who left Ur for the land promised him by Yahweh, continued longing for a land they could call their own before, during, and after their sojourn as captives in Egypt. The anticipated conquest imagined God fulfilling his promise by granting the land (Gen. 12:1–3, 15:1–8, 17:1–27; see the more pointed hope in Exod. 3:8), and such a hope was probably tempered only by the reality of how things went with the actual conquest.

The second phase would have involved *the conquest itself.* Within this historical phase, the time of the events being narrated, we still have the central question before us: did *God* command the killing of the Canaanites in some way similar to the final reporting of the events six hundred years later? Put otherwise, did people perceive the voice of God to be commanding the killing of the Canaanites, however they might have construed the divine voice of Yahweh? This is not an impossibility. Certainly, the Israelites would have felt that God wanted to deliver them into the land, and they would have experienced divine assistance, and perhaps even a divine mandate, to carry out the clearing of the land. Even if this were the case, though, experientially and historically, we are still left with the theological question as to the degree to which the transcendent and loving God of the universe ever desired one tribe to eradicate neighboring clans and tribes, for whatever reason.

Was this Israeli foreign policy projected on God, or God's mandate to "his people"? If the latter is true, then whose people were those poor Canaanites who were living peaceably in the land until the Israelites wreaked arbitrary havoc upon them? Is not God the God of the whole universe and all "his dear children"? What were the Israelites thinking, anyway? It is likely that some reflection would have taken place by some wise and sensitive folk in the Israeli community, depending, of course, on how things went. In other words, some Israelites must have felt universalistic passion and compassion for those other human beings, and most of the Israelites must have wondered why, if all of this was divinely ordained, some campaigns went well and others did not. In any case, theological conjecture would have played a formative role early in the subsequent presentation and narration of the historical events. This phase, however, would not have been the last opportunity for crafting the role of God's direction in the matter.

A third phase in the history of tradition would have involved the oral narration of war stories, complete with the exaltation of heroic figures and events, and the denigration of the less worthy. Within this oral stage of narrative transmission, several features arise within the material and contribute to its elaboration. Stories sometimes get duplicated, or interesting points from one narration become attached to another; actual numbers and accounting get rounded off into general groupings and figures; moralizing comments get added along the way, as events in the past become patterns for the future; and tribal features emerge within the narrations as a means of furthering tribal prosperity and success. Within this early tradition stage, "our tribe versus their tribe" would certainly have played a role in the formation of the memory. Within that stage, and it continued until the material was finalized, probably in the middle of the sixth century B.C.E., the "voice of Yahweh" would have played a significant role in the emerging destiny of the nation.

In particular, explaining *why* things did or did not go well in the past becomes a didactic platform for addressing contemporary issues six hundred years later when the narratives are being reedited into an official story line, and these become the basis for imagining and structuring the future. Several exhortative themes can be seen to have developed within this phase: (a) the conviction that God had promised to deliver them into the land; (b) the memory of at least partial success whereupon God, not Israel, deserved the glory; (c) the memory of at least partial failure whereupon Israel and her failings, not God, deserved the blame; and finally, (d) the emerging tension resultant from the fact that they had been delivered into the promised land, but that land was fraught with difficulties and their memory was fraught with their own horrendous bloodshed.

As regards their religion, they faced temptations to resort to Baal worship and to follow Canaanite pagan customs, evoking this sort of existential question: *"How could God have delivered us into the land, but at the same time have given us a land that had its seemingly entrenched temptations and trials?"* Answer: It was not God's fault; it was Israel's. When we followed God fully, the enemy was delivered into our hands. When we did not, however, the conquest was incomplete, and that's how the root of later "problems" might best be explained.

A psychoanalyst, of course, would have some important insights here regarding the degree to which the Israelite temptation to identify with the local Canaanite inhabitants, evidenced by their commerce and intermarriage with them as well as their sharing of the Canaanite religious devotion, might reflect an unconscious level of embarrassment and bad conscience regarding how badly they had abused the Canaanites, purportedly at the command of Yahweh. Why not seek Baal, who had apparently afforded his people peace and prosperity until Yahweh and his bunch came along and wreaked such uncivilized havoc on the settled Canaanite civilizations? Who would want to stick with that kind of Yahwist god for the long run?

That speculation aside, of course, a fourth phase in the preservation of Israel's history would have involved preserving the material in more standardized forms and units, at times producing written traditions and at times formalizing oral ones. Interest in preserving the memories of particular aspects of the conquest and the geographical progress, explaining also the reason a place had the name it did or served as a reminder of a particular event, would likely become increasingly important as distance from the heroic conquest events increased. Here especially we see the value of historical narrations providing a pattern for faithfulness in the future. Especially in Judges, for instance, the cycles of disobedience, hardship, and punishment, followed by repentance and recovery of prosperity, provide instructive lessons for later generations, motivating them to be ever more vigilant and faithful. In particular, making peace with the pagan neighbors was frowned upon, and this served to motivate presumed or claimed religious and ethnic purity in Israel as compared with her neighbors, from the conquest to the Babylonian exile. The emphasis should be upon the phrase "presumed or claimed," since in practical fact Israelite behavior was no more sanctified than that of the nations around Israel. The Israelite prophets themselves make this truth plain.

A final stage in the material's composition before being finalized by the Deuteronomistic editors, then, would have been the writing of complete books and narratives. On this matter, Deuteronomy, Joshua,

Judges, and Samuel each had their own relative autonomy, but many similarities and connections also can be traced through all of these traditions. Of special importance in each of these historical narrations is the connection between what happened "back then," namely, in the earlier, remembered history of conquest and consolidation, and its implications for a later generation. In that sense, interpretative modifications probably never stopped collecting around these ancient memories until these works were standardized in the sixth century B.C.E.

These are very broad strokes with which to paint the tradition-development landscape, but why is this speculation about the development of Israel's traditional history important for the consideration of the present topic? Given the theological implications of the presentation of the divine voice of God commanding the killing of individuals and entire groups of people, the contextual question presents itself as an extremely important matter. If we can make some good guesses about the contexts out of which the presentation of God's command to kill Canaanites might have developed, we might gain a clearer sense of how much of this motif goes back to God and how much of it resulted from either an anthropomorphic projection of the divine will in relation to the needs of Israel at the time, or even the degree to which it simply serves as a literary device. This being the case, narrating the voice of God commanding the killing of neighboring tribes and individuals will have different meanings and associations in different stages in the narratives' tradition history. The answer to our question regarding God as the source of such mandates may finally be inaccessible, but we may gain clearer insights into ways such a presentation was represented and passed on within Israel's developing tradition history. Moreover, this may be crucial in helping us understand how the ancient traditions are being consciously or unconsciously applied in Israeli foreign policy toward the Palestinians at our present moment in history.

Meanings and Associations within Israel's Developing Tradition

With regard to the presentation of God's role in the killing of the Canaanites, several features of Israel's warfare deserve consideration. They will provide the background for a better understanding of how to regard the "voice of Yahweh" in commanding mass killings.

First, Israel's wars are not portrayed as hers; they are portrayed as Yahweh's wars, with Yahweh receiving the glory for the triumphal results.[4] Because of this, Yahweh uses all means at his disposal. He uses the forces of nature (see Exod. 15), he uses Israel as an agent of battle, and he even employs other nations to do his bidding, sometimes to discipline Israel. Yahweh fights for Israel and invites her to join him in his work.[5]

Second, Yahweh alone gives the battle into Israel's hands, and this is a factor of her faithfulness to Yahweh.[6] Yahweh's presence goes forth as a victorious feature in Israel's conquest, and whenever the Ark of the Covenant is with them, they are invincible in battle. A result of Yahweh's fighting for Israel is that the enemy loses courage, and the battle is often won readily.[7] In Israel's faithfulness to Yahweh, she must first of all trust, and the reliance on Yahweh alone is often portrayed as the obverse of relying on chariots or weapons of war.[8]

Third, particular stipulations are to be associated with the ways Yahweh's Holy War is to be fought. (a) Combatants are to dedicate themselves in purity to Yahweh and to fight for him alone. This may have involved a ritual cleansing (Josh. 3:5), and holy warriors were expected to be sexually chaste (1 Sam. 21:4–5; 2 Sam. 11:6–17). (b) They were not allowed to keep any booty or spoils of war (as in the case of Achan, Josh. 7), or even take prisoners (as in the case of Saul, 1 Sam. 15) because the mission was to clear the land rather than to amass gain. This is called "the ban." (c) Then again, reports were not always consistent on these matters. Deuteronomy 20, for instance, prescribes a variety of approaches, and this fact suggests a fair amount of unevenness in the ways the Israelites carried out their campaigns. When attacking a city, they were to make an offer of peace, and if the inhabitants surrendered they would be spared and could work as their servants (vss. 10–11). If the inhabitants resisted the men were to be killed, but the rest of the people, the livestock and their valuables could be taken as spoils. At least cities at a distance could be treated this way (vv. 12–15). However, the nearby cities were to be destroyed completely (vv. 16–18), and an interesting reason is listed. If they are not, they will corrupt the Israelites with their religion and detestable practices and will cause Israel to fall away from God. The trees, however, are to be saved (v. 19).

Fourth, we see a variety of results in how things are reported to have happened. Where Israel trusted Yahweh fully, success was sweeping and grand. However, where the Israelites failed in faith or faithfulness, disaster ensued. Von Rad rightly points out how the suc-

Saul Attacking David, by Giovanni Francesco Barbieri Guercino. The Art Archive/Palazzo Barberini Rome/Dagli Orti (A).

cesses of people like David, Gideon, Deborah, and Moses serve as narrative examples of how things went right in Yahweh's wars.[9] On the other hand, things also went awry, and not only did Israel lose heart at times,[10] but she or her leaders sometimes disobeyed the instruction of Yahweh. Achan failed by collecting and hiding valuables under his tent, and because of this sin, three dozen Israelite soldiers were routed at Ai (Josh. 7). Saul failed by sparing the king of the Amalekites and his livestock (1 Sam. 15), and because of this Yahweh eventually removed Saul as king of Israel.

Eventually, several things brought an end to Holy War in Israel. The appointing of Saul as a king was the beginning of the end according to the Samuel tradition, because from that time on, Israel abandoned Yahweh as her king and began to establish standing armies and instruments of war. This was entirely contrary to the ethos of fighting alongside Yahweh as the divine warrior. It constituted a shift from a theocracy to a monarchy, in the view of the chief religionist of the time, Samuel, who had everything to lose and nothing to gain by this change. Another development was the devastation of Israel and Judah by the Babylonians and the Assyrians. The devastating failures to oppose the enemy in those wars forced Israel to reconsider her understanding of Holy War. Nonetheless, the memory lived on, and even within the prophetic and poetic traditions of Israel, the lore of Yahweh's battles lived on.

Two theological considerations follow the preceding survey of Israel's Holy Wars. First, one of the things we see is Israel projecting her need for a provider and protector upon Yahweh. People of all religious persuasions will always construct an image of the Deity in ways consonant with their needs and situation, and Israel was no different. Dianne Bergant, in her excellent essay "Yahweh, A Warrior God?" (see note 4), points out how the Israelites during these sojourning years would have yoked the metaphorical character of theological language to their sustenance needs at the time. They clearly regarded Yahweh as their patron protector, and against the dangers of hostile tribes and territories, they interpreted Yahweh's deliverance and help in patriarchal warlord sorts of ways. Does this mean, however, that God is a male and a male only? Of course not! God also provides nurturing and sheltering support for Israel, and the God of Israel transcends gender representations.

Theologically, this consideration is important. It clarifies the legitimacy of Israel's experience and representation of Yahweh as a warrior, without necessitating an ontological identification of God as such. That being the case, Yahweh's clearing the land of its obstacles, including socioreligious ones, takes precedence over the concern to love Israel's neighbors and to treat them well, a notion that seems to still prevail today in Israeli perceptions—as well as in Palestinian perceptions and policy.

A second theological inference emerges from considering why the divine voice of Yahweh was required as part of Israel's narrated history on this matter. Why, for instance, is Yahweh the one portrayed as commanding the killing, even genocidal killing on the local level? The answer relates first of all to the question of why Yahweh was commanding the clearances to begin with. In Deuteronomy 20:18 the *why* comes to the surface. If you do not completely destroy the Hittites, Amorites, Canaanites, Perizzites, Hivites, and Jebusites from the land, declares Yahweh, they will corrupt you with their detestable worship practices and you will fall into sin! Putting that concern in reverse makes the point clearly.

The conquest narratives also respond to the later questions in the sixth to the tenth centuries B.C.E.: *"Why do we still have corrupting pagan influences in the land, despite a perfect God bringing us faithfully into it?"* The answer according to the historians is *not* that it is Yahweh's fault. They might have put it this way: "Look, Yahweh tried to warn Israel to be devout and thorough so that the land could be cleared once and for all, but Israel failed to live up to her end of the bargain. When she did so faithfully and effectively, things went fine, and the land was cleared. However, due to several kinds of failure, the clearances were ineffective, and that is why we have the temptations and the troubles that we do in our lands today!" In that sense, Yahweh's commands to clear the land thoroughly explain the failed panacea, which explains, in turn, the interreligious tensions and violence suffered by Israel over the next six centuries until these traditions were finalized.

Can the God of Jesus and the God of the Conquest Be One and the Same?

Now we return to our original question: can the God of Jesus and the God of Israel's conquest ever be considered one and the same? The teachings of Jesus, in the name of the God of Israel, seem clear on the matter. We are commanded to love our neighbors, and even to love our enemies. This is not a program, however, of doormat passivity; rather, it represents a radically subversive goal of challenging the domination systems of the world, which tend to be bolstered by the myth of redemptive violence. Jesus challenges that myth with the proclamation of the domination-free order of God, using Wink's language, and he invites humanity to attend and respond to the active leadership of God in the world.

These views, however, would not have been foreign to the ancient Israelites entirely. Indeed, six out of the Ten Commandments deal with horizontal concerns, the love of neighbor. Hospitality is required especially for the alien in the camp, as illustrated by Lot's hospitality to the angelic strangers (Gen. 19) and the tragic story of the Levite and his concubine (Judg. 19). We even see people using nonviolent alternatives to conflict resolution here and there in Hebrew Scripture, and in those ways, Jesus reflects more continuity with the God of the Old Testament than some scholars and religious leaders have thought. Bishop Oxnam's claim that the God of the Old Testament is a big bully and is in no sense the God of love and peace that we see in the face of Jesus is a trivial and trivializing comment. Even the deliverance of Israel into the land can be seen as a means to the end of Yahweh's blessing the earth through the seed of Abram

(Gen. 12:1–3), and in that sense, Jesus was also seeking to further the same.

The preceding analysis also raises the question sharply as to whether the God of the Hebrews *ever* actually strove for the death of Israel's neighbors, who were also created in the divine image. This question may be impossible to answer finally, but three factors must give us pause before claiming to *know* that he did: first, discerning the divine voice is always a challenging endeavor, and we might simply keep in mind the difference between a direct leading and declaration of God and human perceptions of such. Tribal loyalties, perceptions of God's special and exclusive calling of the Hebrew nation, needs for provision and deliverance in the land—all of these may have figured in perceiving or misperceiving the divine voice.

Second, the instruction of God to clear the land of its inhabitants must have served literary and socioreligious, as well as aggressive political, functions along the way, as the tradition matured and was preserved. Given Israel's needs for protection and sustenance, it is perfectly understandable but hardly justifiable that Israel would have cast God's provision and protection in ways commensurate with the prime figure of strength in their culture, the warrior-lord figure. Reducing the eternal God to such a construct, however, is simply not fitting. Finally, the presentation of Yahweh as commanding genocide in the Hebrew conquest narratives served the function of setting the stage for explaining why the conquest was an incomplete one. As a means of answering the existential and irritating questions of their interreligious setting, the conquest historians may also be explaining whose fault it was that there were still pagan inhabitants in the land. "It is not God's fault," they might have claimed. "God commanded a thorough cleansing, but it was Israel's lack of faith and faithfulness that contributed to the ambiguous situation we face now, centuries later!" None of the post-exilic editors seems to have tumbled to the notion or had the temerity to suggest that those Israelites who, in the end, moved for accommodation and integration were more "on the side of the angels," so to speak, than a monster killer-god.

This being the case, the real God of the Old Testament might not be so far from the God of the New. In both cases, God's love for his children is evident, and God's provision is sure. In both parts of the Bible, narrators of the past are trying to deal with the meaning of emerging situations, bringing the great events in the past into the light of the present day. However, can the God of the Israelites be construed as the same God represented by Jesus? Indeed, human perceptions of God grow over time, and God may grow with them. On the other hand, if we recognize the anthropomorphic projections involved in the narrative traditions, God's consistent and loving character comes through in both of these disparate parts of the Bible. If the presentation of God can be taken to be addressing issues faced by the emerging community of faith at the time, these two renderings of God might not be so far apart as some might have thought.

In the end, the way one looks at these things and the manner in which one interprets these matters depends completely upon one's theology of sacred scripture. Most of the problems in religion and social ethics in the last five thousand years in the Western World result directly from an inadequate theology or philosophy of sacred scripture in which the human cultural-historical matrix that carries "the voice of God" for us is not adequately distinguished, within each of our faith traditions, from the word of truth that the matrix carries for our benefit. To read the Hebrew Bible, the New Testament, or the Qur'an correctly, as J. Harold Ellens (cf. introduction to volume 1) has constantly claimed for three decades, requires the ability to distinguish the voices of humans in sacred scripture from the voice of God. To use Ellens' language, it requires the ability to separate the garbage from the gospel; the cultural metaphors from the divine meanings.

Notes

1. See my fuller treatment of the issue in "Jesus and Peace," *The Church's Peace Witness*, Marlin E. Miller and Barbara Nelson Gingerich, eds. (Grand Rapids: Eerdmans, 1994), 105–130, especially 105–109.

2. See "Jesus and Peace," 109–120.

3. Walter Wink, *Engaging the Powers* (Minneapolis: Fortress, 1992).

4. See Millard Lind, *Yahweh Is a Warrior: The Theology of Warfare in Ancient Israel* (Scottsdale: Herald Press, 1980); Peter Craigie, *The Problem of War in the Old Testament* (Grand Rapids: Eerdmans, 1978); Lois Barrett, *The Way God Fights: War and Peace in the Old Testament* (Scottsdale: Herald Press, 1987); Patrick Miller, *The Divine Warrior in Early Israel* (Cambridge: Harvard University Press, 1973); Susan Niditch, *War in the Hebrew Bible: A Study in the Ethics of Violence* (New York: Oxford, 1993); Gerhard von Rad, *Holy War in Ancient Israel*, Marva Dawn, trans. and ed. (Grand Rapids: Eerdmans, 1991); Ben Ollenburger, "Peace and God's Action Against Chaos in the Old Testament," in *The Church's Peace Witness*, Marlin Miller and Barbara Nelson Gingerich, eds. (Grand Rapids: Eerdmans, 1994), 70–88; and Dianne Bergant, "Yahweh: A Warrior God?" in *The Church's Peace Witness*, Marlin Miller and Barbara Nelson Gingerich, eds. (Grand Rapids:

Eerdmans, 1994), 89–103. There are even references to the "Book of Yahweh's Wars" upon which latter narratives are constructed (Num. 21:14).

5. See von Rad, 44–45; Exodus 14:4, 14, 18; Deuteronomy 1:30; Joshua 10:14, 42; 11:6; 23:10; Judges 20:35; 1 Samuel 14:23.

6. See von Rad, 42–44; Joshua 2:24; 6:2, 16; 8:1, 18; 10:8, 19; Judges 3:28; 4:14; 7:9, 15; 18:10; 20:28; 1 Samuel 14:12; 17:46; 23:4; 24:4; 26:8; 1 Kings 20:28.

7. See von Rad, 46–49; Exodus 15:14–16; 23:27–28; Deuteronomy 2:25; 11:25; Joshua 2:9, 24; 5:1; 10:2; 11:20; 24:12; 1 Samuel 4:7–8. As a result, the enemy is thrown into what von Rad calls "divine terror"—Exodus 23:27; Deuteronomy 7:23; Joshua 10:10–11; 24:7; Judges 4:15; 7:22; 1 Samuel 5:11; 7:10; 14:15, 20.

8. See von Rad, 45; Exodus 14:13–14; Deuteronomy 20:3; Joshua 8:1, 10:8, 25; 11:6; Judges 7:3; 1 Samuel 23:16–17; 30:6; 2 Samuel 10:12.

9. See von Rad's chapter on "Holy War in the Post-Solomonic Novella," 74–93.

10. See von Rad, 47; Leviticus 26:36; Joshua 7:5; 1 Samuel 17:11; 28:5.

CHAPTER 4

Beyond Just War and Pacifism: Jesus' Nonviolent Way

Walter Wink

A four-volume recital of the destructive power of religion could give the impression that religion is irremediably evil, unless we at least acknowledge that it also can be one of the best means for overcoming evil. No doubt religion bears a heavy burden of blame for the woes of humanity. But religion is also the cure for many of these woes. A perfect example of the ambivalence of religion is Jesus' message about nonviolent resistance to evil. "You have heard that it was said, 'An eye for an eye and a tooth for a tooth,' but I say to you, 'Do not resist one who is evil; but if anyone strikes you on the right cheek, turn to him the other also; and if anyone would sue you and take your coat, let him have your cloak as well; and if anyone forces you to go one mile, go with him two miles. Give to him who begs from you, and do not refuse him who would borrow from you'" (Matt. 5:38–42). In this sermon we can see, simultaneously, a traditional understanding that utterly falsifies Jesus' meaning, and a buried interpretation that gives fresh meaning to this, one of the most revolutionary teachings Jesus ever spoke.

Contrary to that traditional understanding, the new reality Jesus proclaimed was nonviolent. That much is clear, from not just the Sermon on the Mount, but also his entire life and teaching and, above all, the way he faced his death. His was not merely a tactical or pragmatic nonviolence seized upon because nothing else would have worked against the Roman empire's near monopoly on violence.

Rather, he saw nonviolence as a direct corollary of the nature of God and of the new reality emerging in the world from God. In a verse quoted more than any other from the New Testament during the Church's first four centuries, Jesus taught that God loves everyone and values all, even those who make themselves God's enemies. We are therefore to do likewise (Matt. 5:45; cf. Luke 6:35). The Reign of God, the peaceable Kingdom, is, despite the monarchical terms, an order in which the inequity, violence, and male supremacy character- istic of dominator societies are superseded. Thus nonviolence is not just a means to the Kingdom of God; it is a quality of the Kingdom itself. Those who live nonviolently are already manifesting the trans- formed reality of the divine order now, even under the conditions of what I call the Domination System.

The idea of nonviolent resistance was not new. The Hebrew mid- wives; the Greek tragedians; and Jainism, Buddhism, Hinduism, Lao- Tzu, and Judaism were all, to various degrees, conversant with nonviolence as a way of life and, in some cases, even as a tactic of social change. What was new was the early Church's inference from Jesus' teaching that nonviolence is the *only* way; that war itself must be renounced. The idea of peace and the more general rejection of violence can be found before Christianity and in other cultures, says Peter Brock, but nowhere else do we find practical antimilitarism leading to the refusal of military service.[1]

When, beginning with the emperor Constantine, the Christian Church began receiving preferential treatment by the empire that it had once so steadfastly opposed, war, which had once seemed so evil, now appeared to many to be a necessity for preserving and propagat- ing the gospel.

Christianity's weaponless victory over the Roman empire eventu- ated in the weaponless victory of the empire over the gospel. No defeat is so well disguised as victory! In the year 303 C.E., Diocletian forbade any member of the Roman army to be a Christian. By the year 416, no one could be a member of the Roman army *unless* he was a Christian.

It fell to Augustine (d. 430 C.E.) to make the accommodation of Christianity to its new status as a privileged religion in support of the state. Augustine believed, on the basis of Matthew 5:38–41, that Christians had no right to defend themselves from violence. But he identified a problem that no earlier theologian had faced: what Augustine regarded as the loving obligation to use violence if neces- sary to defend the innocent against evil. Drawing on Stoic just war principles, he articulated the position that was to dominate church teaching from that time right up to the present.

Ever since, Christians on the left and on the right, in the East and in the West, have found it exceedingly easy to declare as "just" and divinely ordained any wars their governments desired to wage for purely national interests. As a consequence, the world regards Christians as among the most warlike factions on the face of the earth. Little wonder; two-thirds of the people killed in the last 500 years died at the hands of fellow Christians in Europe,[2] to say nothing of those whom Christians killed in the course of colonizing the rest of the world.

As Gandhi once quipped, "The only people on earth who do not see Christ and His teachings as nonviolent are Christians."[3] The time has come to look again to the rock from which we were hewn. The key text remains Jesus' statement about resisting evil (Matt. 5:38–42 NRSV; see also Luke 6:29–30).[4]

Christians have, on the whole, simply ignored this teaching. It has seemed impractical, masochistic, suicidal, an invitation to bullies and spouse batterers to wipe up the floor with their supine Christian victims. Some who have tried to follow Jesus' words have understood this teaching to mean nonresistance: let the oppressor perpetrate evil unopposed. Even scholars have swallowed the eat-humble-pie reading of this text: "It is better to surrender everything and go through life naked than to insist on one's legal rights," to cite only one of scores of these commentators from Augustine right up to the present.[5] Interpreted thus, the passage has become the basis for systematic training in cowardice, as successive generations of Christians are taught to acquiesce in evil.

Cowardice is scarcely a term one associates with Jesus. Either he failed to make himself clear, or we have misunderstood him. There is plenty of cause to believe the latter. Jesus is not forbidding self-defense here, only the use of violence. Nor is he legitimating the abandonment of nonviolence in order to defend the neighbor. He is rather showing us a way that can be used to intervene on behalf of justice for our neighbors, nonviolently.

The classical interpretation of Matthew 5:38–42 and Luke 6:29–30 suggests two, and only two, possibilities for action in the face of evil: fight or flight. Either we resist evil, or we do not resist it. Jesus seemingly says that we are not to resist it; so, it would appear, he commands us to be docile, inert, compliant, to abandon all desire for justice, to allow the oppressor to walk all over us. "Turn the other cheek" is taken to enjoin becoming a doormat for Jesus, to be trampled without protest. "Give your undergarment as well" has encouraged people to go limp in the face of injustice and hand over the last thing they own. "Going the second mile" has been turned into a platitude meaning nothing more than "extend yourself." Rather than encourage the oppressed to counteract their oppressors, these revolutionary statements have been transformed into injunctions to collude in one's own despoiling.

That interpretation excluded a third alternative: active nonviolent resistance. The word translated "resist" is itself problematic; what translators have failed to note is how frequently *anthistemi* is used as a military term. Resistance implies "counteractive aggression," a response to hostilities initiated by someone else. Bible dictionaries and concordances generally define *anthistemi* as to "*set against* esp. in battle, *withstand.*" Ephesians 6:13 is exemplary of its military usage: "Therefore take the whole armor of God, that you may be able to withstand [*antistenai*, literally, to draw up battle ranks against the enemy] in the evil day, and having done all, to stand [*stenai*, literally, to close ranks and continue to fight]." The term is used in the *Septuagint (LXX)*, that is, the ancient Greek translation of the Hebrew Bible or Old Testament, primarily for armed resistance in military encounters (forty-four out of seventy-one times).[6] Josephus uses *anthistemi* for violent struggle fifteen out of seventeen times, Philo four out of ten. Jesus' answer is set against the backdrop of the burning question of forcible resistance to Rome. In that context, "resistance" could have only one meaning: lethal violence.[7]

Stasis, the noun form of *stenai*, means "a stand," in the military sense of facing off against an enemy. By extension it came to mean a "party formed for seditious purposes; sedition, revolt." The NRSV translates *stasis* in Mark 15:7 as "insurrection" (so also Luke 23:19, 25), in Acts of the Apostles 19:40 as "rioting," and in Acts of the Apostles 23:10 as "violent dissension."[8]

In short, *antistenai* means more in Matthew 5:39a than simply to "stand against" or "resist." It means to resist *violently*, to revolt or rebel, to engage in an insurrection. Jesus is not encouraging submission to evil; that would run counter to everything he did and said. He is, rather, warning against responding to evil in kind, by letting the oppressor set the terms of our opposition. Perhaps most importantly, he cautions us against being made over into the very evil we oppose by adopting its methods and spirit. He is saying, in effect, "Do not mirror evil; do not become the very thing you hate."

In the three examples that follow in Matthew, Jesus illustrates what he means.

Turn the Other Cheek

"If anyone strikes you on the right cheek, turn the other also." Why the *right* cheek? A blow by the right fist in that right-handed world would land on the *left* cheek of the opponent. An open-handed slap would also strike the left cheek. To hit the right cheek with a fist would require using the left hand, but in that society the left hand was used only for unclean tasks. Even to gesture with the left hand at Qumran carried the penalty of ten days' penance.[9] The only way one could naturally strike the right cheek with the right hand would be with the back of the hand. We are dealing here with insult, not a fist-fight. The intention is clearly not to injure but to humiliate, to put someone in his or her place. One normally did not strike a peer thus, and if one did the fine was exorbitant. The Mishnaic tractate *Baba Qamma* specifies the various fines for striking an equal: for slugging with a fist, 4 *zuz* (a *zuz* was a day's wage); for slapping, 200 *zuz*; but "if [he struck him] with the back of his hand he must pay him 400 *zuz*." But damages for indignity were not paid to slaves who were struck (8:1–7).

A backhand slap was the usual way of admonishing inferiors. Masters backhanded slaves; husbands, wives; parents, children; men, women; Romans, Jews. *We have here a set of unequal relations, in each of which retaliation would be suicidal.* The only normal response would be cowering submission.

Part of the confusion surrounding these sayings arises from the failure to ask who Jesus' audience was. In all three of the examples in Matthew 5:39b-41, Jesus' listeners are not those who strike, initiate lawsuits, or impose forced labor, but their victims ("If anyone strikes *you* . . . wants to sue *you* . . . forces *you* to go one mile . . ."). There are among his hearers people who were subjected to these very indignities, forced to stifle outrage at their dehumanizing treatment by the hierarchical system of caste and class, race and gender, age and status, and as a result of imperial occupation.

Why then does he counsel these already humiliated people to turn the other cheek? Because this action robs the oppressor of the power to humiliate. The person who turns the other cheek is saying, in effect, "Try again. Your first blow failed to achieve its intended effect. I deny you the power to humiliate me. I am a human

Mahatma Gandhi, 1946. Library of Congress.

being just like you. Your status does not alter that fact. You cannot demean me."

Such a response would create enormous difficulties for the striker. Purely logistically, how would he hit the other cheek now turned to him? He cannot backhand it with his right hand. One need only try this to see the problem.[10] If he hits with a fist, he makes the other his equal, acknowledging him as a peer; but the point of the back of the hand is to reinforce institutionalized inequality. Even if the superior orders the person flogged for such "cheeky" behavior (this is certainly no way to *avoid* conflict!), the point has been irrevocably made. He has been given notice that this underling is in fact a human being. In that world of honor and shaming, the oppressor has been rendered impotent to instill shame in a subordinate.[11] He has been stripped of his power to dehumanize the other. As Gandhi taught, "The first principle of nonviolent action is that of noncooperation with everything humiliating."[12]

Give the Undergarment

The second example Jesus gives is set in a court of law. Someone is being sued for his outer garment. Who would do that, and under what circumstances? The Hebrew Scriptures provide the clues.

> When you make your neighbor a loan of any sort, you shall not go into his house to fetch his pledge. You shall stand outside, and the man to whom you make the loan shall bring the pledge out to you. *And if he is a poor man,* you shall not sleep in his pledge; when the sun goes down, you shall restore to him the pledge that he may sleep in his cloak (*himatio*) and bless you. . . . You shall not . . . take a widow's garment (*himation*) in pledge. (Deut. 24:10–13, 17; see also Exod. 22:25–27; Amos 2:7–8; Ezek. 18:5–9)

Only the poorest of the poor would have nothing but a garment to give as collateral for a loan. Jewish law strictly required its return every evening at sunset.[13]

Matthew and Luke disagree whether it is the outer garment (Luke) or the undergarment (Matthew) that is being seized. But the Jewish practice of giving the outer garment as a pledge, since it alone would be useful as a blanket for sleeping, makes it clear that Luke's order is correct, even though he does not preserve the legal setting. In all Greek usage, according to Liddell-Scott, *himation* is "always an outer garment . . . worn above the *chiton,*" whereas the *chiton* is a "garment worn next to the skin."[14] Consistent with this usage, the Greek translation of the Old Testament (*LXX*) reads *himation* in the passages just cited. S. Safrai and M. Stern describe normal Jewish dress: an outer garment or cloak of wool and an undergarment or tunic of linen.[15] To avoid confusion I will simply refer to the "outer garment" and the "undergarment."

The situation Jesus speaks to is all too familiar to his hearers: the debtor has sunk ever deeper into poverty, the debt cannot be repaid, and his creditor has summoned him to court (*krithenai*) to exact repayment by legal means.

Indebtedness was endemic in first-century Palestine. Jesus' parables are full of debtors struggling to salvage their lives. Heavy debt was not, however, a natural calamity that had overtaken the incompetent. It was the direct consequence of Roman imperial policy. Emperors had taxed the wealthy so stringently to fund their wars that the rich began seeking nonliquid investments to secure their wealth. Land was best, but it was ancestrally owned and passed down over generations, and no peasant would voluntarily relinquish it. Exorbitant interest, however, could be used to drive landowners ever deeper into debt. Debt, coupled with the high taxation required by Herod Antipas to pay Rome tribute, created the economic leverage to pry Galilean peasants loose from their land. By the time of Jesus we see this process already far advanced: large estates owned by absentee landlords, managed by stewards, and worked by tenant farmers, day laborers, and slaves. It is no accident that the first act of the Jewish revolutionaries in 66 C.E. was to burn the Temple treasury, where the record of debts was kept.[16]

It is to this situation that Jesus speaks. His hearers are the poor ("if any one would sue *you*"). They share a rankling hatred for a system that subjects them to humiliation by stripping them of their lands, their goods, finally even their outer garments.

Why then does Jesus counsel them to give over their undergarments as well? This would mean stripping off all their clothing and marching out of court stark naked! Imagine the guffaws this saying must have evoked. There stands the creditor, covered with shame, the poor debtor's outer garment in the one hand, his undergarment in the other. The tables have suddenly been turned on the creditor. The debtor had no hope of winning the case; the law was entirely in the creditor's favor; but the poor man has transcended this attempt to humiliate him. He has risen above shame. At the same time he has registered a stunning protest against the system that created his debt. He has said in effect, "You want my robe? Here, take everything! Now you've got all I have except my body. Is that what you'll take next?"

Nakedness was taboo in Judaism, and shame fell less on the naked party than on the person viewing or causing the nakedness (Gen. 9:20–27).[17] By stripping, the debtor has brought the creditor under the same prohibition that led to the curse of Canaan. Much as Isaiah had "walked naked and barefoot for three years" as a prophetic sign (Isa. 20:1–6), so the debtor parades his nakedness in prophetic protest against a system that has deliberately rendered him destitute. Imagine him leaving the court naked: his friends and neighbors, aghast, inquire what happened. He explains. They join his growing procession, which now resembles a victory parade. The entire system by which debtors are oppressed has been publicly unmasked. The creditor is revealed to be not a legitimate moneylender but a party to the reduction of an entire social class to landlessness, destitution, and abasement. This unmasking is not simply punitive, therefore; it offers the creditor a chance to see, perhaps for the first time in his life, what his practices cause, and to repent.

The Powers That Be literally stand on their dignity. Nothing depotentiates them faster than deft lampooning.[18] By refusing to be awed by their power, the powerless are emboldened to seize the initiative, even where structural change is not immediately possible. This message, far from being a counsel to perfection unattainable in this life, is a practical strategy for empowering the oppressed, and it is being lived out all over the world today by powerless people ready to take their history into their own hands.

Jesus provides here a hint of how to take on the entire system by unmasking its essential cruelty and burlesquing its pretensions to justice. Here is a poor man who will no longer be treated as a sponge to be squeezed dry by the rich. He accepts the laws as they stand, pushes them to absurdity, and reveals them for what they have become. He strips naked, walks out before his fellows, and leaves this creditor, and the whole economic edifice that he represents, stark naked.

Go the Second Mile

Jesus' third example, the one about going the second mile, is drawn from the relatively enlightened practice of limiting to a single mile the amount of forced or impressed labor (*angareia*) that Roman soldiers could levy on subject peoples.[19] The term *angareia* is probably Persian and became a loanword in Aramaic, Greek, and Latin. Josephus mentions it in reference to the Seleucid ruler, Demetrius, who, in order to enlist Jewish support for his bid to be king, promised, among other things, that "the Jews' beasts of burden shall not be requisitioned (*angareuesthai*) for our army" (*Ant.* 13.52). We are more familiar with its use in the Passion Narrative, where the soldiers "compel" (*angareuousin*) Simon of Cyrene to carry Jesus' cross (Mark 15:21//Matt. 27:32). Such forced service was a constant feature in Palestine from Persian to late Roman times, and whoever was found on the street could be compelled into service.[20] Most cases of impressment involved the need of the postal service for animals and the need of soldiers for civilians to help carry their packs. The situation in Matthew is clearly the latter. It is a matter of requisitioning not animals but people themselves.

This forced labor was a source of bitter resentment by all Roman subjects. "*Angareia* is like death," complains one source.[21] The sheer frequency, even into the late empire, of legislation proscribing the misuse of the *angareia* shows how regularly the practice was used and its regulations violated. An inscription of 49 C.E. from Egypt orders that Roman "soldiers of any degree when passing through the several districts are not to make any requisitions or to employ forced transport (*angareia*) unless they have the prefect's written authority,"[22] a prescription clearly made necessary by soldiers abusing their privileges. Another decree from Egypt from 133–137 C.E. documents this abuse: "Many soldiers without written requisition are traveling about in the country, demanding ships, beasts of burden, and men, beyond anything authorized, sometimes seizing things by force . . . to the point of *showing abuse and threats to private citizens*, the result is that the military is associated with arrogance and injustice."[23] To minimize resentment in the conquered lands, at least some effort was made by Rome to punish violators of the laws regarding impressment.

The Theodosian Code (438 C.E.) devotes an entire section to *angareia*.[24] Among its ordinances are these:

1. If any person while making a journey should consider that he may abstract an ox that is not assigned to the public post but dedicated to the plow, he shall be *arrested with due force* by the rural police . . . and he shall be haled before the judge [normally the governor]. (8.5.1, 315 C.E.)

By this interdict We forbid that any person should deem that they may request packanimals and supplementary posthorses. But if any person should rashly act so presumptuously, *he shall be punished very severely.* (8.5.6, 354 C.E., ital. added)

2. When any *legion* is proceeding to its destination, it shall not hereafter attempt to appropriate more than two posthorses (*angariae*), and only for the sake of any who are sick. (8.5.11, 360 C.E.)

Late as these regulations are, they reflect a situation that had changed little since the time of the Persians. Armies had to be moved through countries with dispatch. Some legionnaires bought their own slaves to help carry their packs of 60 to 85 pounds (not including weapons).[25] The majority of the rank and file, however, had to depend on impressed civilians. There are vivid accounts of whole villages fleeing to avoid being forced to carry soldiers' baggage, and of richer towns prepared to pay large sums to escape having Roman soldiers billeted on them for the winter.[26]

With few exceptions, the commanding general of a legion personally administered justice in serious cases, and all other cases were left to the disciplinary control of his subordinates. Centurions had almost limitless authority in dealing with routine cases of discipline. This accounts for the curious fact that there is very little codified military law, and what we have is of late recording. Roman military historians are agreed, however, that military law changed very little in its essential character throughout the imperial period.[27] No account survives to us today of the penalties to be meted out to soldiers for forcing a civilian to carry his pack more than the permitted mile, but there are at least hints. "If in winter quarters, in camp, *or on the march*, either an officer or a soldier does injury to a civilian, and does not fully repair the same, he shall pay the damage twofold."[28] This is about as mild a penalty as one can find, however. Josephus' comment is surely exaggerated, even if it states the popular impression: Roman military forces "have laws which punish with death not merely desertion of the ranks, but even a slight neglect of duty" (*J.W.* 3.102–8). Between these extremes there was deprivation of pay, a ration of barley instead of wheat, reduction in rank, dishonorable discharge, being forced to camp outside the fortifications, or to stand all day before the general's tent holding a clod in one's hands, or to stand barefoot in public places. The most frequent punishment by far was flogging.[29]

The frequency with which decrees were issued to curb misuse of the *angareia* indicates how lax discipline on this point was. Perhaps the soldier might receive only a rebuke. But the point is that the soldier *does not know what will happen.*

It is in this context of Roman military occupation that Jesus speaks.[30] He does not counsel revolt. One does not "befriend" the soldier, draw him aside, and drive a knife into his ribs. Jesus was surely aware of the futility of armed insurrection against Roman imperial might; he certainly did nothing to encourage those whose hatred of Rome was near to flaming into violence.

But why carry his pack a second mile? Is this not to rebound to the opposite extreme of aiding and abetting the enemy?[31] Not at all. The question here, as in the two previous instances, is how the oppressed can recover the initiative and assert their human dignity in a situation that cannot for the time being be changed. The rules are Caesar's, but how one responds to the rules is God's, and Caesar has no power over that.

Imagine then the soldier's surprise when, at the next mile marker, he reluctantly reaches to assume his pack, and the civilian says, "Oh no, let me carry it another mile." Why would he want to do that? What is he up to? Normally, soldiers have to coerce people to carry their packs, but this Jew does so cheerfully, and *will not stop!* Is this a provocation? Is he insulting the legionnaire's strength? Being kind? Trying to get him disciplined for seeming to violate the rules of impressment? Will this civilian file a complaint? Create trouble?

From a situation of servile impressment, the oppressed have once more seized the initiative. They have taken back the power of choice. The soldier is thrown off balance by being deprived of the pre-dictability of his victim's response. He has never dealt with such a problem before. Now he has been forced into making a decision for which nothing in his previous experience has prepared him. If he has enjoyed feeling superior to the vanquished, he will not enjoy it today. Imagine the situation of a Roman infantryman pleading with a Jew to give back his pack! The humor of this scene may have escaped us, but it could scarcely have been lost on Jesus' hearers, who must have been regaled at the prospect of thus discomfiting their oppressors.

Jesus does not encourage Jews to walk a second mile in order to build up merit in heaven, or to exercise a supererogatory piety, or to kill the soldier with kindness. He is helping an oppressed people find a way to protest and neutralize an onerous practice despised through-out the empire. He is not giving a nonpolitical message of spiritual world transcendence. He is formulating a worldly spirituality in which the people at the bottom of society or under the thumb of imperial power learn to recover their humanity. Instead of being impressed into service against his will by the Roman soldier, and thus in a subservient posture with regard to the soldier's power, the Jew is, instead, in the position of the one giving charity to the soldier out of his goodwill. That puts the Jew into a position of power and con-descension toward the soldier, who is now a recipient of charity, as are the poor, powerless, and indigent.

One could easily misuse Jesus' advice vindictively; that is why it must not be separated from the command to love enemies, integrally connected with it in both Matthew and Luke, but love is not averse to taking the law and using its oppressive momentum to throw the sol-dier into a region of uncertainty and anxiety where he has never been before. Of course, the line is a fine one here between genuine charity and passive-aggressive demeanment of the soldier by the Jew who is carrying his pack a second mile.

The Consequences

Such tactics can seldom be repeated. One can imagine that within days after the incidents that Jesus sought to provoke, the Powers That Be would pass new laws: penalties for nakedness in court, flogging for carrying a pack more than a mile! One must be creative, improvising new tactics to keep the opponent off balance.

To those whose lifelong pattern has been to cringe before their masters, Jesus offers a way to liberate themselves from servile actions and a servile mentality. He asserts that they can do this *before* there is a revolution. There is no need to wait until Rome has been defeated, or peasants are landed and slaves freed. They can begin to behave with dignity and recovered humanity *now*, even under the unchanged conditions of the old order. Jesus' sense of divine immediacy has social implications. The reign of God is already breaking into the world, and it comes not as an imposition from on high, but as the leaven slowly causing the dough to rise (Matt. 13:33//Luke 13:20–21). Jesus' teaching on nonviolence is thus of a piece with his proclamation of the dawning of the reign of God.

In the conditions of first-century Palestine, a political revolution against the Romans could only be catastrophic, as the events of 66–73 C.E. would prove. Jesus does not propose armed revolution, but he does lay the foundations for a social revolution, as Richard A. Horsley has pointed out. A social revolution becomes political when it reaches a critical threshold of acceptance; this in fact did happen to the Roman empire as the Christian Church overcame it from below.[32]

Nor were peasants and slaves in a position to transform the economic system by frontal assault, but they could begin to act from an already recovered dignity and freedom, and the ultimate consequences of such acts could only be revolutionary. To that end, Jesus spoke repeatedly of a voluntary remission of debts.[33]

It is entirely appropriate, then, that the saying on debts in Matthew 5:42//Luke 6:30//Gospel of Thomas 95 has been added to this saying block. Jesus counsels his hearers not just to practice alms and to lend money, even to bad risks, but to lend without expecting interest or even the return of the principal. Such radical egalitarian sharing would be necessary to rescue impoverished Palestinian peasants from their plight; one need not posit an imminent end of history as the cause for such astonishing generosity. Yet none of this is new; Jesus is merely issuing a prophetic summons to Israel to observe the commandments pertaining to the sabbatical year enshrined in Torah, adapted to a new situation.[34]

Such radical sharing would be necessary to restore true community. For the risky defiance of the Powers that Jesus advocates would inevitably issue in punitive economic sanctions and physical punishment against individuals. They would need economic support; Matthew's "Give to everyone who *asks* (*aitounti*, not necessarily, *begs*) of you" may simply refer to this need for mutual sustenance. Staggering interest and taxes isolated peasants, who went under one by one. This was a standard tactic of imperial "divide and rule" strategy.[35]

Jesus' solution was neither utopian nor apocalyptic. It was simple realism. Nothing less could halt or reverse the economic decline of Jewish peasants than a complete suspension of usury and debt and a restoration of economic equality through outright grants, a pattern actually implemented in the earliest Christian community, according to the Acts of the Apostles.[36] Jesus' alternative to both fight and flight can be graphically represented by a chart:

Jesus' Third Way

Seize the moral initiative.

Find a creative alternative to violence.

Assert your own humanity and dignity as a person.

Meet force with ridicule or humor.

Break the cycle of humiliation.

Refuse to submit or to accept the inferior position.

Expose the injustice of the system.

Take control of the power dynamic.

Shame the oppressor into repentance.

Stand your ground.

Make the Powers make decisions for which they are not prepared.

Recognize your own power.

Be willing to suffer rather than retaliate.

Force the oppressor to see you in a new light.

Deprive the oppressor of a situation where a show of force is effective.

Be willing to undergo the penalty of breaking unjust laws.

Discard fear of the old order and its rules.

Seek the oppressor's transformation.

Flight	Fight
Submission	Armed revolt
Passivity	Violent rebellion
Withdrawal	Direct retaliation
Surrender	Revenge

Gandhi insisted that no one join him who was not willing to take up arms to fight for independence. They could not freely renounce what they had not entertained. One cannot pass directly from "Flight" to "Jesus' Third Way." One needs to pass through the "Fight" stage, if only to discover one's own inner strength and capacity for violence. We need to learn to love justice and truth enough to die for them, by violence if nothing else.[37]

Jesus, in short, abhors both passivity and violence. He articulates, out of the history of his own people's struggles, a way by which evil can be opposed without being mirrored, the oppressor resisted without being emulated, and the enemy neutralized without being destroyed. Those who have lived by Jesus' words, Leo Tolstoy, Mohandas K. Gandhi, Martin Luther King Jr., Dorothy Day, César Chavez, Mother Theresa, Adolfo Pérez Esquivel, point us to a new way of confronting evil, the potential of which, for personal and social transformation, we are only beginning to grasp today.[38]

Beyond Just War and Pacifism

Just war theory was founded in part on a misinterpretation of "Resist not evil" (Matt. 5:39), which Augustine regarded as an absolute command to *nonresistance* of evil. No Christian, he argued, can take up arms in self-defense, therefore, but must submit passively even to death. Nor can Christians defend themselves against injustice, but must willingly collaborate in their own ruin. But what, asked Augustine, if my neighbors are being thus treated? Then the love commandment requires me to take up arms if necessary to defend them.[39]

Jesus did not teach nonresistance. Rather, he disavowed *violent* resistance in favor of *nonviolent* resistance. Of course Christians must resist evil! No decent human being could conceivably stand by and watch innocents suffer without trying to do, or at least wishing to do, something to save them. The question is simply one of means. Likewise Christians are not forbidden by Jesus to engage in self-defense, but they are to do so nonviolently. Jesus did not teach supine passivity in the face of evil. That was precisely what he was attempting to overcome!

Pacifism, in its Christian forms, was often based on the same misinterpretation of Jesus' teaching in Matthew 5:38–42. It too understood Jesus to be commanding nonresistance. Consequently, some pacifists refuse to engage in nonviolent direct action or civil disobedience, on the grounds that such actions are coercive. Nonresistance, they believe, only licenses passive resistance. Hence the confusion between "pacifism" and "passivism" has not been completely unfounded.

Jesus' third way *is* coercive, insofar as it forces oppressors to make choices they would rather not make; but it is *nonlethal*, the great advantage of which is that, if we have chosen a mistaken course, our opponents are still alive to benefit from our apologies. The same exegesis that undermines the scriptural ground for traditional just war theory also erodes the foundation of nonresistant pacifism. Jesus' teaching carries us beyond just war *and* beyond pacifism, to a militant nonviolence that actualizes already in the present the ethos of God's domination-free future.

Out of the heart of the prophetic tradition, Jesus engaged the Domination System in both its outer and spiritual manifestations. His teaching on nonviolence forms the charter for a way of being in the world that breaks the spiral of violence. Jesus here reveals a way to fight evil with all our power without being transformed into the very evil we fight. It is a way, the only way possible, of not becoming what we hate. "Do not counter evil in kind." This insight is the distilled essence, stated with sublime simplicity, of the meaning of the cross. It is time the church stops limping between just war theory and nonresistant pacifism and follows Jesus on his nonviolent way.

Notes

1. Peter Brock, *The Roots of War Resistance: Pacifism from the Early Church to Tolstoy* (Nyack: Fellowship of Reconciliation, 1981), 9. Brock finds no known instance of conscientious refusal to participate in war prior to the Christian era. Even as late as the nineteenth century, he says, actual noncooperation with war was confined solely to those within the Christian tradition.

2. Ruth Leger Sivard, *World Military and Social Expenditures 1991* (Washington: World Priorities), 20.

3. Dale W. Brown, *Biblical Pacifism* (Elgin: Brethren Press, 1986), ix.

4. The core of Matthew's logion is 5:39b–42, though verse 42 may not belong to the original cluster. In verses 39b–41, the focus is first on what an oppressor does and then on what the hearers can do back; in 42, the focus shifts to the hearers and what they should do when another would beg or borrow. The more original version of verse 42 is probably preserved in Luke 6:35, "but lend, expecting nothing in return," and Gospel of Thomas 95, "If you have money do not lend at interest, but give . . . from whom you will not get them (back)." What in Matthew seems to be the bland encouragement of almsgiving and money lending appears in Luke and Thomas in a form as shocking as the injunctions that precede it in Matthew: lend without hope even of interest, lend even to those who cannot pay it back at all. "The follower of Jesus is not merely to lend without interest, but to *give*. If this be so, the very radicalism of the saying might suggest its authenticity" (R. McL. Wilson, *Studies in the Gospel of Thomas*, London: Mowbray, 1960, 128).

Luke's version (6:29–30) lacks Matthew's introduction, thesis statement, and the saying about forced labor. Luke has made a number of alterations to the Q version. He regards the striking as armed robbery and the response as submission: offer the other cheek to be pummeled. Consequently, he drops Matthew's "right" cheek, apparently not recognizing that "right" specifies the type of blow, and that it is intended not as attack or injury, but as humiliation. In the same way he regards the taking of the coat as theft; disciples are supposed to offer to the thieves their last remaining covering. In verse 30 he preserves Matthew's injunction to give to beggars, but in the second half of the saying he returns to the theme of brigandage: if anyone forcibly seizes your goods, do not seek to recover them, as if one could! Since he has read virtually the whole passage as a response to armed robbery, Luke simply has no use for the saying about how to respond to the enforced carrying of military baggage, so he drops that altogether. Luke correctly preserves the original sequence of the taking of garments, however: first the *himation* (outer garment, cloak), then the *chiton* (undergarment, shirt).

In the analysis that follows I treat Matthew's version of the core of the discourse (5:39b–42) as substantially original but regard Luke 6:35//Gospel of Thomas 95 as more authentic than Matthew's verse 42. I assume that Jesus is the source of these sayings, but only the plausibility of the interpretation will bear that out.

For a structural analysis of this logion, see John Dominic Crossan, "Divine Immediacy and Human Immediacy," in *Semeia* 44 (1988): 121–140. On the Q form of this unit, see John Kloppenborg, *The Formation of Q* (Philadelphia: Fortress, 1987), 173–180. On the meaning of the passage as a whole, see Gerhard Lohfink, "Der ekklesiale Sitz im Leben der

Aufforderung Jesu zum Gewaltverzicht (Matt. 5, 39b–42/Luke 6, 28f)," *Theologische Quartalschrift* 162 (1982): 236–253. He incorrectly identifies Jesus' audience as the disciples rather than inferring from the text itself who his audience was: those who are struck, sued, and impressed, the common people of the land. See also Jean Lambrecht, S.J., "The Sayings of Jesus on Nonviolence," *Louvain Studies* 12 (1987): 291–305, one of the better treatments of the text; W. Wolbert, "Bergpredigt und Gewaltlosigkeit," *Theologie und Philosophie* 57 (1982): 498–525; and Jürgen Sauer, "Traditionsgeschichtliche Erwägungen zu den synoptischen und paulinischen Aussagen über Feindesliebe und Wiedervergeltungs-verzicht," *Zeitschrift für die Neutestamentliche Wissenschaft* 76 (1985): 1–28.

5. Eduard Schweizer, *The Good News according to Matthew* (London: SPCK, 1976), 130.

6. Sjef van Tilborg grasps the proper sense of *antistenai:* "A manly word is used: if you fight do it as a soldier who stands fast in war" (*The Sermon on the Mount as an Ideological Intervention*, Assen: Van Gorcum, 1986, 71). The following are examples of the military use of *anthistemi:*

"power to *stand against* your enemies"—Leviticus 26:37

"he *attacked* you"—Deuteronomy 25:18

"to *stand before* your enemies—Joshua 7:13

"no one has been able to *withstand* you"—Joshua 23:9

The verbal stem *histemi* ("to stand") is compounded in a wide variety of terms denoting violent warfare, attack, revolt, rebellion, insurrection, and revolution:

aphistemi: "Judas the Galilean *rose up*"—Acts of the Apostles 5:37

ephistemi: "they *attacked* Jason's house"—Acts of the Apostles 17:5

epanistemi: "children will *rise up against* parents"—Mark 13:12// Matthew 10:21

katephistemi: "the Jews made a united attack"—Acts of the Apostles 18:12

exanistemi: "*rise up* from the ambush and seize"—Joshua 8:7

antikathistemi: "*resisted* to the point of shedding blood"—Hebrews 12:4

sunephistemi: "the crowd joined in attacking"—Acts of the Apostles 16:22.

The following compounds of *histemi* are sometimes used as technical terms for military formations and strategy: *kathistemi* (1 Macc. 10:32); *apokathistemi* (2 Macc. 15:20); *periistemi* (2 Macc. 14:9); *sunistemi* (Num. 16:3).

7. James W. Douglass, *The Non-Violent Cross* (New York: Macmillan, 1968), 193.

8. *Stasis* is also compounded in myriad ways frequently associated with war, violent uprisings, insurrection, sedition, rebellion, and revolution:

akatastasia: "wars and insurrections"—Luke 21:9

apostasia: "rebellion"—2 Thessalonians 2:3

dichostasia: "dissension"—Romans 16:17

stasiotes: "partisans"—Josephus, *Antiquities of the Jews* 13:403

stasiodes: "revolution and *sedition*"—Josephus, *Jewish Wars* 1:198

stasiopoios: "*sedition* and revolution—Josephus, *Life* 134

stasiopoieo: "dissension"—Josephus, *Antiquities of the Jews* 17:117

stasiazo: "they *rebelled*"—Judith 7:15

epistasis: "*onslaught* of evil"—2 Maccabees 6:3

apostasis: "rebellion"—Joshua 22:22

apostatis: "rebellious"—1 Esdras 2:18

apostatein: "revolt"—1 Maccabees 11:14

apostates: "rebel"—2 Maccabees 5:8

sustasiazo: "rebel"—Josephus, *Antiquities of the Jews* 17:285

sustasiastes: "fellow-rebels"—Josephus, *Antiquities of the Jews* 14:22

prostateuo: "a military 'protector' "—1 Maccabees 14:47.

See also *stasioteia; stasiarchia; stasiarchos; stasiastichos; stasiasis; stasiastes; stasiasmos; stasiopoiia; sustasis.*

9. 1 QS 7. "Right" must not be regarded as an insertion into Matthew's text, whatever other tendencies one may find in the tradition (against Crossan, "Divine Immediacy"). Otherwise the type of blow is not specified, and it is regarded as a slug, not a backhand (Luke). "Hit on the right cheek" here is effectively a technical term; it is not merely descriptive of anatomy. (So also Lapide, *The Sermon on the Mount*, 121, whose work independently confirms some of the conclusions of this analysis.)

Didache has generally been regarded as dependent on Matthew, Luke, or both, but Aaron Milavec has presented compelling evidence that it had access to the Jesus tradition independent of the Synoptics ("The Didache as Independent of the Gospels," paper presented at the Jesus Seminar, Sonoma, Calif., March 1–3, 1991). For this saying, in fact, *Didache* 1:4 preserves the best and quite possibly earliest version extant: (1) he specifies the right cheek, following Matthew; (2) yet he follows Luke (correctly) in the order "cloak/shirt"; and (3) he agrees with Matthew against Luke by including the saying about the second mile.

10. The TEV translation, excellent in this passage in other respects, misses when it reads, "Let him slap your left cheek too." But this is precisely what he *cannot* do, unless he abandons the backhand altogether.

11. "Landowners look for respect since what counts to them as well as to their tenants is honor; landowners need the 'status support' that only their tenants can give them" (Bruce J. Malina, "Patron and Client, The Analogy behind Synoptic Theology," *Forum* 4 [1988], 3).

12. Gandhi, in *Harijan*, March 10, 1946; cited by Mark Juergensmeyer, *Fighting with Gandhi* (San Francisco: Harper & Row, 1984), 43.

13. The rights of the poor debtor are thus protected by Scripture. On the other hand, the creditor is permitted to harass and shame the debtor by demanding the outer garment each morning. The Mekilta de R. Ishmael on Exodus 22:25–27 shows creditors intensifying their demand by taking a night garment by day and a day garment by night. See also T.B. Tem. 6a; T.B. Mes. 31b, 113ab, 114ab; T.B. San. 21a.

14. H. G. Liddell and R. Scott, *A Greek-English Lexicon* (Oxford: Clarendon Press, 1958), 829.

15. W. Safrai and M. Stern, *The Jewish People in the First Century* (Philadelphia: Fortress, 1987), I.2. 797–798; J. M. Myers, "Dress," *IDB* 1:869–71. See also Mekilta de R. Ishmael on Exodus 22:27, *"For that Is His Only Covering.* This refers to the cloak. *It Is the Garment for His Skin.* This refers to the shirt." Matthew is not the only evangelist who confuses these terms. Mark, for example, uses *chiton* for the high priest's mantle in 14:63 whereas Matthew, following *LXX* usage, has *himation.*

16. Josephus, *Jewish Wars* 2:427. See Martin Goodman, *The Ruling Class in Judaea* (Cambridge: Cambridge University Press, 1987), 55–58.

17. Augustine certainly understood Jesus to be speaking of nudity: "Whoever wishes to take away thy tunic, give over to him *whatever clothing thou hast"* (*Sermon on the Mount* I.19.60). The *Pseudo-Clementine Homily,* which in 15.5 cites Matthew 5:40, changes the word here for "undergarment" in order to avoid the suggestion that the person becomes naked. For, comments the *ANF* translator, A. Cleveland Coxe, the person who lost both cloak and tunic would be naked altogether; and "this, the writer may have imagined, Christ would not have commanded" (*ANF* 8.310). Another indication that Matthew 5:40 refers to nakedness is provided by Gospel of Thomas 21, which appears to be a gnosticizing development of Jesus' saying about stripping naked. When the owners of the field come to reclaim it, the children take off their clothes before the owners and "are naked in their presence," an excellent nonviolent tactic, here unfortunately distorted to mean stripping off the body after death in the presence of the evil Archons.

Nudity is abhorrent to the conventional because it violates the system of classification by which one can identify a person's place on the social map. Without clothes, the boundaries by which society is ordered and guarded are dissolved. Clothing signifies one's social location, gender, and status (Jerome H. Neyrey, "A Symbolic Approach to Mark 7," *Forum* 4, no. 3 [1988]: 72). Thus Jesus depicts the wounded person by the side of the road as naked, so that the priest and Levite have no claim laid on them by his social rank or status, but only his humanity (Luke 10:30). Therefore, to strip naked voluntarily before the creditor and magistrate, precisely in a context intended to shame the poor into repayment, is to defy the hierarchical system of classification in its entirety.

18. One of the immediate causes of the Jewish War of 66 C.E. was public ridicule of the Roman procurator Florus for his raid on the Temple treasury, under the pretext of paying tribute that was in arrears. "Some of the malcontents . . . carrying round a basket begged coppers for him as for an unfortunate destitute" (Jos., *J.W.* 2:295). Enraged, he demanded that the Jewish leaders hand over the mockers. Their refusal to do so led to bloodshed (296–308).

19. See B. H. Isaac and I. Roll, "A Milestone of A.D. 69 from Judaea: The Elder Trajan and Vespasian," *Journal of Roman Studies* 66 (1976): 15–19. There is, so far as I can tell, no surviving Roman law limiting *angareia* to one mile, but scholars have almost universally inferred from the wording of the text (correctly, I believe) that some such rule was in force.

20. M. Rostovtzeff, "Angariae," *Klio. Beitrage zur alten Geschichte* 6 (1906): 249-58. In one Aramaic version of the Book of Tobit, Tobit is unable to go fetch the gold deposited in Rages because "in those days the *angareia* had increased," and therefore "the travelers had disappeared from the streets out of fear" (*The Book of Tobit. A Chaldee Text from a Unique MS in the Bodleian Library*, A. Neubauer, ed. [Oxford: Clarendon, 1878], p. 4, lines 7–9) (mistranslated "tribute," xxviii). Other early references to *angareia* are found in Pap. Teb. I 5, 178ff. and 252ff. (second century B.C.E.). The former commands soldiers and others who are on official business neither to impress (*angareuein*) any of the inhabitants of the province or their beasts of burden for their own personal needs nor to requisition calves, and the like. Similarly also *Orientis Graeci Inscr. Selectae* I 665.21 (W. Dittenberger, ed.).

21. T.B.Mes. 6.3,11a, cited by Paul Fiebig, "angareuo," *ZNW* 18 (1918): 64–72. For additional Jewish references, see *"angaria"* in Gustaf Dalman, *Aramäisch-neuhebräisches Handwörterbuch*, 2d ed. (Frankfurt: J. Kauffmann, 1897–1901), 105; and Marcus Jastrow, *A Dictionary of the Targumim* (New York: Pardes, 1950), 81; for Greek, *"angareia"* in Liddell-Scott; for Latin, *"angaria, angario"* in *Thesaurus Linguae Latinae* (Lipsiae: B. G. Teubneri, 1940–46), 2.43. See also August Wünsche, *Neue Beiträge zur Erläuterung der Evangelien aus Talmud und Midrasch* (Göttingen: Vandenhoeck & Ruprecht, 1878), 64–65; L. Goldschmid, "Impôts et droits de douane en Judée sous les Romains," *Rev. d. it. juives* 34 (1897): 207–208; Friedrich Preisigke, "Die ptolemäische Staatspost," *Klio* 7 (1907): 275–277; Ulrich Wilcken, "Transport-Requisitionen für Beamte und Truppen," L. Mitteis und U. Wilcken, *Grundzüge und Chrestomathie der Papyruskunde* (Leipzig/Berlin: B. G. Teubner, 1912), 1.374–376; Vincente Garcia de Diego, "Notas etimológicas: Angaria," *Boletín de la Real Academia Española* 40 (1960): 380–399; T. Henckels and H. G. Crocker, *Memorandum of Authorities on the Law of Angary* (Washington: Government Printing Office, 1919), 25–30; J. Le Clère, *Les mesures coercitives sur les navires de commerce étrangers* (Paris: Librairie générale de droit et de jurisprudence, 1949), 19–21, 35–36; Adolf Deissmann, *Bible Studies* (Edinburgh: T. & T. Clark, 1901), 86–87; A.-H.

Schröder, *Das Angarienrecht* (Hamburg: Forschungsstelle für Völkerrecht und ausländisches öffentliches Recht der Universität Hamburg, 1965), 15–18; Joshua Gutmann and Daniel Sperber, "Angaria," *Encyclopaedia Judaica* 2 (1971): cols. 950–51; D. Sperber, *Nautica Talmudica* (Ramat-Gan: Bar-Ilan University, 1986), 115–118; Sperber, "Angaria in Rabbinic Literature," *L'Antiquité Classique* 38 (1969): 164–168; G. E. M. de Ste. Croix, *The Class Struggle in the Ancient Greek World* (Ithaca: Cornell University Press, 1981, 14–16); and I. A. Solodukho, "Podati i povinnosti v Irake v III-V vv. nashi ery" ("Taxes and Obligations in Iraq in the Third to Fifth Centuries of Our Era"), *Sovetskoe vostokovedenie* 5 (1948): 69, section 9 and note 1.

22. *Corp. Insc. Gr.* no. 4956, A21, cited by Edwin Hatch, *Essays in Biblical Greek* (Amsterdam: Philo, [1889] 1970), 37. Hatch suggested that Matthew 5:41 should not be translated "whosoever shall compel thee to go one mile," but "whosoever shall compel thee to carry his baggage one mile," but few versions have followed his advice. TEV comes closest: "If one of the occupation troops forces you to carry his pack one mile," though in Galilee it might have been one of Antipas' militia doing the compelling.

23. PSI 446 (133–137 C.E.), cited by Ramsay MacMullen, *Soldier and Civilian in the Late Roman Empire* (Cambridge: Harvard University, 1963), 89 n. 42, it. added.

24. *The Theodosian Code*, Clyde Pharr, ed. (Princeton: Princeton University, 1952), sections 8.5.1, 2, 6, 7, 8.1, 11, 66. See in addition *The Digests of Justinian*, Th. Mommsen, ed. (Philadelphia: University of Pennsylvania, 1985), sections 49.18.4; 50.4.18.21-22 and 29; 50.5.10, 11; and Justinian's *Novella* (Constitutions) 16.9, 10; 17.1, 9, 22; *The Civil Law*, S. P. Scott, trans. (Cincinnati: Central Trust, 1973).

25. According to Tacitus, slaves and camp followers outnumbered the soldiers in the army that Vitellius marched to Rome (*Hist.* 2.70). In Acts of the Apostles 10:7, the centurion Cornelius counts at least two servants and a soldier "among those that waited on him." See for a later period MacMullen, *Soldier and Civilian*, 106 n. 29, 126–127.

26. See Michael Grant, *The Army of the Caesars* (London: Weidenfeld & Nicolson, 1974), xxi–xxx; Fiebig, "angareuo," especially Lev. R. Par. 12; T.B. Sanh. 101b; T.B. B. Qam. 38b; T.B. Sota 10a; T.B. Ber. 9b; T.B. Yoma 35b; T.B. Ned. 32a. Vegetius, *De re militari* gives a graphic picture of the contents of a Roman soldier's pack and the rigors of a forced march (tr. in *Roots of Strategy*, T. R. Phillips, ed. (Harrisburg: Military Service Publications, 1955), 76–88. Josephus states that "an infantry man is almost as heavily laden as a pack-mule" (*J.W.* 3:95).

27. "It was the centurion who formed the backbone of Roman military discipline, and he did so by intensely personal coercion" (C. E. Brand, *Roman Military Law*, Austin: University of Texas, 1968, 42, 81). The centurion was responsible for giving judgment in any complaint brought by civilians

against the excesses of soldiers (Roy W. Davies, *Service in the Roman Army*, New York: Columbia University Press, 1989, 37, 51, 57, 174). See also Robert R. Evans, *Soldiers of Rome* (Washington, D.C.: Seven Locks, 1986), 74; G. W. Currie, *The Military Discipline of the Romans from the Founding of the Empire to the Close of the Republic* (Bloomington: Indiana University, 1928), 10, 12, 161; Abel H. J. Greenridge, "The *Provocatio Militiae* and Provincial Jurisdiction," *Class. Rev.* 10 (1896): 226; Richard E. Smith, *Service in the Post-Marian Roman Army* (Manchester: Manchester University Press, 1958); Robert O. Fink, *Roman Military Records on Papyrus* (Cleveland: Case Western University Press, 1971), esp. 383–386; Michael P. Speidel, *Guards of the Roman Armies* (Bonn: Rudolf Habelt, 1978).

28. Maurice, *Strategica* 7:3, ital. added; cited by Brand, *Roman Military Laws*, 21. See also 4.10, 195.

29. Brand, *Roman Military Laws*, 104–106. In any case military law was always more severe in its punishments than civil law. Of the 102 instances where the punishment of a soldier is mentioned, 40 resulted in the death penalty (Currie, *Military Discipline*, 38).

30. Jesus' saying does not reflect a situation of daily occupation by Romans, but rather the occasional relocation of the legions guarding the empire's eastern flank. Josephus' *Antiquities of the Jews* 18:120–124 gives an instance of a legion passing through Judea and the lengths Jewish leaders went to prevent it. Even in Jerusalem, Galilean pilgrims would have been treated to scenes similar to that enacted by the impressment of Simon of Cyrene to carry Jesus' cross. Herod had raised auxiliaries in Samaria that continued to be garrisoned in Caesarea; and in Galilee, his son, Herod Antipas, organized his army along Roman lines, which would no doubt have included the right of impressment. Palestine was on the route between Egypt and Syria, which involved frequent dispatches of mail, troops, and supplies. Roman soldiers also accompanied caravans and acted as police in suppressing robbers. See George Leonard Chessman, *The Auxilia of the Roman Imperial Army* (Hildesheim: Georg Olms Verlag, 1971), 161–163.

31. Epictetus provides an example of passive submission to impressment that is the polar opposite of Jesus' advice in Matthew. "You ought to treat your whole body like a poor loaded-down donkey . . . and if it be commandeered (*angareia*) and a soldier lay hold of it, let it go, do not resist (*antiteine*) or grumble. If you do, you will get a beating and lose your little donkey just the same" (*Disc.* 4.1.79). For the degeneration of *angareia* to plain extortion by soldiers, see Ramsey MacMullen, *Soldier and Civilian*, 85–86; and M. Rostovtzeff, *The Social and Economic History of the Roman Empire*, 2d ed. (Oxford: Clarendon, 1957), 1.424 and 2.721–723, notes 45–47.

32. *Jesus and the Spiral of Violence* (San Francisco: Harper & Row, 1987), 318–326.

33. See Sharon H. Ringe, *Jesus, Liberation, and the Biblical Jubilee*, Overtures to Biblical Theology Series (Philadelphia: Fortress, 1985).

34. That Jesus proposed such behavior in concrete situations is illustrated by the story of the rich young man (Mark 10:17–22 par.). The same kind of liberating generosity is envisioned in Luke 7:41–42; 10:35; Mark 10:23–31. See Douglas E. Oakman, *Jesus and the Economic Questions of His Day* (Lewiston: Edwin Mellen, 1986), 166, 215–216.

35. Horsley, *Jesus and the Spiral of Violence*, 32.

36. Acts of the Apostles 2:43–47; 4:32–5:11; 6:1. These reports may be idealized but they are by no means pure fiction. The well-established poverty of the Jerusalem Church may have been one of the unintended results of mixing Jesus' stringent program of redistribution of wealth with the Church's apocalyptic belief in an immediate end of history. Hence the early community liquidated capital and lived off the proceeds rather than sharing in communitarian economic arrangements, and quickly found itself destitute.

37. A. J. Muste insisted that one must be a revolutionary before being a pacifist. "A non-revolutionary pacifist is a contradiction in terms" ("Pacifism and Class War" [1928], in *The Universe Bends Toward Justice*, Angie O'Gorman, ed., Philadelphia: New Society Publishers, 1990, 113).

38. I have attempted a practical application of Jesus' teaching on the "third way" to the situation in South Africa in *Violence and Nonviolence in South Africa* (Philadelphia: New Society Publishers, 1987). An extended treatment of the whole topic appears in my *Engaging the Powers* (Minneapolis: Fortress, 1992). It would be anachronistic to regard "nonviolence" as a full-blown philosophical option in first-century Palestine. Gandhi seems to have been the first person to develop nonviolence into a total way of life, philosophy, and strategy for social change. But all the elements of that synthesis were present in Jesus' life and teaching. See Ched Myers, *Binding the Strong Man* (Maryknoll: Orbis, 1988), 47.

39. Augustine, Sermon on the Mount I.19.56–68; *Reply to Faustus the Manichaean* 22.76; *On Lying* 27; *Letters* 47.5, *NPNF First Series*, 1:293. Reinhold Niebuhr exactly mirrored this view in *Christianity and Power Politics* (New York: Charles Scribner's Sons, 1940), 10; and in *An Interpretation of Christian Ethics* (New York: Harper, 1935), 50, 62–83.

CHAPTER 5

GOD DOES NOT REQUIRE OBEDIENCE; HE ABHORS IT!

Rafael Chodos

Introduction

What is it to hear God's voice, and to respond to His command? Does God issue commands? And if He does, is "obedience" the proper word to describe our highest response to them?

There is a dark linkage, which stretches across the centuries, between the Judeo-Christian conception of God as a Being that gives commands that must be obeyed, and programmatic violence. Programmatic violence is not the random sort of violence that bursts out when its perpetrator loses control. Instead, it is deliberate, planned, often organized, and its perpetrator believes it is justified. One of the most common types of justification offered for this sort of violence is that it is being perpetrated in obedience to God's command: "I do what I do because God commands me to do it." And, "You must do what I tell you to do because God has commanded us to do it."

But God does not require obedience: only people do. Indeed, the kinds of obedience that can be required, or compelled, or coerced, or commanded—these kinds of obedience are abhorrent to God and repugnant to true religious feeling. If there is any obedience possible in the relationship between a person and God, it is an entirely different kind of obedience.

We live in an age when this point tends to be forgotten. The social collective has become so dominant in our consciousness that it has intruded itself even into the relationship between God and humankind. We tend strongly to see our relationship with God through the lens of our relationship to our fellow humans: we see God as a King of Kings; as a Heavenly Father; as a Lawgiver. Thinking of God this way, we tend to think that He requires obedience in the same way that a king requires it, or a father, or a lawgiver. But God is something else, and His voice is unlike any other voice, and His command requires a response different from any other command.

I write this chapter from my belief that authentic religious experience is necessarily private, and that to cast religion in the role of a socializing force is at one and the same time a corruption of religion and a violation of one of our most fundamental political beliefs: the separation of church and state.

I write also as one who was raised in a Jewish household, and who grew up with certain images of obedience that were held up to me with approval as models to be emulated: the image of Abraham and Isaac on their way to Mount Moriah; the image of the Orthodox Jew who observes, with *"kavono,"* intention, the 613 commandments each day; the story of the Jewish people who accepted God's law even before they knew what it was; the story of Moses, who accepted God's command to defy Pharaoh. Images of disobedience were held up to me as well: of Adam and Eve in the Garden, of Jonah running away to Tarshish, of Korah questioning Moses' authority. I write this chapter partly to sort out this jumble of images.

So I invite you to follow me as I reconsider obedience in all its forms and manifestations, and reach the conclusion that the attitude of obedience is ultimately inconsistent with the highest form of conversation with God.

The Grammar of Obedience[1]

We begin with an analysis of the notion of obedience as it appears in a variety of contexts, and start with what we may call the "word field" of obedience.[2] From an examination of the word field, we may glean some understanding of the concept.

The Word Field of Obedience

I have set out this word field in the following list. Subtle variations in the notion of obedience come into the foreground as we explore this word field.

> COMMAND, request, urge, importune, encourage, exhort, affirm,
>
> forbid, enjoin, enjoin upon, prohibit,

obey, disobey, comply, be in compliance with, be out of compliance with,

obedience, disobedience,

obedient, disobedient, compliant, unruly, servile, slavish,

grudging obedience, grudging compliance,

willing obedience, voluntary obedience,

involuntary obedience, coerced obedience,

obedience to . . . law, commands, orders,

compliance with . . . laws, statutes, commands, orders, injunctions, prohibitions,

complying with orders; following instructions,

blind obedience, slavish obedience,

civil disobedience,

orders, one-time orders, standing orders,

commands, commandments.

Obey/Disobey, Obedience/Disobedience, Obedient/Disobedient

As we move from the verb forms (obey/disobey), to the noun forms (obedience/disobedience), and then to the adjective forms (obedient/ disobedient), there are shifts in the sense of the underlying notion. *Obey* and *disobey* focus our attention on a particular act of obedience or disobedience: one obeys or disobeys a particular order, command, or person, while the nouns *obedience* and *disobedience* feel general and require helping words, such as "a particular act of," to instantiate them. The adjectives *obedient* and *disobedient* describe people and in their simplest form are general qualities of character, as in "He is an obedient child." If we want to tie "obedient" or "disobedient" to particular orders or commands or persons, we use the forms *"obedient to"* or *"obedient toward"* and *"disobedient to"* or *"disobedient toward,"* as in "He was always obedient to his teacher." In this usage, we are no longer using the words to describe someone's *character*; instead, we are using them to describe someone's *behavior*.

Obedience and Compliance

In their simple form, "obedient" and "disobedient" are semantically similar to "compliant," "servile," and "unruly," but the quality referred to is slightly different in each case.

There is a difference between obeying commands, or being obedient to law, and complying with regulations, statutes, laws, injunctions, or prohibitions. Being obedient connotes an element of voluntariness or deliberateness that is something more than being merely compliant: one might be compliant without intending to be, or without wanting to be, while being obedient suggests an intention, or a desire to comply. Of course, we do speak of "grudging obedience" and "grudging compliance," but these phrases themselves have different connotations. Grudging obedience refers to one's attitude, one's state of mind: one obeys without wanting to obey. But "grudging compliance" suggests that objectively, the compliance meets only the minimum standard of what is required, or that it is delayed or late in coming. This is consistent with the point that "obedience" has to do with one's moral or ethical stance, whereas "compliance" seems to focus more objectively on behavior.

The fact is, it is possible to comply with a command without being obedient to it, and it is possible to be out of compliance with a command while still being obedient to it. The parent might punish his son by saying, "Go to your room and stay there all day." The son might go, thinking to himself, "Well, the fact is, I want to stay in my room today, since I have things I want to do here. This is no punishment." When this son stays in the room, he complies but he is disobedient. The parent might tell the child, "Return by midnight." The child might intend to return, might plan to return, and might actually try to return by the deadline; but she might be hijacked, or diverted. She would thus fail to comply, but we would not call her disobedient.

Being either "obedient" or "compliant" is considered superior to being "servile" or "slavish," terms that connote weakness, or lower social standing. "Unruly," on the other hand, is a term of disapprobation that describes someone's behavior as being difficult to control.

The Objects of Obedience

These distinctions bring us to realize that there are different kinds of things toward which one might be obedient. One can obey a particular command, or order, as when we say, "Smith ordered Jones to leave the room, and Jones obeyed." One can obey a particular person, as, for example, a good soldier always obeys his superior. But we also use the words to describe one's behavior or attitude with regard to a system of rules or a hierarchy of persons. So when we say, "Socrates was obedient to law," we are not referring to any particular law, but rather we are describing Socrates' attitude toward the whole system of law. Likewise, when we say that someone is an obedient child, we are describing her behavior or attitude with regard to her parents, teachers, and elders in general: only in special circumstances would we interpret that statement as describing the child's behavior or attitude toward the speaker, or toward another particular person.

Intermediate between the particular command and the system of commands is what we sometimes call the "standing order": take attendance at the beginning of the class, do not murder, do not eat meat with milk, pray three times a day, honor your father and your mother. These commands, or "commandments" (a strange locution), are not tied to any particular occasion, nor are they delivered to any particular person They are of general application and they are part of a system of rules. Yet they are less abstract than a "system of rules": they are instead particular rules. A coherent collection of particular rules makes up a system of rules.

Commands, Orders, and Instructions

Is there any difference between obeying an order, following an order, carrying out an order, complying with an order, and responding to an order? To obey an order suggests that the order is clear and that the obedience is rendered in one clear time frame. Following an order, on the other hand, suggests that some process is needed, as if the order might be one of a series of orders, or as if one might have to go through a series of steps to follow the order. Carrying out the order suggests that the person who does the carrying out needs to exercise some initiative of his own: the order needs to be fleshed out, and more is required than simply following it. Complying with an order is similar to obeying it, but as we discussed previously, it requires no particular commitment or state of mind. Finally, responding to an order has two senses: in the simpler sense, one might respond to an order by punching the one who issued it in the nose, or by ignoring it; these would be "responses" even though neither of them would be what the person who issued the order had in mind. But in a more complicated sense, to "respond" to an order means to be sympathetic toward it, to vibrate in harmony with it, and in that state of mind, to obey it.

Now does any of this change if we substitute "commands" or "instructions" for "orders"? "Commands" and "orders" are issued by persons in a position of power,[3] from inside some hierarchy. So we have orders in the military, and orders from courts and governmental agencies. Of the two words, "commands" is probably the older, and it carries with it overtones of royalty: kings issue commands, but nowadays almost no one else does, except possibly God. Instead, most of what would have been called "commands" in older times are now called "orders." Instructions, on the other hand, may come from someone who is attempting to transfer knowledge to, or convey some benefit on, the one to whom they are given. So when one "carries out instructions" or "follows instructions," he may be doing it for his own benefit, not necessarily for the benefit of the person who gave the instructions. But when he "follows orders" or "carries out orders" or "obeys commands," he is doing it for the benefit of the person who gave the order or command.

I say, "Not necessarily": I might be ordered to carry out a task, and this order might have been issued for the benefit of the person who gave it, not for my benefit. But once the order has been issued, and once I undertake to carry it out, I may require help in the form of instructions. The act of giving instructions is at the very least for the benefit of both the one giving and the one receiving the instructions: if a benefit is intended only for the one who issues the instructions, we would say instead that he would issue detailed orders that the one who receives them would then carry out.

Requiring, Coercing, Compelling, Inspiring . . . Obedience

There are many ways that one person can bring about obedience in another: one can require it, coerce it, compel it, or inspire it. What are the differences among these?

To require obedience is to announce in advance that one will insist on a certain hierarchical relationship: the king requires obedience of his subjects; the commander requires obedience of his soldiers. To coerce obedience is both to require it and to use force to obtain it. So one has to coerce obedience when she encounters resistance of some kind, and the term sometimes connotes the use of physical force. To compel obedience is very much like coercing it, but the term connotes less physical force. To inspire obedience is of course different: one who inspires obedience has no need of force, but rather receives willing obedience from the ones she inspires.

These words suggest a range of different attitudes toward obedience on the part of the one who is obedient: voluntary obedience is different from coerced obedience; grudging obedience is different from joyous obedience.

The Concept of Obedience

From the word field, we move to an analysis of the concept.

The Basic Schema: A Is Obedient to B with Respect to C

The fully instantiated concept, that is, the concept in its native form, with all the loose ends tied down, is a three-place predicate: A is obedient to B with respect to C. B is a person who issues a command, C, and A obeys it. This is what I call the "basic schema."

So when we say simply that A is obedient to B, we mean that he has a tendency or habit of obeying all the commands, C, that B issues. When we say simply that A is obedient, we probably mean that in general he is ready to obey all commands C issued by persons B entitled to issue them. When we say he is servile, we mean that he is ready to obey commands issued by anyone, without regard to whether they are entitled to issue them. But the full-blown concept involves three elements: a person obeying; a person to whom obedience is rendered; and a command, order, or instruction issued by the second person to the first one.

Particular to General

The sense of obedience changes as its objects, the person to whom obedience is rendered, or the command with respect to which the obedience is rendered, move from the particular to the general.

What B?

In the most particular sense, we use obedience to refer to particular acts in relation to particular commands. So when A obeys B's order, or injunction, it is a particular order that is being obeyed, and a particular person who issues the order. But when we speak of A's obedience to parents, or teachers, or superiors in a hierarchy, we are speaking no longer of particular acts, but of a general pattern of behavior in relation, not to a particular person, but to a class of persons. The obedience is one aspect of a social hierarchy: it is the people who are being obeyed, and the commands are validated because they are issued by the people upstream in the hierarchy. Here the B in our basic schema no longer refers to an individual person, but rather to a group of people.

What C?

Similarly, there is such a thing as obedience to law, or to systems of commands. This sort of obedience is not obedience to people, but rather obedience to principles. This is a sort of obedience that many great thinkers claimed to have demonstrated: Socrates claimed to have respected the law and to have followed it even when the Athenians misapplied it. Antigone refused to follow Creon's order but rather claimed to be obedient to a higher law. Here the C in our basic schema refers no longer to a particular command, but rather to something more general and more abstract: a system of commands. To be called a system, these commands must be organized around some principles. If there are no principles, then the obedience is merely to a list of unrelated imperatives, and we have not yet encountered, in the history of our species, anyone who claims to be obedient to a list of unrelated imperatives. Instead, even if we may think the imperatives are unrelated, the person who is obedient to them will discern in them some system.

We see some of these points more clearly when we consider the concept of disobedience. A child may disobey a particular command given by his parent but may still be an obedient child in general, which would mean that he usually does not disobey his parents' commands. One may exercise "civil disobedience," which is principled disobedience to law, or to the will of those in power. These examples show that as the objects of obedience become generalized, either the person or the commands to whom obedience is rendered, issues of principle and social cohesion come to the foreground.

The Cognitive Aspect of Obedience

In order to obey a command, one must understand it. "Know thyself!" looks like a command, but in fact it is too hard to understand: we cannot tell what is being required of us, nor can we tell whether we have complied. "Leave the room!" works much better.

Sometimes it is necessary to deliver instructions with a command, to fill the cognitive gap. "Build an ark!" was the command, but to carry out that command, Noah required lengthy instructions.

When obedience is rendered to a system of rules, it is necessary to understand how the system is coherent. This becomes the cognitive gap, and to fill it, it is necessary to rationalize each rule or command with other commands in the system. What is required in order to fulfill the biblical injunction "Thou shalt not seethe the kid in its mother's milk" (Deut. 14:21)? How close must a man be standing to the synagogue in order to be counted as one of the ten men needed for a *minyan?* If these questions are to be taken seriously, prodigious feats of cognitive exertion are required to answer them.[4]

The Difference between Following Orders and Following Instructions

We have already touched on the difference between obedience to one's superior in a hierarchy and obedience to the instructions one receives from her doctor, or from her teacher, for example, in learning to play the piano, or martial arts. The doctor issues orders only to benefit the patient. The teacher issues orders and instructions only to benefit the student; this is not true of the superior in the hierarchy. The two kinds of obedience are often confused because all the teachers we encounter in childhood are in fact our superiors in a hierarchy. But when one adult offers to teach another a skill, or a body of knowledge, then there is no social hierarchy; instead, there is only the bond of trust that arises from the student's conviction that the teacher's intention is to benefit him and that the teacher is able to benefit him. As hard as it may be to remember when we are actually in the doctor's office, there is no hierarchy there, either; the doctor is giving instructions for our benefit, which we may follow if we wish to achieve the result he intends.

We may ask whether God's commands are like orders issued by our superiors in a hierarchy, or whether they are more like instructions issued by our teachers or our doctors. "Get up and leave your land, your birthplace, and the house of your father, and go to a place which I will show you." Which sort of command was this? For whose benefit was it issued? We might like to say that God issued this command for Abraham's benefit and not for His own. But of course, the authors of the Book of Genesis had the idea that God had His own agenda, a desire to see history unfold in a certain way, and Abraham was a key player in that unfolding. So if Abraham had refused to obey that particular command, how could the whole history of the Jewish people have unfolded? We will keep this question in mind as we go further.

Involuntary Obedience versus Voluntary Obedience

We have already noted that obedience is bound up with affect because both the person who issues the command and the person to whom the command is given have an affective response to the command. For this reason the obedience of humans is something quite different from the obedience of robots or computers, who obey without affect. (But the person who issues commands to robots or computers does have an affective response.) Our obedience may be voluntary, or it may be involuntary. But these kinds of obedience may have affective shadings.

Dogs have much to teach us on the subject of voluntary obedience. We see that for them, to be obedient to their masters is a joyous process; it is the way they communicate with us and express their love toward us. When we teach a dog to sit, we are not imposing our will on the dog; we are explaining ourselves to him, bringing him to understand us, and offering him a pathway of communication with us. He craves this communication, he thrives on it. If he is disobedient, it is not because he wants to do something different; it is only because he has not yet understood what it is that we want. Take the time someday to watch those agility trials in which dogs race through hoops and nets, around and over obstacles, under ground, and when they have finished the course, they wag their tails in joy. Having struggled to understand the commands given to them, they obey the commands with exuberance. Their obedience is voluntary, and in fact it is joyous. We must ask ourselves: Is their obedience the model we should emulate in our relationship with God? Or is their kind of voluntary obedience special to them, something they can carry off gracefully just because they are dogs? Is it that they are innocent and free from existential doubt? They do not ask whether the commands are worth following, or for whose benefit the commands are given. Is that why their obedience is so joyous? If humans were to act the same way, might we consider them thoughtless, slavish, or even prideful? In fact, might we not even call such people "duty proud"?

Perhaps for us humans, it is involuntary obedience toward which we ought to strive. The story is told of Rabbi Elimelekh of Lizhensk, a great Hasidic master, that he rose up the day before Yom Kippur and told his students, "You may not fast tomorrow." "But Rabbi," his students said, "we are commanded to fast on Yom Kippur, and even the Baal Shem Tov fasted on Yom Kippur. Why do you forbid us to fast?" And Rabbi Elimelekh answered, "Three days before Yom Kippur, the Baal Shem Tov would leave his village and go into the forest to pray. He took with him a sack containing three small loaves of bread, one for each day, since he planned to return on the eve of Yom Kippur. But when he returned to his village he found that his sack still had the three loaves in it. Absorbed in his intense prayer, he had forgotten to eat. Fasting such as this is permitted: all other fasting is forbidden!"[5]

Kinds of Involuntary Obedience

The Baal Shem Tov's obedience was not innocent, but it was "involuntary" in the sense that he obeyed the command without intending to obey it. His attention was focused not on the command to fast, but rather on his prayer, and unintentionally, involuntarily, naturally, he carried out the command.

This is reminiscent of a kind of virtue toward which Buddhists strive: a becoming one with the Universe, so that one is in complete harmony with the divine. If one achieves this sort of harmony, then everything she does is in accordance with the divine command; there is no discord, no possibility of disobedience. When one's nature has become perfected, one obeys naturally.

The Baal Shem Tov's obedience was like that but a little different. He was passionate, he was striving, his prayer was passionate: it did not come from stillness, nor did it move toward stillness. He would surely have wanted to be obedient, and if you had asked him he would have said so. But his focus was elsewhere, so his obedience became a side effect of his prayer, an incidental consequence. The Buddhist ideal is different: when one achieves that sort of harmony with the divine, one can escape the cycle of karma, and it is no longer necessary to be reborn. Obedience then becomes irrelevant, a concept that is no longer meaningful.

A medieval *piyyut,* a liturgical poem, is still sung in most Jewish synagogues today as part of the morning prayers. Some of the verses go like this:

Good are the lights that our God has created, . . .
They are joyous when they rise and they rejoice when they set,
　　They carry out with awe the will of their Creator.
They give splendor and honor to His name,
　　jubilation and joyous song in honor of his Kingship.
For He called out to the sun and it glowed with light,
　　He saw the moon and fashioned its form.

This vision of the heavenly lights—the sun, moon, and stars—moving about in the heavens in natural obedience to God's command is one more model of involuntary obedience. Here the parties rendering obedience are merely elements of nature, not human beings; but still they are seen as obeying, with joy and awe, the will of God. The planets, again, are different from the Buddhist masters, but there is something similar in them.

Can we aspire to this sort of obedience? Can we bring ourselves into complete compliance with God's law, so that we become simply an aspect of His creation? In fact, do we have any choice in this matter, or are we already nothing more than that: aspects of His creation, like planets, sun, moon, and stars? Perhaps we have no choice but to be obedient to God's command and even when we think we are disobeying, we are in fact obeying. Perhaps even Adam and Eve were obeying when they thought they were disobeying. In this way, we might be like complicated computer programs: we always do exactly what God has programmed us to do, and even when He is surprised at the results, or dissatisfied with them, He has only Himself to blame. He must tinker with us, modify us, improve us, until we perform as He wishes. In that process, He will be forced to clarify His own thinking. Perhaps this is the way we must inevitably relate to God's commands: we are in interaction with Him, we engage Him in a learning process in which both of us achieve clarity and raise our consciousness.

The Ethics of Obedience

Obedience is different from compliance partly because it has a strong ethical component: obedience is deliberate, conscious, and purposive, whereas compliance may be inadvertent. The same goes for disobedience: to disobey an edict or command is different from merely being out of compliance with it, and the difference is that the disobedience is purposive and deliberate.

We have spoken of disobedience so far as if it were correlative with obedience—as if obedience were merely the lack of, or opposite of, disobedience and disobedience were merely the lack of, or opposite of, obedience. But that is much too simple a formulation.

Obedience, Disobedience, and the Possibility of Obedience and Disobedience

First, it is clear that the possibility of disobedience is the ethical precondition of obedience. If it were not possible for Adam and Eve to have eaten of the forbidden fruit, what would be the point of God having commanded them not to eat? And what would be the point of their having foreborne to eat? To obey a command becomes an ethical act only when it is possible to disobey it. Obedience takes on its moral character when we reject disobedience and decide, affirmatively, to obey. That decision has a certain affect, a flavor, a feeling to it, a social psychological aspect.

Likewise, to disobey a command becomes an ethical act only when it is deliberate and purposive, and that means when there is the possibility of obeying it. "Leave the room!" is a command that can be obeyed or disobeyed, and either of those responses communicates something. But "Don't ever leap over the Empire State Building!" cannot be obeyed, and therefore it cannot really be disobeyed in any ethical sense of the term.

An imperative that looks like a command may turn out to be something different when we consider whether obedience is possible. For instance, "Love thy neighbor as thyself!" sounds like a command, but it is not really. Instead, it is an aspirational injunction, or a precept. Part of what takes it out of the category of commands is that the possibility of obeying it is problematical. There is also the fact that it is a "standing order" whose application to particular situations is unclear; these features too take it out of the category of command. Similar to it is "Know thyself!" This also is something different from a command, and it is not quite possible to "obey" it: it gains its force from the fact that until we think about it we might be under the impression that it is impossible to *disobey* it.

Civil Disobedience

And this brings us to a discussion of civil disobedience, a subject important to Sophocles' *Antigone,* and to Socrates in the *Crito.* For civil disobedience is purposive and deliberate, but this is something it has in common with other kinds of ethical disobedience. When a parent orders a child into his room, or orders him to return home by midnight, and the child disobeys, his disobedience has that "ethical" quality of which we spoke. This is not to say that the disobedience is admirable or praiseworthy; it is merely to say that it was more than mere noncompliance, and that it sent some kind of an interpersonal message.

What distinguishes civil disobedience from other forms of ethical disobedience is that the actor seeks to justify it by appeal to a higher authority than the authority that issued the command she is disobeying. So Antigone told Creon that she was burying her brother's corpse despite his command, because in doing so she was obeying an authority higher than his. And the sit-ins and protests of the 1960s in our own country echoed this motif: the law was disobeyed, the protesters all said, in an effort to awaken the country to its highest ideals. Local laws were disobeyed to dramatize how inconsistent they were with constitutional principles. In a media-saturated political commu-

Socrates standing before a seated group of men; the figure of Justice stands behind him. Illustration in Cooper, *The Life of Socrates*, London, 1750. Library of Congress.

nity, one's actions are sometimes more persuasive to the majority than any words he can utter.

Antigone was an early advocate of civil disobedience. Socrates was an early critic of it. In the *Crito*, Socrates considers this kind of disobedience but rejects it explicitly. He asks, quite directly, if one is subjected to an unjust command, or, more precisely, to a command that he believes to be unjust, what must he do? Must he simply obey, stifling his resentment and keeping his opinions to himself? Or may he disobey and justify his disobedience on the grounds that the command was unjust? Socrates suggests that neither of these is the right way to respond. Instead he suggests an intermediate course: he must attempt to persuade the party who issued the command to revoke it or modify it. This persuasion may be successful or unsuccessful; that will depend, of course, not only on the excellence of the arguments advanced, but also on the willingness and ability of the one to whom they are advanced to understand them and assimilate them. But if the attempt to persuade fails, then obedience is required. Socrates demonstrated his commitment to these principles by arguing his case (in the *Apology*) and then drinking the hemlock (in the *Phaedo*).

What Socrates' arguments and behavior dramatized was his unshakeable commitment to live as a law-abiding citizen of Athens. If the unjust command had come from an invading tyrant, perhaps his view of his responsibilities would have been quite different. But because he was being put to death under the laws of his own city, Athens, after a trial in which he had spoken to a jury of his fellow citizens in his own defense, he felt that his integrity required him to act in obedience to those laws.

Socrates, then, did not believe that civil disobedience was a legitimate response to an unjust command. He was not a revolutionary, and he did not believe that Athens' treatment of him was a proper occasion for revolution. He remained in conversation with the citizens of Athens, and with the Laws of Athens, even in his death.

We may compare Socrates' attitude toward unjust laws with Job's attitude toward an unjust God. Job also submitted to God's actions, after acknowledging that there was no way to view them as anything but unjust. Just as Socrates argued in the *Apology* that his conduct was not unlawful and that his intentions had always been most noble, so Job argues with his interlocutors and insists that he did not deserve the punishment God had meted out to him. And just as Socrates ended up submitting, on principle, to the judgment of his fellow citizens, even though he disagreed with it, so Job abandoned himself to God, even though he was convinced that God's actions were not justified. Neither of these two great ethical figures was a revolutionary.

Obedience and the Power Gradient

The giving of a command assumes a perceived power gradient: one who commands is perceived to have the power, or the authority, to issue orders to the one who is commanded. The word "gradient" means that the one who issues the command is perceived to have more power or authority, at least with respect to the transaction in which the command is given, than the one to whom the command is given.

The gradient need not be of political, military, or physical power; it may be a gradient of moral authority. So the aged seer can give commands even to the king; and the teacher can give commands to his pupil.

The act of giving a command emphasizes this gradient, on which it depends. To command is therefore to do violence to the one commanded. Where the gradient is one of political or physical power, the threat of using it is what "backs up" the command,[6] and to threaten to use power is a form of violence. And where the gradient is merely one of moral authority, the command is a sign of disrespect for the other's integrity. For if the integrity of the person to whom the command is given were really respected, then one would not command him; instead, he would seek to persuade him.

The power gradient may nevertheless be benign or malignant; when a beloved parent gives a command, it feels different from when a stranger issues even the same command. The power gradient may be something with which both parties feel comfortable (as in a healthy parent–child relationship), or with which neither feels comfortable (as in an unhealthy parent–child relationship, or when a senior executive appoints one member of a corporate department to manage it, when neither she nor anyone else in the department thinks it is a good choice), or it may be something imposed on one of the parties against his will. The power gradient need not be a permanent one; it needs only to be established with respect to the transaction or situation in which the command is given.

The power gradient is the source of much of the affect of obedience.

Obedience as the Bond that Holds Society Together

1. It would be naive indeed to ignore the role that obedience has played in human society since the dawn of time. We humans are pack animals, like the apes from which we sprang, and not unlike wolves, lions, elephants, birds, bees, or ants. We have always lived in groups: we are born into groups, and we die away from groups. I have always been struck by Freud's reference to the "primal scene" in his discussion of the Wolf Man Case History. This is the scene imprinted on the infant's memory, of his parents copulating, a scene that Freud said induced a neurosis we must struggle all our lives to resolve. Perhaps it is so, but I have imprinted on my own memory a different scene that I think is much more truly called "primal."

In this scene I am in a small group. We are sitting inside a cave, and there is a fire burning at the mouth of the cave to keep wild animals away. We are all naked. We sit in a circle, looking at each other, in fear. We are bonded to each other but I cannot tell you the nature of the bond. We have hunted together, we have helped each other ward off attacking lions or wolves. We eat in each other's presence. One of us is our leader: I cannot tell you who. It is not necessarily the strongest, or the oldest. It is not even necessarily a man. But this is the person who tells us when to get up and when to sit down, and gives permission for us to leave the cave.

This scene, I would submit, is engraved much more deeply in our minds than the one Freud speaks of, and it is from this primal scene that we must struggle to escape in order to become individuated. In this primal scene we are hopelessly enmeshed in a pack. We are bound together by fear. And we live always under the watchful eye of authority. In this scene there is no place for God. We might sing together, pray together; we might bury our dead with a shared sense of solemnity. But God cannot come into this scene because He cannot find in it an individual with whom He might converse.

Nevertheless, we can readily see that this primal group is bonded together in a hierarchical structure, and that obedience is an important part of the "glue" that holds the group together. As populations grow the group becomes larger, but many of its fundamental qualities remain unchanged. There is still a hierarchy. Soon there is a king, and then an emperor. Face-to-face surveillance is no longer possible, but bureaucratic structures are elaborated, and systems of economy and taxation arise. The fear that occasioned the fire at the mouth of the cave was in no wise diminished as the groups grew into nations; instead it fathered forth armies and wars. The cave was no longer sufficient to house the nation; cooperative projects of construction, irrigation, farming, all these social enterprises depended to some extent on obedience. For obedience is a mechanism of cooperation: responsibility is distributed, information is distributed, and so orders, commands, and instructions are given and obeyed so that the result that all the participants desire can be achieved.

2. Obedience is an expression of trust: unless you are forcing me to do your will, I obey you because I trust you. This point was dramatized most interestingly by Stanley Milgram in his experiments at Yale conducted in the early 1960s. Participants were asked to play the role of "teachers" to a "learner" who was strapped into a mini electric chair. The learner was read a list of word pairs and then was asked to produce the second word of the pair when he heard the first word later on in the experiment. If he failed to produce the correct second word, the teacher was told to administer a progressively more intense electric shock to him. The putative point of the experiment was to see how effective pain was in inducing learning. But the real purpose was to see how far the teachers would go in administering painful shocks to the learner even after he started to exhibit symptoms of intense pain and discomfort. As the teachers expressed unwillingness or reluctance, the experimenter would reassure them that although the shocks were painful they were not harmful and that

the experiment required them to proceed until the maximum voltage had been administered.

The results of these experiments were that most people complied with the experimenter's directions and ignored the learner's expressions of intense pain. Milgram thought that this dramatized what he called "the problem of obedience," and he drew parallels between this sort of obedience and that exhibited by Nazi personnel in the death camps. Only a small percentage of the people who participated as teachers exhibited what Milgram thought would be a "normal" or healthy reaction to the situation: they refused to administer shocks even if the experimenter urged them to go on, or told them to go on, once the subject evidenced pain. Milgram also observed that when the experimenter was not actually present in person, compliance with the instructions fell off, and when three teachers were participating in the same room, two of them "plants" who refused to follow the experimenter's orders, the third teacher would also generally refuse to follow, thus showing that obedience is undermined when there is discord in the group.

The teachers in Milgram's experiments were the real subjects of the experiment. They were given limited information about the situation, and the experimenter asserted to them that his purpose was to advance human knowledge by developing laboratory data on the effectiveness of pain in promoting memory and learning. This is of course an entirely legitimate purpose, and one way we can interpret the results is that the subjects' trust in the legitimacy and good intention of the experimenter was not shaken even when they saw the learner writhing in pain. The teachers were not told that they were the real subjects of the experiment, nor were they told that the learner was in fact an actor who was only pretending to be in pain.

If anyone had told the teachers that they were the real focus of the experiment, or that the person who introduced himself as the experimenter, the chief scientist responsible for carrying out the experiment, was actually an impostor, or merely an actor, then presumably the results would have been entirely different. The obedience was rendered partly as an expression of trust in the experimenter and in the whole scientific apparatus in which the experimenter presented himself.

Obedience as an Abdication of Personal Responsibility

Milgram observed that to render obedience to another can sometimes be a way of evading personal responsibility. The "Eichmann

Defense," the argument that because one is just carrying out orders given by another it is that other who alone is responsible, is raised in a variety of contexts, and it is an expression of one persistent aspect of obedience. We saw this defense raised recently in the context of the Enron accounting scandals. Milgram conjectured that the teachers in his experiments did not feel responsible for inflicting pain on the learners because they were just carrying out the orders given by the experimenter.

1. As a general legal proposition, it is no defense to either criminal or civil liability to say that one acted under orders. The law does recognize the defenses of coercion and duress: if you put a gun to my head and order me to shoot a third party, and if I do it, I act under duress, and this will be a defense to criminal liability. But there is always the factual question of how much duress I was under. Merely being told that I will lose my job if I do not carry out your order to commit a criminal act does not constitute duress. If that is the only threat I am facing, the law requires me to refuse obedience, and it then allows me to sue you for retaliatory termination if you fire me because I disobeyed this order.

The law distinguishes, however, between acts that I know to be criminal (such as when I am ordered to kill someone) and acts whose criminal character may not be apparent to me because I lack full information. It is likely that many of the people involved in the Enron scandal carried out orders that they might not have known to be improper or illegal. What may protect them from liability is not that they were carrying out orders but that they did not know their conduct was criminal. What is at issue is the *mens rea*, the guilty knowledge: as a general rule, one who acts innocently, not knowing that her conduct was criminal, is not criminally liable. But of course, there may be a duty on the part of the one who receives the orders to question them. This will depend on whether the orders appeared regular and proper in all respects, or whether there was something about them that should have raised a question. In each actual case, a court will have to evaluate what may be a complicated factual predicate to decide if liability should attach.

There is a big difference between the way responsibility flows *inside* a group, or collective, and the way it flows from inside to *outside*. If I order you to commit a tort, to steal someone else's property, for instance, and you carry out my order, you are responsible to the party whose property you stole, but you may have a claim against me for indemnity. The third party can sue both of us, however, since we cooperated to steal his property and acted jointly in the enterprise. In other words, "following orders" is not a defense, but it may be the basis of a claim for indemnity. The basic idea is, if you choose to follow the orders given inside the group, you are responsible for that choice. You are liable for the consequences, even though you may have a right to force the person inside the group who gave the order to "cover" you.

The existence of the collective has additional effects. If you are my employee and, without being ordered to do so, still commit a tort that injures a third party, he may sue both you and me. He may sue you because you committed the tort; but he may sue me because you are my employee, a member of my enterprise; under the time-honored doctrine of *respondeat superior*, I may be liable. And you still will have a claim against me for indemnity, provided that you were acting in the course and scope of your employment and your conduct was not intentionally wrongful.

2. These general principles do not apply in the military. There, absolute obedience is required, and the soldier to whom a command is given is neither required nor entitled to question its validity. He is free, even required, to question its authenticity (that is, to verify that it really is a command from his superior), but once he has ascertained that the command is authentic, he must carry it out. Every soldier is deemed to be under duress because, if he fails to carry out the orders, serious consequences, including loss of life, may come to him. Therefore we do not punish him for carrying out his orders, even if in doing so he murders, steals, and destroys property. We might say that in the military context, the scope of personal responsibility is defined by obedience. But this is another way of saying that a soldier has diminished ethical responsibility; he is excused from the duty that we have in normal life, of questioning the commands given to us and making personal decisions about whether to accept or reject any particular command.

The legal appeal of the Eichmann Defense, when Eichmann advanced it, was that he was a soldier operating in a military context. One problem with his defense was that his conduct started before there was any declaration of war, and that it had no obvious military objective. Not only do individuals appeal to "war" as an excuse from ethical requirements, but also our own government is now appealing to "the war on terror" as an excuse from constitutional requirements, which may be seen as the ethical constraints on a government. If we are to believe our present political leaders, people can be arrested and held indefinitely without arraignment, Fourth Amendment rights can be diminished, all because "we are at war."

These are ways in which obedience can be seen as an abdication of personal responsibility.

Obedience as a Way of Coming Closer to God

1. Growing up in a Jewish household I recited countless times a week the benedictional formula "Blessed art Thou, O Lord our God, King of the Universe, who has sanctified us by His commandments, and has commanded us to . . . [do this or that]." This is the formula recited when putting on the prayer shawl or the phylacteries, or when lighting the Sabbath candles, or when eating the *matzo* on Passover, and when performing many other rituals. What does it mean that God "sanctified" us by His commandment? Is it possible that commandments might be given, not to modify the behavior of the one to whom they are given, but to sanctify him? The underlying idea is that the commandments emanate from God and are therefore holy; by addressing them to us, God includes us in His holiness and thereby sanctifies us.

There is an interesting passage in the Babylonian Talmud, *Kiddushin* 31a, in which the commandment "Honor thy father and thy mother" is being discussed. One of the discussants, R. Hanina, tells the story of a non-Jew, the son of a prominent jeweler, who lived in the city of Ashkelon. The leaders of the Jewish community came to him to purchase jewels for the Torah crown. They offered to purchase jewels at a great profit, and although the son was eager to make the sale, he sent them away because his father was sleeping and the key to the jewel chest was under his father's pillow. God rewarded this man: a few months later a red heifer, something of even greater value than jewels, was born to him in his herd. The leaders of the Jewish community came to him to purchase it, and they would have paid any price; but he said to them, "Just give me the profit I lost through my father's honor!" R. Hanina observed on this story, "If one who is not commanded to honor his father and his mother [i.e., the non-Jew], yet does so, is thus rewarded, how much more so one who is commanded and does so. For he who is commanded and fulfills the command, is greater than he who fulfills it though not commanded." Do we agree with this idea? The jeweler's son honored his father deliberately, purposively, yet he was not subject to the commandment. R. Hanina thought that fulfilling the commandment while being subject to it is nobler than fulfilling it without being subject to it.

2. Although there is truth to the idea that obedience to God's commandments brings us closer to Him, the development of this idea into a complicated network of rules and rituals that must be observed on a daily basis seems to carry the idea too far. The orthodox Jew performs 613 *mitzvot*, commandments, each and every day. Even as a child I asked myself whether a lifetime of that kind of ritualized obedience could possibly find favor in God's sight. Could God possibly care how we tie our shoes, or what we eat, or what benedictions we recite? Would He not prefer to see us devote our attention to more constructive pursuits? And can He possibly approve of the sort of obedience that is routinized, mindless, and repetitive? Or does He not prefer the kind of obedience that Abraham rendered to him on Mount Moriah: the passionate obedience that transcended ethical constraints and brought Abraham into direct communication with Him?

Is Obedience a Virtue or a Fault?

Surely, without more, we cannot say whether obedience is a virtue or a fault. It depends—but on what? *On three factors*, which are the three elements of the "schema" discussed previously, and also comprise the elements of an interesting "scoring" system:

1. Obedience to whom?
2. Obedience from whom?
3. Obedience to what?

If the source of the command is sufficiently exalted, we approve of obedience without further analysis. So if a command emanates from God, no one will be faulted for obeying it. If it emanates from a king, some further inquiry may be required.[7] And if from a parent, or a teacher, or a supervisor, perhaps more inquiry is required.

The further inquiry will begin with the question "To whom is the command addressed?" If the person being commanded is a child, perhaps it will be a virtue in him to obey without further question the commands of his teachers and parents. But if the person is an adult, he may be required to question the command and inquire: from whom does it emanate, and what is being commanded?

If the command is to do something that is generally thought to be morally neutral, or morally noble, then obedience will be deemed virtuous no matter who issued the command and no matter to whom it was issued. But if the command is to do something that is morally distasteful, then obedience will be a fault unless the command issues from a high source or the status of the person being commanded is such that obedience is always a virtue (soldier, slave).

Blind Obedience versus Unconditional Obedience

Blind obedience is surely a fault, but unconditional obedience has been said to be a virtue. When we say someone acted out of "blind obedience," we mean that she obeyed a command without questioning it, when she ought to have questioned it. But this is something different from "unconditional obedience," which means a determination to obey the commands of the person or authority in question, even after questioning them and even after disagreeing with them.

Socrates argued, in the *Crito* (50a and ff.) that every Athenian citizen owed unconditional obedience to the Laws of Athens. But no one would say that the obedience Socrates encouraged was "blind" obedience. To the contrary, he insisted on questioning the law and trying to improve it; what he insisted on was simply unconditional obedience. The undertaking to obey the laws was not conditioned on the laws' acting "justly": there was no provision in the "agreement" between Socrates and the Laws of Athens that he could ignore judgments that he thought to be unjust (*Crito* 50c). Instead, he was bound to submit to the judgments of the Laws whether or not he thought them just.

There is a Jewish *midrash* based on Exodus 24:7, *na'aseh v'nishmah*, "We will do and we will hear." The verb "to hear" used in this context probably means "to obey," but the *midrash* interprets it to mean simply "to hear," and tells this story whose purpose is to explain how Israel came to be God's Chosen People: that after the Torah was completed God went around the nations looking for one of them to accept it and adopt the Torah as its law. Every nation he went to asked God, "What is written in your law?" To one he said, "Thou shalt not murder," and they said, "Oh, we murder regularly, and in some cases, we encourage murder. We could not possibly accept this Torah." To another he said, "Thou shalt not commit adultery," and they said, "But we believe in having many wives and mistresses, and we could not possibly accept such a law." And each nation that he went to found something in the Torah that was unacceptable and refused to adopt it, until God came to the Jewish people and they responded immediately, *na'aseh v'nishmah*; we will agree to accept it as our law, and then we will hear what laws it contains. Because of this expression of unconditional obedience, God "chose" the Jewish people as His own.

Unconditional obedience may be a virtue if it is rendered toward a power or authority that is sufficiently lofty—toward God, or toward the Laws of Athens. Even if it is rendered to a power or authority of lesser stature, it has some moral strength and may be seen as a virtue. This was the condition of Oliver North, the devoted servant of President Reagan who carried out orders to sell arms to Iran during the so-called Iran-Contra Affair, and helped the president to violate laws and congressional edicts. Colonel North was proud of his unconditional obedience, and many people admired him for it. Others thought that the president was not so high an authority as to be entitled to that sort of unconditional obedience, and they viewed North's obedience as a fault. But the fact is that deliberate, voluntary, thorough-going, unconditional obedience lends a kind of strength to the personality that it might otherwise lack.

The Binding of Isaac: Obedience and Courage

There is a linkage between obedience and courage. It may sometimes take courage to obey a command; it may sometimes take courage to give a command. This is an unexpected consequence of the fact we have discussed previously, that "obedience" is more than mere "compliance": one may be able to enforce compliance with his commands, but after all he may not be able to enforce obedience to them, because obedience involves the ethical stance of the one to whom the command is addressed.

The story of the *Akedah*, the Binding of Isaac, in Genesis 22, can be read as a short compendium of the varieties of obedience. Read at its most literal level, the story is about Abraham's obedience. Because he was ready to obey God's command, even to the point of sacrificing his only son, God rewarded him. But Kierkegaard read the story as being about courage: in *Fear and Trembling* he awakened us to the qualities of character that Abraham exhibited in responding to God's voice in this instance: he transcended human moral categories, he made the "leap into faith," he demonstrated a marvelous level of integrity. For Kierkegaard, the point of the story was Abraham's courage, not his obedience.

In this story, we have at least four different types of obedience presented: the obedience of Abraham, which took courage, and which was active; the obedience of Isaac, which was an expression of unconditional trust and was passive; the obedience of the slave who was told to wait at the bottom of Mount Moriah, which obedience was merely socially determined; and the obedience of the angel who conveyed God's commands without having a will of his own, as if he were just a force of nature. All four are examples of obedience, but only Abraham and the angel heard God's voice, and only Abraham responded to it with courage.

This leads us to ask: is courage a uniquely human virtue, or does God also have courage? We might say quickly that, of course, God lacks courage because He has no need of courage. This would not be to say that God is a coward, just that courage and cowardice are not categories that apply to the Divine. For in order to exhibit courage, one must transcend fear, and God has no fear; in order to exhibit courage, one must endure risk, and God does not encounter risk.

But this is not so: the story of the *Akedah* begins with a reminder that God wanted to *test* Abraham, as if He were not sure how Abraham would react. And God was pleased when Abraham reacted by obeying the command. We are reminded when we come to this story that God did take risk, a great moral risk when He created the world. His act of creation took courage, and it took courage for God to issue the terrible command to Abraham. How would the world unfold? How would Abraham respond to that command? These are things that God could not know until the events unfolded. The story thus demonstrates the way in which the transaction of giving a command and responding to it implicates the courage and integrity of both parties, the one who gives the command and the one who receives it.

The character of Abraham, like that of any man who hears and responds to God's unmediated command, is *courageous*, which is quite the opposite of the character of the man who accedes to the authority of one who claims to know what God has commanded. To declare, "I do what I do because God has commanded me to do it!" is the declaration of one who is either a lunatic or a Knight of Faith, as Kierkegaard argued so persuasively. Such a person is quite the opposite of one who declares, "You must do what I say because God has commanded us to do it." This other type of person is a representative of an orthodoxy, some problems of which we discuss in the following section.

Obedience to God's Command

The ethical aspects of obedience that we have discussed so far concern themselves with psychological qualities—integrity, consistency, resolve, commitment, and with social relationships—power gradients, hierarchies, and the cohesion of a society. We have only hinted so far at the relationship between humans and God, asking ourselves whether we could analogize God's commands to commands that arise in interpersonal settings. But now we must ask directly: What is it to be obedient to God's command?

Commandments and Commands

We note immediately that there seem to be two kinds of commands that issue from God: what we might call *commandments*, or standing orders, and one-time *commands*, which come always in epiphanies. How utterly different these two are!

Commandments Are Orders of General Application

Commandments are issued to everyone and purport to be valid in all contexts. "Do not murder," "do not steal," "do not do harm to your fellow human," "keep your word," "do not cook the meat of the kid in the mother's milk." For these reasons, they require interpretation, explication, and energetic application to specific settings. Because they are so general they may conflict with one another, and it requires intellectual effort to reconcile the contradictions that sometimes arise between them. The whole enterprise of law, the resolution of particular cases in the light of general principles, the evolving of rules to cover cases that were not anticipated earlier while attempting to reconcile the new rules with existing ones, this enterprise is a response to "commandments" or general principles.

Commands Are Noumenal

When God said to Abraham, "Take your son, your only son, Isaac, the son whom you love, and go to the land of Moriah and offer him there for a burnt offering upon one of the mountains which I will point out to you," this was a very special command. It was issued to Abraham only and was not of general application. It was not necessary or even possible for Abraham to question its source; it was not open to Abraham to question its validity. The same goes for the command issued to Moses out of the burning bush: "Go unto Pharaoh and tell him, Let my people go!" The burning bush symbolizes the noumenal quality of the command: the command was delivered by God in direct conversation with Moses, in an epiphany.

When we long to hear God's voice and to respond to His command, what we are longing for is a noumenal experience. For we need not long to hear God's commandments: to relate to them what is needed is not longing, but study and intellectual industry. However longing, *sehnsucht*, the intense craving, the rapture of hearing God's voice, these are passions appurtenant to the *noumenal*.

The Dramaturgy of Exodus: Commands Transformed into Commandments

Having understood the distinction between commands and commandments, we realize that one of the most important features of the Old Testament story found at Exodus 21, the story of the giving of the Ten Commandments, is that the *commands* that God gave to Moses in their encounter on Mount Sinai, those very commands, became the *commandments* that were delivered to all of the rest of us. "Moses received the Torah from Sinai, and transmitted it to Joshua; and Joshua to the Elders; the Elders to the Prophets; and the Prophets transmitted it to the men of the Great Assembly."[8]

This dramatic idea, the transformation of what God said to Moses in their intimate encounter at the top of Mount Sinai into a message delivered to the whole community—this is an idea of unequaled dramatic power. The juxtaposition of the noumenal with the quotidian, of the intimate with the communal, and the transformation of the direct Word of God into an indirect communication from God, into commandments—this is an overwhelmingly powerful idea.

But is it a plausible idea? The character of one who hears God's command directly is diametrically opposed to the character of one who hears it indirectly. To hear God's voice directly, unmediated, requires courage. As Kierkegaard taught us, God's voice is terrifying, and one must be a "Knight of faith" to respond to it. But to obey what your elders tell you, or to go along with the accepted norms of behavior promulgated in your community, and even to be a promulgator of those norms—that requires a much different personality. Do we really believe that by obeying the Ten Commandments we are somehow participating in Moses' conversation with God at the top of Mount Sinai? Is not Moses, in the way, an intrusive figure who disrupts our own conversation with God? Was not Korah correct?

Religious Orthodoxy and Its Anomalies

The dramatic idea at the core of the Book of Exodus lies at the root of all religious orthodoxy. For what is said to have happened at Mount Sinai is the predicate for every authoritarian figure who declares, "You

must do as I say because God has commanded us to do it." Not that
there was no orthodoxy before Mount Sinai; it appears that the
Egyptians and the Babylonians already had orthodoxies much earlier,
and that it is a feature of human societies that they tend to elaborate
orthodoxies just like some bacteria elaborate enzymes, and like blood
vessels form plaque. Orthodoxies arise in a wide variety of contexts:
there are religious orthodoxies, academic and scientific orthodoxies,
political orthodoxies. But it is with religious orthodoxy that we will be
concerned, because of all the forms of orthodoxy that we might think
of, it is religious orthodoxy that is associated most strongly with obedience and with violence.

Such orthodoxies—all of them—exhibit certain anomalies.

The First Anomaly: The Epistemological Problem

When the Chief Rabbi, or the Cardinal, or the Ayatollah, comes to
me and says, "You must do as I say because God has commanded us
to do it," what will he do if I respond, "That's odd; I spoke to God this
very morning, and He told me to do quite the opposite!"? He will call
me a heretic, and he may use violence against me. He purports to
assert God's authority, but he is actually asserting his own authority
and the authority of the orthodox hierarchy of which he is a representative. He says he is reporting God's words, but the only voice he
can produce is his own voice. The obedience he demands is obedience
to himself and to the hierarchy in which he functions: obedience to
people, not to God. This is an epistemological problem that cannot be
resolved. It leads the orthodox into denial, and the denial leads them
into anger, and the anger leads them to violence. This is part of the
"dark linkage" I spoke of at the beginning.

I call this an epistemological problem: how can I know that the
assertion "God said . . . [this or that]" is true? Even if I myself have
heard God say it, I might be tormented by doubt; but at least if I
heard God's voice directly, unmediated, the epistemological problem
might be solved. But if you tell me that God said this or that, how can
I know you speak the truth? If you claim to have heard God directly,
then I will be caught up in issues of authentication: Are you authentic or are you a charlatan or a huckster? Do you have the ability to
hear God's voice? Is your report of what was said accurate, or were
you so carried away that you misheard? All these issues will trouble
me. But it will be much worse if you do not claim to have heard God's
voice yourself, but are rather merely reporting what you heard from

someone else, who heard it from someone else, who claims to have heard it directly from God.

This kind of problem can never be solved satisfactorily, except in fiction. In Numbers 16, the story is told of Korah and his kinsmen who came forward to challenge Moses' authority. They claimed that the whole congregation was holy and that it was wrong of Moses and Aaron to set themselves up as leaders; all of them had just as good access to God as Moses and Aaron. But in that narrative, God himself intervened to settle the dispute. He caused the earth to swallow up Korah and all those who stood with him, and thus He reinforced Moses' authority. But surely this story has to be seen as a high-class form of political propaganda: the authors of the Five Books of Moses were interested in validating Moses' law and in legitimizing the kingdom in which they lived by tracing its lineage back through history to Moses. Perhaps a different Bible would have been written by scribes loyal to Korah. In real life, the claims to legitimacy and authority of the orthodox hierarchy are not vindicated by Divine intervention: if they are vindicated at all, it is by force and violence.

The Second Anomaly: The Logical Problem

The founder of every new religion must reject the old religion. As a matter of historical fact, it appears that all great religions were founded by individuals who were led reluctantly to reject the orthodoxy of their time and place. Abraham left his land and his birthplace and his father's house in order to go to a place that the Lord would show him. Moses left Egypt and found God in the Burning Bush. Jesus rejected the Jewish orthodoxy of his day. Buddha rejected some of the key doctrines of Jainism and Hinduism. Muhammad rejected the polytheism of his milieu. Kuukai, the ninth-century Japanese priest who brought Esoteric Buddhism to Japan, rejected the orthodox Buddhism of his day.

These great innovators were not merely rebellious; all of them went through an intense struggle before they could leave the established ways of thinking in which they were brought up. Out of a desire to be obedient, they were led to a form of disobedience. In the life story of each of these innovators, there is a drama of struggle: Moses resists the command at the Burning Bush; Abraham has to leave his father's house; Muhammad is forced to "proclaim" after resisting the angel twice. Kuukai, the story goes, had to swallow a star and only then went out to establish his new religion; Jesus struggled in the desert, and on the cross.

But this is not just a historical fact, it is a logical necessity. For in order to found a new religion, one must leave the old religion. This creates an anomaly for all forms of orthodoxy: the authority they claim derives from a religion that was once new. The newer it was, the more recent was the memory of its founder, and of his generative act of creative disobedience. The older and more entrenched a given orthodoxy, the greater the distance it has traveled from its founder and the less it is entitled to claim his authority.

State Religion: Church and State

How All Three Judeo-Christian Religions Became "State Religions"

Because human collectives have a tendency to form orthodoxies, religions have tended throughout their history to be co-opted by the political power structure. This is true of Judaism, Christianity, and Islam. But the histories of each of these religions are different from one another, particularly their histories as state religions.

Christianity began its life as the very opposite of a state religion. It was not until the fourth century, when the Emperor Constantine declared it to be Rome's official religion, that it became anyone's "official" religion. It had three hundred years of growth and development before it was a state religion, and those three hundred years have served it in good stead.

The transformation of Christianity into a state religion has been much discussed and bemoaned. The Vatican itself has been said to be the spiritual heir, not of Jesus, but of the Roman Empire. The transformation of the religion into a state religion spawned the monastic movements of the fourth and fifth centuries, and Christianity had its Luther a thousand years later. Throughout its history, the religion has benefited from an energetic sectarianism that has kept the issue of personal versus state religion well in focus.

The transformation of Islam from Muhammad's private revelation into a state religion took place, amazingly, during the lifetime of the Prophet himself. Islam had no time to develop before it was commingled with the political enterprise of the Prophet. But even so, Islam has its Sufis, who represent an inward, personal, esoteric kind of religious passion that separates itself from the more communal state religion and its orthodoxy.

Judaism too underwent this transformation, and as with Islam, it occurred at an early point in its life cycle. But because, unlike Islam, it has existed only in diaspora throughout most of its history, and because it has endured such persecution over the centuries, Judaism is not usually thought of as a state religion. Yet the truth is that the Judaism of the Old Testament is the most virulent possible form of state religion. The Five Books of Moses document the transformation of Judaism from a bucolic, personal religion to a state religion with a clear political agenda. The Book of Genesis depicts a series of personal relationships with God: that of Adam and Eve, of Cain and Abel, of Noah, of Abraham, Isaac, and Jacob. Nowhere do we find in that Book anything like general laws. Instead, what we read in Genesis are moral tales, tales of ethical action and development, stories of personal encounters with God.

But in the Book of Exodus, as soon as the Ten Commandments have been handed down from Mount Sinai, we see a proliferation of rules and commandments, and the bucolic religion of Abraham is gone from the narrative. In its place we have a state religion, a priestly bureaucracy with Aaron at its head and with rules of succession, and we have an orthodoxy. And most significantly, we have a political–military agenda: we have the whole people of Israel on a mission to occupy the Land of Israel. The nexus between the One God, the One People, and the One Land—this passionate nexus that informs the whole of the Old Testament—this is something the narrative prepares us for when God promises it to Abraham, but the whole feeling of what it is to be a Jew changes radically from Genesis to Exodus.

Judaism was thus the first passionate state religion, more passionate than the earlier religions of Egypt and Babylon, which may also have been state religions, because Judaism was formed partly by the writing of the Old Testament. This use of the Old Testament narrative to justify the state religion gave Judaism an intensity that the older religions, which had formed over the course of centuries, did not need and did not have. It was the binding of the religious to the narrative aesthetic that gave Judaism a uniquely powerful aspect.

What Happens When a Real Religion Becomes a State Religion?

A great deal has already been said about how the state is contaminated when it adopts a religion: the separation of church and state was identified as an aspirational ideal in the American constitution. I call it an aspirational ideal because we can hardly say that a complete separation of church and state has been achieved, even in our country. Even at the beginning of the twenty-first century we are struggling with national holidays, trying, for instance, to pretend that Thanksgiving and Christmas are times of shared sentiment. Indeed, we still believe in spite of ourselves that shared sentiment is something the state should encourage and that it has a right to want. We still have not sloughed off the vestiges of ceremony, or even of the sort of kingship against which our Founding Fathers rebelled so nobly: our public officials still strike poses and adopt forms of rhetoric appropriate to medieval monarchs.

These aspects of our society have become worse since the explosion, in the mid-twentieth century, of the mass media. For the media adopted the existing forms and cultural stereotypes, choosing to present all its subjects in the light of celebrity and majesty, in order to pander to the desires of the viewers. Nevertheless, despite all this most of us would agree that having any state religion is bad for the state.

But how many of us realize that it is also bad for the religion? The state is for everybody; religion is not. It is only for those who are prepared to encounter God, and who have the courage to hear His voice. When Moses assembled the entire people of Israel at the foot of Mount Sinai and delivered the Ten Commandments to them, he allowed his political ambitions to overcome his religious sensibilities. Looking at their faces, he must have known that from among the whole congregation of Israel only a few could possibly understand what God was, and what the Ten Commandments were. This is no criticism of the People of Israel; it is very much similar to observing that only a few people really have the talent to love great music, or great art. We should not criticize a person for lacking a talent, but to pretend that everyone has the talent is to betray the music and the art. When a religion becomes a communal thing, it is betrayed in that way.

The proper office of religion is to provide each of us a pathway toward God. This pathway leads away—it must lead us away from the community into a private encounter with God. When religion purports to bring us into the community it has lost sight of its proper function, and it has become vulgarized and debased.

Conclusions

We have outgrown the religion of our ancestors, but we are afraid to admit it. The God of the classical Judeo-Christian religious texts, the Old and New Testaments, and the Qur'an, and of their liturgies, is a king, clothed in majesty, more powerful than any earthly king. It is quite natural to think of a king as issuing commands because the king is at the pinnacle of the social hierarchy, and at one end of the power gradient. In that frame of mind, it is natural to think of obedience toward God, something modeled on social obedience, which we have discussed here.

But there is a problem with this God: we no longer believe in kings. Kings are comical figures today, laughable anachronisms whom nobody can quite take seriously. Can we today possibly think of God as a King? Even if we could separate Him from the common failings of earthly kings, from pride, arrogance, cruelty, and narcissism, we would have to explain why He wanted or needed subjects, or intermediaries, or bureaucracies. If we separate Him from all these things, and see God as having only some glowing, unearthly regal grace and dignity, then we will not perhaps need to call Him a King at all, nor will we need to think of Him as speaking in commands.

He might still speak to us in the imperative mood, but not every use of the imperative mood is a command. Many uses of the imperative voice sound like commands but they in fact are not. There are precepts, such as "Know thyself!" "Love thy neighbor as thyself!" "Do not envy!" There are exhortations, such as "Justice, justice shalt thou pursue!" There are encouragements, such as "Run, Johnny, run!" or the *midrash* "Behind each blade of grass, an angel stands whispering, 'Grow! Grow!'" And there are affirmations, like "Be fruitful and multiply." When God said, "Let there be light!," we might take those words as a command, but perhaps they were more in the nature of an *affirmation*. The First Commandment, "I am the Lord thy God . . ." might also be heard as an *affirmation* rather than a command. "Honor thy father and thy mother" is probably an *exhortation* or a *precept* more than a command. "Leave your land, and the place of your birth, and your father's house, and go to a land which I will show you . . ." is as much an exhortation, and an encouragement and an affirmation, as it is a command.

The conversation we strive to hold with God will not involve any small talk. And it will not involve or require even the exchange of information since our intimacy with Him will obviate the need for the exchange of information. One model of a conversation like that, the best model that our ancestors could come up with, is that it will consist of God's commands and our obedient responses to His commands. For commands are not associated at all with small talk or with information exchange: they are a different type of discourse that is involved with the ongoing act of creating the world and perfecting it.

But in the real conversation with God, we will be ethical equals. He will still be all-powerful and we will not be, but He will see our integrity and He will respect it, so there will be no "gradient" of authority and no giving of commands. God may use the imperative mood with us, and we may use the imperative mood with Him. We will answer each other, and respond to each other, and we will dance together in the realm beyond time. For His spirit will be fully realized in us, and our spirit will be fully realized in Him.

But when our relationship with God is thus perfected, obedience will be abhorrent to us both.

Notes

1. The term "grammar" is used here in the sense used by Wittgenstein, *Philosophical Investigations* (New York: Macmillan, 1953).

2. This is a term borrowed from Old Testament textual criticism. It refers to the method of trying to get at an underlying concept, for example, the Old Testament concept of sin, by examining the different words that seem to relate to it such as *peshah, avon, averah, toeavah*, and so on. See, for example, Knierim, *The Task of Old Testament Theology* (Grand Rapids: Eerdmans, 1995), at 425–426.

3. This is a temporary oversimplification. See the section under the heading Obedience and the Power Gradient, where it is explained that all that is required is some gradient of perceived power or "authority."

4. See the passages from the Talmud in which these questions are explored (e.g., *Chullin* 108, 113; *Pesachim* 85b).

5. See Buber, *Tales of the Hasidim, The Early Masters* (New York: Schocken, 1947), 45.

6. Indeed, the English philosopher John Austin wrote in the nineteenth century that law is a system of "orders backed up by threats." John Austin, *The Province of Jurisprudence Determined*, W. Rumble, ed. (Cambridge: Cambridge University Press, 1995; first published 1832).

7. In the work mentioned in note 6, John Austin defined law as a system of commands of general application that issue from the legitimate sovereign, identified as the person or persons to whom members of the society render habitual obedience and who render no such obedience to others.

8. Ethics of the Fathers, 1:1; see this passage "debunked" in Boccaccini, *Roots of Rabbinic Judaism* (Grand Rapids: Eerdmans, 2002).

CHAPTER 6

REFLECTIONS ON MONOTHEISM AND VIOLENCE

Charles Mabee

Introduction

The question of the relationship between monotheism and violence is complex and ancient. The subject matter is rich and variegated. This chapter is intended to be an exploration of the question rather than a final answer to it. Although I claim identity with Christianity, the following discussion is not exclusively related to that religious tradition. My intent is to explore the logic of monotheism as a spiritual expression, not to examine the meaning of the behavior of all people who have claimed monotheistic belief. It goes without saying that the monotheists of the world, of all shapes and stripes, have perpetrated acts of violence. In that specific sense, monotheism is ipso facto violent; but that begs the question as to whether monotheism inherently motivates those who hold monotheistic belief to act violently, or even inclines them to do so.

In the age of political correctness, the almost knee-jerk response to this question is yes, monotheistic belief leads inevitably to the legitimation of violence. It is patriarchal and imposing, thus inevitably oppressive. The reasoning often is based on an Aristotelian syllogism that runs in this sort of fashion:

If the one true God that my religion believes in is real
And that which is real characterizes the faith of my religion
Then the one true God characterizes the faith of my religion, and all
 other religions are somehow false.

This implication or claim of the falseness of the faith of others is tantamount to legitimizing violence against them. Even without physical violence, that polemic posture is a violation of the person who holds to any alternative view or faith perspective. Certainly, a logical sequence of this sort has been followed by many who claim monotheistic belief. That cannot be denied, but it misses the larger point: does the logic of monotheism itself inherently incline one to such a violating or potentially violent position?

The Logic of Monotheism

A fruitful and satisfying answer to this issue should begin with a definition of two terms: *monotheism* and *violence*. I employ the term theism synonymously with the acknowledgment of God, and understand monotheism as attributing reality exclusively to a particular manifestation of God. Of course, this need not imply the denial of other concepts of the divine being within the divine economy. In fact, monotheistic religions frequently populate the divine realm with a plethora of lesser divine, or at least heavenly, beings and manifestations. This can include the eventual incorporation within the divine economy of other divine beings, who were worshipped as gods by other people and religious cultures. In the interesting case of Hindu monotheism, lesser gods are acknowledged as real, at least to those who believe in and worship them, because they are understood to point to and incorporate attributes of the one Ultimate Reality that underwrites the sacred sphere. However, it is this Ultimate Reality (Brahman) that establishes the context for the existence of the lesser deities, not the other way around. Because they incorporate the divine essence of Brahman, the lesser gods are lesser only in the sense that they assume different form, we may almost say masks, to accommodate the limitations of their human subjects.

However, this rather straightforward and simplistic view of monotheism is not without ambiguity. You may ask: what part of "My God and only my God exists" is a violation of others? The problem is that this claim says very little about the *content* of monotheistic belief. Logically, monotheism as such does not determine the nature of the god who is claimed. "The One True God" can be benevolent and kind or arbitrary and vindictive. The logic of monotheism as such does not demand one or the other affirmation. So the term *monotheism* should have the accent on the *mono* rather than the *theism*. Monotheism is a concept that defines theism only against those who claim the existence of more than one god. Monotheism is fundamentally a denial of any other type of theism, whether monotheism, henotheism, or atheism.

In claiming the reality of only one God, nothing is said about the nature of this God, except that God is exclusive. Is this God malevolent? Is this God malicious? Is this God arbitrary and unpredictable? Is this God full of grace? Nothing, strictly speaking, in the claim of monotheism itself eliminates any of these possibilities. Monotheistic belief does not inherently ensure the dominance of love over hate, peace over war, or nonviolence over violence. Such refined questions are still unanswered within the logic of the designation. All that is claimed is the denial of the reality of other theisms or gods.

Hence, the simple answer to the question "Is monotheism violent?" is yes and no. Yes, it can be. No, it need not necessarily be. But, while this may be the strict logic of the answer to the question, it surely does not capture the sense behind the question. What is clearly implied here is the further qualification of monotheism by something like "those significant expressions of monotheism in human experience." Does the historical manifestation of monotheism within human history tend toward the violent or the nonviolent? Should we logically welcome the advent of monotheistic belief in the human striving toward a more ethical human universe? The term *monotheism* does not really help us at this point. We cannot really determine a tendency toward violence or nonviolence within it. It is toward an examination of the term *violence* that we now turn for more fruitful guidance in answering the question.

The claim of monotheism may be perceived as violent by those who claim the existence of multiple gods. In addition, should those gods actually exist, then the gods themselves would necessarily feel the sting of violence by virtue of the denial of their existence. Thus it is immediately evident that any claim to inherent *monotheistic nonviolence* can come only from within the framework of monotheism itself. That is to say, within the logic of its denial of the reality of other gods, this denial can be viewed as nonviolent *only if these other gods do not actually exist*. Henotheism, which does not deny the existence of other gods but champions one primary God, does not fall into this logic. From within the logic of monotheism, however, the very opposite point may also be made: the claim for divine status on behalf of a god who does not "truly exist" necessarily does violence to the one God who truly does. Thus, in a very real sense, the question of violence is rooted in the intellectual framework at play in the mind of the beholder. What is violent for one might be construed as liberating by another, and vice versa.

However, the issue is even more complicated. Today we ask questions of religious belief that include the human social and psychological dimensions lying beneath religious conviction. We ask such questions as the following: What role do social structures play in the perpetuation of any sort of monotheistic or non-monotheistic belief? How do belief mechanisms function as a means of power and social control? Can a Marxist analysis that uncovers economic forces at work in society be totally ignored in theological analysis? How *real* are we to consider theological formulation of any sort, especially if they are separated from human practical or operational realities of daily life? Are theological statements really psychological statements in disguise? Is the whole concept of God a surrogate father figure? Freud seemed to think so. What about recent discoveries concerning the healing power of faith? Does it *really* make any difference whether the god(s) we pray to actually exist? Is it enough if we *think* they do? It is no longer possible for theology to ignore what is now a massive and imposing intellectual framework for all contemporary philosophical and theological thought.

As important as the human dimension of the problem of monotheistic violence may be, none of the aforementioned considerations are central to the argument. Raising them here serves primarily to suggest something of the difficulty of the issue at hand. By focusing on the logic of monotheism, we have the possibility of shedding light on the problem of monotheism and violence in human history. Does the historical evidence suggest that monotheistic conviction within the highly evolved life of the world's great religions, such as Judaism, Christianity, Islam, Baha'i, and Sikhism, has resulted in increased violence by the adherents? A similar way to ask this question is: when a Christian performs an action or deed in the name of Christianity, a monotheistic religion, does the evidence suggest that it is monotheistic conviction that is accountable?

A large part of the ambiguity at work here is the inherent ambiguity of the term *religion* itself. Inquiring into the meaning of religion implies that we can not ultimately avoid inquiring into the meaning of theism. Only then can we propose a guide for sorting out the violence and nonviolence at play in the historical manifestation of the world's monotheistic religions. Religion can be authentic or nonauthentic in the same sense that monotheism can be violent or nonviolent. We have a way to distinguish authentic or genuine religious experience from counterfeit religion. It is possible to differentiate an authentic monotheism that is nonviolent from a counterfeit monotheism that perpetrates violence in the name of God.

The central thesis of this chapter is that an authentic monotheism is a rhetoric of religious conviction that has the capacity of lessening human violence and establishing a context for liberating the human spirit. I do not make this claim based on personal conviction. I base it on the underlying intention of the logic of monotheism. Of course, Buddhism seems to offer proof that this nontheism also has inherent characteristics that move one toward nonviolence. So do persons of high ethical stature who ground their worldviews in something other than faith in God. It is ethical action and thought that frame the issue of violence. The rhetoric of authentic monotheistic faith, by claiming an inherent transcendental unity for all the created world, intends to produce a strategy for liberating the whole of society from power structures dominated by elites. Monotheists, in other words, would claim that cultural polytheism historically served as the religious backbone of elitist cultural and societal forms. Such elitism is, by definition, *intrinsically violent*. The difficulty arises in the tension such claims inherently carry with them, suggesting the necessity of *imposing* a "redemptive" monotheism in the place of elitist polytheism.

What is the nature of religion itself that serves as the context for authentic monotheistic belief? I propose a simple formula: $R = B + C + S$. R is religion, B is body (biology), C is culture, and S is spirituality. The active engagement of S in the realms of life controlled by the body and culture is the fourth dimension of religion. The intervention of authentic spirituality is not violent in any absolute sense because it is not initiated for purposes of power and suppression. Authentic spiritual engagement of the biological and cultural givenness of the human situation must interact with the problematic features already present in our material culture before the incursion of monotheistic belief.

Life is short and brutal, and who can doubt the reality of approaching death? Every revolution of the planet brings each of us that much closer to it. *Resignation* at the hopelessness of this reality is *not* the authentic spiritual, and hence religious, response to this perplexing situation. Rather, such religious concepts as God's grace, heaven, resurrection, immortality of the soul, release and absorption into the divine form the rhetoric of authentic spirituality. These are examples of genuine spiritual engagements with our mortality that, while not eliminating death's reality, take away its absoluteness, its sting. When religion engages death in this way, it is doing so not in a violent way, but in a constructive, imaginative way. Theological concepts become violent when they are employed to suppress the faith or life of others, not when they are used to remove the sting of death.

Much the same argument can be made when spiritual conviction actively and aggressively engages other aspects of human culture and experience. Neither God nor the gods create culture; humans do. Authentic spirituality demands that we engage in the deconstructing of culture to break its evolution toward a kind of absoluteness that stultifies individual creativity and spiritual freedom. This deconstruction is not a violent act per se, because it strives to defuse those aspects of culture that strive to dominate our lives, including our moral lives. Cultural deconstruction must occur when culture oversteps its natural boundary of supplementing our biological limitations with the help and power of the community, when it becomes an idol as an end in itself, to use the language of such monotheisms as Judaism, Christianity, and Islam.

Our individual bodies and communal cultures establish the outer framework of our individual possibilities. Culture teaches us that we are not one but many. Culture binds us to one another and offers us fame and institutional immortality to mitigate the reality of individual death. Culture pools the resources of the many for the service of the many. Culture amplifies and extends the power of the individual in a world that is at best indifferent to our individual aims. This process is not inherently violent, but it is susceptible to great perversion and distortion. Addressing those concerns is the work of authentic spirituality.

The Complexities of Authentic Spirituality

History bears witness to the legitimation of violence to fend off greater violence. Most acts of human violence are legitimized by this sort of "fighting fire with fire": a little violence done for the sake of escaping greater violence. History does provide examples of gratuitous violence carried out for its own sake, but gratuitous violence is the exception rather than the rule. Gratuitous violence seems to be rooted in the irrational mind. Most human violence is quite rational. The assault upon the World Trade Center on September 11, 2001, and the intentional downing of the Egypt Air plane into the Atlantic by its copilot the year before were rational acts of persons whose minds were motivated by very specific religious claims. If one concedes the legitimacy of those religious claims, the violence was a rational course of action and consequence.

The rational dimension of such violence arises from notions of reciprocity, a notion of reward and punishment. This inherent concept of reciprocity may be embedded in our psychobiology: "If you do this, this will happen to you," "If you fail to do that, you will suffer these consequences," or "You have done such and such, therefore you have the following coming to you." We live in a world of reciprocal relationships, a world that is just as immediate to us as the very thoughts of our rational mind, a quid pro quo world of psycho-logic.

To the degree that we can speak of human instinct, reciprocity would surely be a primary candidate for defining a key aspect of it, and in the world of everyday life, the violent repercussions of flawed reciprocal behavior readily rend the fabric of our lives. The threat of force makes us careful adults and good citizens. Touch a hot stove, your fingers burn. Is this an act of violence on the part of the stove? Rob a bank, the police track you down and lock you up. Is this inherent violence? If the United Nations declares war on an unjust state, it makes every effort to end the injustice. Are such attempts violent? We may recognize the legitimate claims of reciprocity or get lost in a maze of cultural and moral relativism. The hold of the biological and culture forces that frame all aspects of our lives can be mollified by monotheistic belief, but not eliminated. The biological structure of the human mind, and its extension through the invention of culture, does not disappear in the spiritual quest, though it may be to some extent transcended. Authentic spirituality is as true of the rhetoric of monotheistic belief as it is of any other religious model.

Monotheism as Engaged Spirituality

Thus, in spite of the acts of violence that have been perpetrated by members of all religions, the great monotheistic religions represent a move forward in the human quest for a peaceful world. Belief in one God ultimately carries the psychosocial implication of belief in the oneness of humanity, and ultimately the oneness of the entire created order itself. This perspective is perceived as violent by those who are opposed to such unity because they are sure that their monotheism or polytheism is superior in truth or effectiveness to other theisms, but this violence is not founded on the basis of either gratuitous violence or the violence of oppression. It is often a rational but ungracious application to life's operations of an irrational assumption that a certain specific monotheism can be a particularism, denying the truth of all other monotheisms.

Every one of the great monotheistic traditions, at some time or another, has rationally condoned acts of oppression based upon that irrational assumption. Despite the inherent ambiguity, this was done frequently in the full knowledge that such acts violate the principles of a God of absolute love and forgiveness. Monotheism intends to promote authentic spirituality. Authentic spirituality seeks to be embodied in the realities of the world. Only in its embodiment can it be redemptive. We live in a violent world. A spirituality that refuses to engage the material world of creation and culture promises unrelieved long-term violence to the human spirit, because it fails to transcend the unconscious level quid pro quo dynamics of our individual and communal psychobiology.

So we may say that the solution of the problem of monotheism and violence rests on the question of spiritual engagement with the body. The question is whether monotheism authentically embodies the spiritual, and whether an authentic engagement with the body, the material world of human life and operations, can result in the elimination of human violence. The argument of this brief chapter is that the spiritual rhetoric of monotheism should not be discredited by acts of violence perpetrated by perverse monotheists in the name of God. Monotheists are capable of falling short of the spiritual mandate of authentic monotheism by failing in the enterprise of authentic spirituality, but that does not mean that the human affirmation of a unified and holistic spiritual world is inherently flawed and should be abandoned. The rhetoric of every authentic spiritual tradition shares with monotheism a similar susceptibility to perversion and manipulation by persons with bad assumptions, perverse logic, or evil intentions.

Is the logic of monotheism, with its claim that only one God is the true God, inherently violent in the sense of tending toward oppression and subjugation of all theological models to one worldview? Not inherently! Such misuse of any monotheistic faith tradition is rather a matter of erroneous style and distorted application of faith to life.

CHAPTER 7

FUNDAMENTALISM, ORTHODOXY, AND VIOLENCE

J. Harold Ellens

Introduction

Christian Fundamentalism is a uniquely American heresy. Unfortunately, it has been exported worldwide by industrious mission efforts. Its central objective is the promotion of a strange kind of orthodoxy. Its components are mainly the following five. It holds to a theology of sacred scripture that claims that the Bible is verbally inspired by God so that it is totally inerrant in every word and detail of content, and therefore is to be taken literally as the authoritative foundation of all truth. Second, Fundamentalism subscribes to the apocalyptic worldview that a cosmic conflict between God and the Devil, between cosmic forces of good and evil, rages everywhere and at all times on the battlefields of history and the human heart. Third, it claims that the communities of humans and of transcendental beings such as angels are divided into two camps, namely, the righteous and the unrighteous, and that the temporal blessing and the eternal destiny of each community, and the individuals within it, depend upon the degree to which those beings conform to the law of God. Fourth, Fundamentalism professes that there is a mechanism for escape from the eternal judgment of God upon those who fail to keep his law, namely, confession of sins and correction of behavior. In this case, the justice of God that has been breached by misbehavior is satisfied because the implorations of confession and reformation access the merits of Jesus' sacrifice for human sin in his crucifixion, and that merit balances the scales of divine justice. Fifth, Fundamentalism expects that ultimately God will win the cosmic conflict and subdue what amounts to the evil god, and terminate history in a cataclysm that will damn the unrighteous to eternal hellfire and embrace the righteous into a blissful heaven.

Exposition

Fundamentalism and Orthodoxy are first of all a psychological phenomenon and only secondarily a religious thing. One can find Fundamentalism, of course, in every form of religion in the world. However, Fundamentalism can be identified, as well, in political movements, ethical systems, scientific perspectives, and every type of profession in which humans engage. Lawyers, for example, who are obsessively committed to a strict constructionist interpretation of every law, and function as though the law is an end in itself while human beings exist for the sake of having a population upon which to impose the stringent constraints of the law, are operating with a Fundamentalist psychology. For such folk regulation is everything and freedom is a dangerous condition of inadequate control.

The same psychology may be found in the practice of medicine, dentistry, surgery, and psychology. There are also philosophers who are Fundamentalist in their understanding of the proper answers to the questions of their discipline, chemists who fall into the same psychological category, astronomers who likewise have a counterproductive lack of flexibility in theory and method. An essential component of this psychology is a rigid structuralist approach that has an obsessive-compulsive flavor to it. It is the mark of those who have very limited ability to live with the ambiguity inherent to healthy human life; or have no capacity for that at all. Fundamentalism is a psychopathology that drives its proponents to the construction of orthodoxies in whatever field it is in which those proponents live or work.

We usually think of Fundamentalism and Orthodoxy as terms that apply to religious attitudes, but they apply equally to models for social organization and management, scientific method and objectives, political style and goals, and ethical constructions for human life. Fundamentalism is a psychopathology and Orthodoxy is its product, in whatever field or discipline it is in which one encounters it. Moreover, because this psychopathology and its products always construct a delusional model of reality in terms of which it fashions its worldview, Fundamentalism is inherently a heresy, that is, the source of an unreal picture of the truth about the matter to which it pertains—religion, science, ethics, or the like. Orthodoxy, which claims to be orthodox precisely because it dogmatically insists that it is the one and only possible formulation of the truth, is always, therefore, exactly the opposite of what it claims. It is fundamentally unorthodox, that is, untrue! It is always an erroneous formulation of purported truth and can never be anything other than that because it refuses to be open to any new insight that might be generated by the ongoing, open-ended human quest for understanding.

Fundamentalisms have reared their ugly heads in every field of human endeavor throughout history and have been particularly noticeable in the fields of religion and ethics. One might cite the history of the Spanish monks who mounted the Inquisition of the late Middle Ages, some of the Gnostic forms of early Christianity that sought to suppress others, the Hassidim in Israelite religion, and the framers of the doctrines shaping al Qaeda today. In Christianity, the prominent forms of Fundamentalism arose out of the Great Awakening and the frontier revivals and their psychology, which characterized the eighteenth and nineteenth centuries in the United States. This mind-set has now been exported everywhere in the world. The late Henry Stob, a wise and very generative Christian philosopher and theologian of hallowed memory, who taught for an entire career on the faculty of Calvin College and Seminary, often referred to American Fundamentalism as the most dangerous heresy extant in modern history. Today we would certainly be forced to include in that category of most dangerous movements both Islamic religious Fundamentalism and Fundamentalistic Israeli politics. All three of the great Western religions that derive from the ancient Israelite religion of the Hebrew Bible are plagued by the presence of this sick psychology and its heretical products.

Moreover, no one in our world today, except apparently the Fundamentalists, needs much persuasion to agree that the rigorist mind-sets of the orthodoxies that have taken the world by storm in our time are productive of immense real and potential violence. Whether they are the orthodoxies of the American religious right that supports Zionism for the purpose of hurrying the cataclysm of Armageddon, or of the Islamic terrorists whose dogmatism breeds suicide bombings and WTC assaults, or the Israeli framers of pre-emptive defense who do not desire to negotiate for peace, the sick psychology is in every case the same. The delusions that substitute for truth are very similar. All are caught up in the ridiculous apocalyptic notions of cosmic conflict and the fight against cosmic forces of evil, none of which are real.

Violence is always the product of such worldviews. Whether it is violation of the truth, or violation of persons, property, and appropriate procedures for human social and juridical order, it is violence. Whether it destroys persons, the necessary conditions of healthy human existence, or useful understandings of the real world, it is violence. Whether it corrupts freedom, constrains legitimate liberty, or fouls the human nest with mayhem and bestiality, it is violence. Whether it oppresses persons or peoples with the force and power of empire building, represses hope and the resilience of the human spirit with mass-casualty fear and intimidation, or terrorizes the tranquility of children with media reports of those kinds of mayhem, it is phenomenally destructive violence.

Psychobiology and Fundamentalism

Who generates these Fundamentalisms and Orthodoxies that are so destructive for the human spirit, for the conditions of healthy human life, and for the viability of truth and reality? John Medina published an article in the December 2002 issue of *Psychiatric Times*, titled "Molecules of the Mind: The MAO A Gene and Exposure to Violent Behavior in Childhood." In it he presented some very enlightening data regarding violence. The article reported research on the nurture versus nature debate regarding the sources of aggressive human behavior. Acknowledging that genetic research has swung the pendulum from environmental models to biochemical models of the origins of human violence, Medina insists that the real data show the importance of both. However, in discussing violent behavior in a specific set of human situations, he was forced to report the incredible influence of genetics.

The familiar enzyme monoamine oxidase is important to the "active concentration of neurotransmitters at the synapse" in the brain (10). That is what makes thinking and conscious feeling possible. Two types of genes produce the enzyme. They are very similar in structure and very near each other on the X chromosome, shared by males and females. Because of some interesting things that had been seen in animal behavior when one of these MAO genes, designated A, was knocked out, researchers interested in human aggression began to look for "mutations of this gene in human subjects to see if any correlation could be found between aggression and disrupted MAO A chemistry" (12).

Ten years ago a Dutch family was identified in which numerous generations of adult males were prone to extraordinary, sudden, explosive bouts of aggressive behavior. Examination of the data confirmed the inherited nature of the behavior. The cerebral-spinal fluid of all the subjects indicated a complete lack of MAO A. The mutation in this gene had neutralized its function in the neurotransmitter process. Only in early 2002 were new subjects identified so that the research could go forward. The New Zealand Dunedin Multi-disciplinary Health and Development research program studied the development of over 1,000 children from their births in 1972. "Tragically a specific subset of these children were found to be raised in severely abusive home environments" (12).

Four hundred forty-two male children were selected for the study, which was looking for a significant relationship between behavior and genetics. Fifty-five of those children who had grown up in violent households had both low MAO A levels and highly violent behavior themselves. Violent behavior in children who were from violent households but had high MAO A levels was only about 25 percent of that of children who were from violent households and had low MAO A levels. Children with high or low MAO A levels and stable structured homes all had about 8 percent as much violent behavior as the children with abusive homes and low MAO A levels. These children with 8 percent as much violent behavior were probably reflecting normal levels of aggression.

The import of this research for our concerns here is that, for a proper understanding of the kinds of people who are inclined toward Fundamentalisms and Orthodoxies, genetic studies might prove to be very useful. Fundamentalist psychology is known to produce not only rigid models of thought and worldviews, but also rigidity in other aspects of life, such as regulation of home life and views of professional and personal or family discipline. Fundamentalist Evangelical families produce a higher level of physical and sexual abuse of children than the general population. Moreover, Fundamentalisms tend to run in families and in extended family communities. Orthodoxies tend to form specific discrete communities and these tend to perpetuate themselves throughout generations. It would be of interest to know to what extent this reflects a genetic bias that produces at least a proclivity toward such rigid life and thought and a pathological lack of openness to more universalizing insights or perspectives on truth and life.

Most of all, it would be of interest to know whether such inflammatory leaders as Osama bin Laden, and many like him, who have created isolationistic groups of followers with the objective of wreaking violence upon the world or upon others within their own world, may be persons with low MAO A genetics and highly abusive or rigid and oppressive developmental settings. This would be interesting information because it would provide for a rational understanding of the horrid phenomena with which the world is faced in such persons as Joseph Stalin, Adolf Hitler, Osama bin Laden, Ariel Sharon, Yasir Arafat, and the like. These are people for whom early resort to massive violence as the ultimate solution to all major problems seems an addiction. Arafat and Sharon may seem to be men of different styles, but their methods are the same. Sharon is overtly aggressive in his promotion of massive violence and Arafat is passive-aggressive in his promotion of massive violence, but the outcome is the same. We ought to know why they resort to radical violence as the ultimate solution to every major problem or sociopolitical impasse, so that we can see these kinds of characters coming on the world scene, and also so that we can anticipate the destructive forces of their Fundamentalist Orthodoxies in politics, ethics, or religion before they have opportunity to wreak the havoc of slaughter in Palestinian refugee camps in Lebanon, or exterminate an entire class of citizens in the farming communities of the Ukraine, or commit genocide in the concentration camps of the Jewish Holocaust. Psychobiology may be our hope for the future.

Fundamentalism and its orthodoxies, in whatever field they appear, are inherently violent. The reasons are few, consistently the same in all Fundamentalisms, and straightforward. Fundamentalism is a psychology that insists addictively that its view of reality and truth is the only authentic one, and is the whole truth. Therefore, any other perspective is willfully false, ignorant, and dangerous to the truth. Therefore, it is for the good of the non-Fundamentalists that the Fundamentalist truth be imposed upon them. In religious Fundamentalism it is thought to be the will of God and a favor to all humankind to bring humanity under the umbrella of Fundamentalism. Therefore, it is the imperative of Fundamentalists to impose their model of the truth upon all non-Fundamentalists, by force if they have the predominating power, or by seduction that is usually called evangelism if they do not have the dominant power.

Therefore, those who resist such inclusion in Fundamentalism or who threaten it with repression or opposition must be neutralized, either by isolating, demeaning, or destroying them. This pattern may readily be seen in the history of religions in the violent imposition of Nicene Orthodoxy upon almost all Christian movements in the fourth century and following, with the great destruction of many of the persons and movements that represented Christian alternatives. It is also illustrated by the Inquisition, the Christian Crusades, the witch trials of the American Puritans, the frequent Islamic Fundamentalist crusades against other Muslims throughout history, and now al Qaeda terrorism against the non-Muslim world.

Religious Fundamentalism Worldwide

Martin E. Marty and R. Scott Appleby have done us a great favor in helping us understand religious Fundamentalism worldwide, by the publication of their immense and immensely important volume, *Fundamentalism Observed*. It is the first volume in *The Fundamentalism Project*. It offers a survey of Fundamentalism in all major religious traditions. Sixteen scholars have joined them in trying to achieve both an appreciation and an assessment of Fundamentalisms in American Protestantism, Roman Catholic tradition, Protestant Fundamentalism in Latin America, the Jewish Fundamentalism of the *Haredim*, Jewish Zionist Fundamentalism, Sunni and Shiite Muslim Fundamentalisms, Asian Islamic Fundamentalism, Hindu Fundamentalism, Sikh Fundamentalism, Theravada Buddhist Fundamentalism, Confucian Fundamentalism in East Asia, and political and religious Fundamentalism in Japan. Marty and Appleby call all this the hypothetical family of Fundamentalism, implying the universal underlying psychospiritual commonality that reigns in all of these otherwise quite disparate movements.

> The premise . . . is that religious fundamentalism, a term historically associated with versions of American Protestantism and more recently employed to describe certain expressions of Islam, exhibits generic characteristics which apply to various religious settings. Hence, not only Christianity and Islam but also Hinduism, Buddhism, Judaism, and other religions may be found to have fundamentalist variants. Moreover, an understanding of each of these versions of fundamentalism, . . . will shed light on the phenomenon as a whole. (197)

This encyclopedic work takes as its theme the proposition that Fundamentalism of every kind is a dogmatically asserted and defended ideological system that is, therefore, open to neither review nor critique. It is inflexibly closed to any continued acquisition of truth or insight, modification or expansion. North American Protestant Fundamentalism expresses itself in a nonnegotiable creedal posture and has radicalized both ethics and politics in terms of that ideology. Its aggression has been channeled into an effort to shape national politics through infiltrating the historic system of American political process in efforts to elect Fundamentalists. It is also aggressively saturating the populace with mass media of all types, and focusing upon specific local sociopolitical and ethical battles such as assaults upon abortion clinics. This strategy for getting Fundamentalist ideology into the forefront of national life and significantly increasing its influence upon the mind-set of the populace has been surprisingly successful. Moreover, no effective critique has been offered to counter it since the typical liberal approach has been "The less said the better. Maybe it will go away." Of course, it will not. Only the open arena of dialogue, informed with good ideas founded in truth and reality, will maintain a decent balance and ward off the very real dangers that attend any significant rise of Fundamentalism anywhere.

A Fundamentalist fringe group of one sort or another has existed in Roman Catholicism since the beginning of its long history. Some of those groups became orders of monks or nuns within the church, eventually received papal consecration, and were domesticated into fairly mainline enterprises. Largely in response to the *aggiornamento* (updating) that Pope John XXIII brought into the Roman Catholic communion by convening the Second Vatican Council in 1962–1965, and shepherding it through its aggressively innovating agenda, a countermovement of Fundamentalism resurged in the church. Archbishop Marcel Lefebrve claimed the Church had lost its moorings in its creeds and traditions by the liberalizing openness of Vatican II, and so he ordained three bishops into a new movement to reestablish the historic traditions of the church. This was an act that violated the order of the Church, so he, his bishops, and their followers were excommunicated.

> The emergence of a "traditionalist" . . . movement spearheaded by a "rebel" archbishop indicates the scope of the conflict that has divided Catholics . . . of hierarchical leadership . . . who claim the high ground of Catholic orthodoxy. The rise of the traditionalist movement also illustrates how Catholicism's troubled encounter with modernity has spawned movements and ideological orientations closely paralleling

those associated with Protestantism's own fundamentalist reactions to the modern world. . . . Lefebvre's brand of Roman Catholic traditionalism is a militant and organized reaction against the intellectual and cultural inroads of modernism . . . to arrest and reverse religious change . . . and to preserve the ideological, organizational, and cultic patterns altered, abandoned, or discredited . . . , a protest against the blurring of Catholic identity and the loss of Catholic hegemony. . . . (67)

This Catholic traditionalist movement is worldwide today and at least loosely organized as a fraternity. The Church's response to this kind of dissent over the centuries has generally been surprisingly wise. It has tended to move with extreme patience, giving some room for the dissent to work itself out without enough pressure on it to produce overt violence or ruptured relationships, and then eventually it has tended to co-opt the unconventional movement. Frequently this very process has energized the inner spiritual drivers of the whole Church. Particularly in the United States, such an approach has worked rather well for the last forty years with regard to the absorption of this traditionalist movement back into the mainstream of the church.

In Latin America, on the other hand, the Roman Catholic Church, traditionally the dominant religious force in culture, politics, society, and liturgy, has lost a great deal of ground to Protestant Fundamentalism, exported from North America by Evangelical Fundamentalist missions. This is thought by some to be the result of a rather arid formalism having permeated the Roman Catholic Church in Latin America from the sixteenth century to the mid-twentieth century, together with the rather unsuccessful strategies of Liberation Theologies in all of the mainline denominations in South America. With the demise of the USSR the Marxist Liberation Theologies have lost much of their impetus. The vacuum has been filled in Latin America with Fundamentalism in the Christian traditions but also Fundamentalist mystery religions with quasi-African roots instead of Christian foundations.

Within Judaism, worldwide, an ultra-orthodox scion has grown up called the *haredim*. Fundamentalist Orthodoxy has always been a significant presence in Judaism, as well as in ancient Israelite religion. These Jews hold to the ideology that *their* religious truths, precepts, and formulations have been and must be an unbroken tradition from Abraham to the present moment and on through the future until the Messiah arrives. "To these Jews the past is the great teacher: today is never as great as yesterday, and the best that tomorrow can promise is a return to the great days of yesteryear" (197). The name by which they are called means "Those who tremble at the word of the Lord." They are sure that they are the only ones to whom God pays attention. Historically the term *haredim* referred to those who were scrupulous or obsessive about religious punctiliousness. It is interesting that one of the sins that the Roman Catholic Church named in the Middle Ages was scrupulosity. To call it a sin and require confession for it was a hedge against the psychological illness that is manifested in or incited by obsessive religiosity or self-discipline. In this is the typical rigidity of Fundamentalism evident in the *haredim*. It is true of their approach to theology, biblical study, ethics, social controls, and personal habits. Judaism worldwide has been radicalized to a significant degree by the forces of this movement. This is particularly true in Israel itself, where the ultra-Orthodox have managed to achieve significant political power by manipulating the various coalition governments, made necessary by the increasingly divided society.

I have mentioned Zionism frequently in the four volumes of this present work. Historically it was a relatively general term referring to the Israelite longing for a homeland in Palestine. In the late 1960s it was radicalized by a small group of people who, armed with military weapons, militantly began to force the occupation of Palestinian territories by Jewish settlers, at the same time wreaking havoc upon the persons and property of Palestinians. The current memory is that this movement arose in response to a sermon by Rabbi Kook the Younger, on the nineteenth anniversary of Israeli independence. In the sermon at a Jerusalem religious academy, Merkaz Harav Yeshiva, Kook emphasized passionately several messianic tenets of his mystical system that he claimed would constitute the spiritual base of the revolutionary Jewish-Zionist movement.

Kook claimed that divine redemption of Israel was in process at that very moment, nationally and politically, since Israel had been established and successfully maintained as a nation for nearly two decades, but that what was lacking was a corollary religious and ethical redemption. Most Israelis were secular, and the moral and ethical codes of the society were not those of the Torah or Talmudim but were merely utilitarian ethics of secular Western society. This launched the course that the Israeli nation has come to follow into the tragic mayhem of perpetual violence and mutual destruction of Palestinians and itself. Moreover, this form of violent Jewish Fundamentalism has produced the current general world crisis in and regarding the Near East.

According to the Jewish scholar Gideon Aran, at the outset few people in Israel took the Jewish-Zionist drive seriously and most Israeli were greatly offended by its violence, injustice, and ideological dogmatism.[1] This movement promoted the illegal establishment of Israeli settlements in the land properly belonging, by treaty and title, to the Palestinians. Moreover, it claimed that the territories from the Tigris to the Nile properly belonged to Israel, as in the golden age of David's and Solomon's kingdoms. This bizarre ideology became a driving undercurrent in Israeli politics and social ferment until an increasing number of Israelis began to endorse the vision. General Sharon and the Israeli Defense Force took advantage of this perspective in support of the invasion of Lebanon, and progressively the movement gained political power until it can now essentially manipulate the government. It is of some considerable help to the movement that General Ariel Sharon is now Prime Minister Ariel Sharon. It is largely in response to this abusive form of Jewish Fundamentalism that the Islamic Fundamentalism of al Qaeda and the militant Palestinians has become increasingly focused, unified, and aggressive against the United States, the primary ally of Israel.

As a result of Anwar Sadat's rapprochement with Israel, Sunni Egyptian Fundamentalists shot and killed their president on October 6, 1981. They were carrying out a jihad that they believed was mandated by God. That was, for many of us, the opening gun of the militancy of Islamic Fundamentalism and its worldwide battle against all those who do not agree with their religious ideology. Their spirit is the same spirit as that of the Israeli Zionists whom they oppose. Both groups are destructive Fundamentalists, though they have different religions and are on opposing sides of the conflict. The pathology of each draws out the sick and evil reaction of the other. The momentum of this violently destructive Islamic religious movement has increased weekly since that day two decades ago when Sadat fell victim to the supposed divine mandate. Its victims now number in the tens of thousands and are fast moving to the hundreds of thousands, in Europe, Asia, India, Africa, Israel, Kurdic Iraq, the Mediterranean basin, and the Americas. Their violent guerrilla-type warfare has been carried out on land, in the air, and on the sea. It has been targeted mainly against civilian noncombatants, demonstrating the inherently unethical barbarism and cowardly abusiveness of these psychopaths.

Their movement is referred to as Islamic Fundamentalism because it is their attempt to reaffirm the foundational principles that they

A gunman fires an automatic weapon into the reviewing stand during an attack that took the life of President Anwar Sadat and five others in a Cairo suburb on October 6, 1981. AP/Wide World Photos.

think shaped original Islam and should shape the structures and laws of Muslim society, religion, and ethics everywhere today. Just like those in the Jewish-Zionist movement, these Sunni Muslims wish to recall fellow Muslims to the correct path of their religion, which they, of course, feel divinely appointed to define. All Muslims hold to the authority and life-shaping claims of their sacred scriptures, but the Fundamentalists have an exclusivist and literalist interpretation of the message, mandates, and moral program of the Qur'an, from which they derive a rigorist pattern for social and political regulation of life in Islamic nations. "Islamic fundamentalism is . . . a distinctive mode

The Ayatollah Khomeini at a press conference in 1979. AP/Wide World Photos.

of response to major social and cultural change introduced either
exogenous or indigenous forces and perceived as threatening to
dilute or dissolve the clear lines of Islamic identity, or to overwhelm
that identity in a synthesis of many different elements" (346). Like
their Jewish counterparts, these Fundamentalists are eager to resort
to armed violence and open assault upon civilian or military targets
to gain their vicious and lawless objectives.

The Ayatollah Ruh Allah Khomeini represented, in his lifetime and
his days of power in Iran, the other branch of Islamic Fundamentalism, that of the Shiites. He came to power on February 1,
1979, after being befriended and promoted by France for fifteen
years, contrary to Western political policy and, as it turned out, contrary to the best interests of the people of Iran. Saddam Hussein, a
secular Arab described by Osama bin Laden, together with Hussein's
fellow Iraqi leaders, as a nest of infidels, made war upon Khomeini

and his Fundamentalist regime in Iran. It was, as we remember, a phenomenally destructive war for both nations. Hundreds of thousands of citizens died on both sides. Hussein's opposition to Islamic Fundamentalism was illustrated at that time by his execution of the noted Shiite leader in Iraq, Ayatollah Muhammad Baquir al-Sadr, on April 9, 1980. Subsequently, Hussein supported the Taliban and al Qaeda in Afghanistan against the USSR, as did the United States, and now Hussein seems to be willing to work with al Qaeda, if it pays off for him in his war with the United States.

One form of Fundamentalism is difficult to distinguish from another, and fundamentalists' willingness to resort to unlawful and barbarous forms of violence together to gain their short-term objectives, with little good vision for the long-term consequences, makes strange bedfellows out of a great variety of Fundamentalists in specific ad hoc situations. One gets the distinct impression that American Fundamentalists, who are bent upon attacking and violently closing abortion clinics, however constructive their objective of decreasing abortions on demand, would welcome an al Qaeda terrorist to assist them by bombing a few such clinics. None of us would be at all surprised if *CNN Headline News* reported tomorrow that American Fundamentalists in Atlanta hired a Palestinian suicide bomber to go into an abortion clinic and set himself off, with the promise that the suicide bomber's family in Hebron would get a check for $25,000 U.S. They all smell the same, look the same, act the same, resort to the same abusive aggression, and invoke the same nonexistent god, namely the ridiculous barbarous god of Fundamentalist dogmatic heresy.

Of course it must be remembered that from the inside of the system, for the Fundamentalist personally, the intention is to establish a structured and secure society, blessed by the order and discipline that Fundamentalists believe God's will and law should impose upon all society, religion, ethical systems, intellectual models, and philosophical worldviews. The Fundamentalist is sure that such a world is not only God's imperative but also the best arrangement for humanity; thus the means of attaining it are justified by the ends achieved. The vicious and barbarous violence is not the legal pattern for the lawful world order to come, but merely the expedient to which one must resort to achieve God's ends and purposes here and now. This is thought by the Fundamentalist to be not only justified, but required by the rubrics of sacred scriptures, whether those are the example of Jesus' violence in the New Testament, the model of Muhammad's military jihad in the Qur'an, or the narrative of the divinely ordered extermination of the Canaanites by the ancient Israelites in the Hebrew Bible.

The Fundamentalist character of a special kind of Hinduism that has arisen with strength in the last quarter century is becoming increasingly evident. This sect is particularly evident in northern India and Kashmir, where it arose in the early 1980s as a response to the Islamic Fundamentalism progressively causing sociopolitical and religious turbulence in that region. Initially it was militant and has subsequently turned murderous. The influence of this barbarously violent Hinduism is now seeding itself throughout India, giving traditional Hinduism generally a new quality and a rigid sharp edge. This could easily turn to generalized violence throughout India, particularly where it can be aimed at Islam. It has unified Hindus of a rigid conservative mind-set and given a new and violent revolutionary tone to the religion and its culture throughout the country. The movement now dominates the leadership of the religion virtually everywhere in India, creating a tinderbox of volatility that could easily move the entire nation into an irrational and destructive revolutionary mood.

The more rational and traditional forces of Hinduism have always been rather low-key, disparate, and scattered in focus. It has tended to be a religion of the individual rather than of communities. This has begun to change under the instigation of what is now called the Arya Samaj, a movement that arose in Mumbai in 1875 as a religious reform and appealed largely to the educated classes. It supported the nationalism movements in the early twentieth century that led to the demise of the British Raj. While quite different from the Arya Samaj, a second movement has had a similar effect upon Hindu India. It is the Rashtriya Svayamsevak Sangh, or RSS, which styles itself as a movement for the reform and renewal of Hindu culture and society, secular in its identity and character. The effect of these two forces, particularly in northern India, where the clash with Islamic religion and culture is a prominent issue, is a reinforcement of destabilizing and frequently violent actions of local communities. Both organizations worked unsuccessfully for caste reform in India. They were more effective in the creation of a network of schools for raising the education level of the citizenry, but the effort has proved to be vastly inadequate for the needs of the whole country.

These Hindu Fundamentalisms continue to flourish in modern India and are "an increasingly growing force in cultural as well as

political life" (575). It is an important question as to what forces perpetuate Fundamentalist religion among Hindus, particularly its frequent recent resort to mob violence. The original energy of these
Fundamentalisms was generated by their resistance to colonialism.
Now the movements seem to be stimulated and energized by the
combination of hostility toward Islam; the rise of a new tribalism
within Hindu culture; and a reaction to the disillusionment of ineffective social, political, and economic structures in Indian society.
These movements have acquired the use of contemporary weapons,
and this has enhanced the lethality of their historical militancy. Daily
reports of vicious and horrible abuse, exterminating human life, are
increasingly the way of Indian life.

There are numerous other manifestations of Fundamentalist psychology in the religions and politics of India. The most prominent is
probably that of the Sikh religious tradition. To a lesser degree
Theravada Buddhism may be encountered in that subcontinent. India
is organized as a secular constitutional democracy, but the Sikh religion, while operating within that setting, does not concede any separation between politics and religion. While its local worshiping
groups are comparable to the Christian churches of the Western
World, the faith communities consciously claim that no dualistic categories or idolatry of either images or creeds is tolerable. Life is a
unity: a spiritual, social, religious, political, military, and economic
unity.

Sikhism was founded upon the precepts of the Adi Granth, also
referred to as the Granth Sahib, the sacred scriptures of this faith
group. The Golden Temple at the center of Sikh worship and consciousness was built by Guru Arjan, the fifth of ten Sikh leaders. He
lived from 1563 to 1606. The temple is called Harmandir, the temple
of god. Arjan's son, Guru Hargobind (1595–1644), built a second
temple the year his father died. It is known as Akal Takht, the throne
of the immortal god, and it faces Harmandir. The religious perspective of these gurus was universalistic. Harmandir has four doors, one
toward each of the points of the compass. Guru Arjan said, "My faith
is for the people of all castes and creeds from which ever direction
they come and to which ever direction they bow" (595).[2] The Golden
Temple was built for the singing of hymns of peace, reflections upon
the sacred scriptures, and listening to the teaching of the gurus
regarding life, god, and godliness. The Akal Takht, however, became
the site for celebration, in song and lecture, of heroism, military

exploits, conquest, and religious instruction that promoted those per-spectives.

A persuasive guru named Bhindranwale led an armed militant movement beginning in the early 1980s to give concrete and opera-tional expression to Sikh "assertion of the political and economic rights and religious prerogatives of the Sikhs," which were thought to be under threat (596). He is generally viewed in India as a Fundamentalist, namely, a leader who has selected a few militant aspects of Sikhism in order to motivate his fellow Sikhs to action. His intended action was purportedly for protecting the rights and inter-ests of Sikhs to promote freely his notion of what Sikhism ought to be. He and his armed band are considered, even by most Sikhs, to be extremists. He created a bizarre Orthodoxy that most Sikhs would consider to be unorthodox in terms of the historic principles of their faith. True Sikh Orthodoxy, it is generally understood, would work against this Fundamentalism, since historic Sikhism was oriented upon peace, ecumenism, and universalistic openness to a great vari-ety of people and ideas and advocated "catholicity and not narrowness of the mind" (596).

In 1983 this band of Fundamentalists barricaded themselves in the temple complex, increasingly reinforcing it militarily over time. They conducted a terrorist campaign in which they murdered and pillaged at will, killing hundreds of innocent Hindus. In 1984 the Indian armed forces, under the command of two Sikh generals and one Hindu general, directed an assault upon the temple complex, killing Bhindranwale and many of his associates. This was the source of great sadness to Hindus and Sikhs alike throughout India, since such violence is contrary to the ethics of both communities, but particu-larly to that of the Sikhs. Moreover, the temple complex was badly damaged by this Operation Blue Star, as it was officially called. While these Fundamentalists considered themselves to be the authentic Sikhs, "defenders of the 'basic teachings' of the Sikh gurus . . . and of the economic interests of the Sikh community . . . ," the government could see them only as terrorists, judged by their behavior and their publicly announced creeds and objectives (597).

The 1984 Fundamentalist crisis took place against the background of numerous preceding violent sectarian clashes within the Sikh com-munity and between Sikhs and Hindus. In 1978 a particularly bloody riot killed members of two battling conservative sects fighting over political party issues. This conflict brought Bhindranwale into

prominence as a religious and political leader and led to the later violence. The difference between the two sects was their view of their
sacred scriptures. One held that nothing could be added to the sacred
scriptures and that they constitute the "written guru" from which all
truth and authority is derived. The other claimed that only living
gurus have authority and each can add to the sacred scriptures as he
is led to understand new insight or revelation. Each claimed, with a
Fundamentalist militant rigidity, that its Orthodoxy was the true historic Sikh Orthodoxy. They resorted readily to murderous terrorism,
and that tradition continues. This has regularly resulted in destructive clashes between Fundamentalist Sikhs and the Hindu majority of
India.

Like all other Fundamentalisms, the Sikh variety depends upon a
radical notion of the authority of their sacred scriptures, selective
emphasis upon elements of the historic faith that promote current
militancy and terrorism, charismatic leaders who are willing to
inflame the community with paranoia and violence, commemoration
of past events that can be made to seem like abuse of Sikh
Fundamentalists by other groups, a cultivated and manipulated sense
of isolation, and aggressive reaction to any perception of constraint
upon Sikh Fundamentalist rights by outside powers. Madan is quite
sure that there is no good sign that Sikh Fundamentalism will abate
in the near run. The fundamental difference between the definition of
the relationship between the state and religion in the secular Indian
constitution, on the one hand, and in the mind of the Sikh Fundamentalists, on the other, is so radical and persistent that it will continue to stoke the fires of dissent, isolation, hostility, paranoia, and
aggressive behavior. This psychology, and the aggression it incites, is
always just a hair's breadth from terrorism in India. It tends to bleed
into other partisan conflicts present in that very complex society and
inflame them further with Sikh Fundamentalist energy.

Two additional Fundamentalist movements complete this cursory
survey of the phenomenon in our modern world: Theravada
Buddhism and Confucianism. Buddha died in 544 B.C.E., and his influence throughout the world has competed aggressively with that of
Jesus of Nazareth for the last two millennia. Theravada Buddhism, a
product of the original Hinayana Buddhism, is a Fundamentalist
form of conservative Buddhism. It arose early in the history of this
faith tradition. It is not quite clear why one should call Buddhism a
religion or faith tradition, since it is really a form of nontheistic ethical philosophy. However, it is regularly listed as one of the great reli-

gions of the world, probably because it takes the form of a humanist spirituality and has a transcendental dimension, the achievement of Nirvana.

Buddhism sprang up quickly and spread widely from the moment of Gautama Buddha's original enlightenment. Nearly simultaneous with the rise of Theravada Buddhism, two other mainstreams of the tradition developed, Mahayana and Vajrayana Buddhism. These are complex philosophical systems in the tradition, which have become widely syncretistic and eclectic, and emphasize the importance of social responsibility and cultural development for the improvement of the quality of human life, as well as the encouragement of all humans to practice Buddhist philosophy and ethics. This is a type of Buddhism that has appealed rather intensely to the Western world. Theravada Buddhism tends to be oriented toward escape from mundane material desire, by meditation that enhances self-transcendence and access to Nirvana. It functions in intense tension, therefore, with its social environment and earthly existence.

The Fundamentalism of Theravada Buddhism is expressed in a claim that its roots are in the original true traditions of Hinayana Buddhism of Buddha himself, and that it has preserved the true form of these traditions. It is rigoristic and rigid in its prescriptions for spiritual and social function, it is militant in whichever culture it finds itself, and it aggressively promotes itself worldwide. It has been very influential throughout history in providing the partisan energy for consolidating the sense of identity and, hence, the unification of nationalism in many countries such as Thailand, Burma, Laos, Cambodia, and Sri Lanka.

In these processes Theravada Buddhism has tended to be terroristic and violent to achieve its ends. It is difficult to discern how this comports with the transcendental orientation of Theravada Buddhism, but it is easy to see its sense of social tension reflected in this aggressive behavior. In Sri Lanka, for example, the Sinhalese are Theravada Buddhists, for the most part, and the Tamil are Hindus. The violent and destructive repression of the Tamils by the Sinhalese has been a virtually uncritical process of the Buddhists for generations. It is quite surprising how terroristic these policies have been. Only in recent years, as a result of the militant rise of the Tamil themselves, has any significant constraint been imposed upon these vicious practices of the Buddhist Fundamentalists.

A great variety of Theravada Buddhisms has developed in the numerous nations in which Buddhism has had significant presence and influence over the centuries. However, this is particularly true in the postcolonialist and now in the postmodern era. Some of these have taken the form of rigorously disciplined, conservative ethical systems, focused upon the eradication of social evils and the demeanment of human life and equality. In his "Fundamentalistic Movements in Theravada Buddhism," in *Fundamentalism Observed*, Donald K. Swearer summarizes the entire matter crisply.[3]

> Fundamentalistic movements . . . (are) frequently led by strong, often militantly aggressive, charismatic leaders whose followers . . . perceive themselves to be variously threatened as individuals, communally, or as a nation. The ideologies embraced by such movements tend to rest upon simplistic, dualistic, and absolutistic worldviews. Often exclusivistic (although . . . evangelistic), the movements reject competing groups . . . as morally evil, spiritually confused, and/or intellectually misguided. Possessed of an almost obsessive sense of their unique role . . . these movements may be quasi-messianic or explicitly millenarian in nature . . . anti-rationalist, anti-intellectual, . . . anti-ritualist . . . open to the criticism that it . . . lacks the depth of its classical predecessors. . . . (678)

Confucius was certain when he died that he had thoroughly failed. Subsequently, and rather quickly after his fifth-century B.C.E. pilgrimage, his philosophy spread throughout East Asia, permanently shaping China and heavily influencing Korea, Mongolia, Japan, and most of the rest of East Asia. Particularly in the last century Confucianism experienced a vigorous revival throughout that area. Confucianism is an ethical philosophy with neither a theistic nor a transcendental orientation. From its beginning in the life and teaching of Confucius it was focused upon the enhancement of the education, social order, economic development, and quality and equality of life for all humans.

The recent revival of Confucianism has taken the form of a quest for the roots and specific precepts of the teaching of Confucius. As a result it has tended toward a Fundamentalist character and psychology. This has driven the quest back to the *Analects* of Confucius himself. In the nineteenth century Japan chose a Westernization process rather than a Fundamentalist resurgence of Confucianism. In China and Korea, the attempts to strengthen Confucianism largely failed to produce workable political and social structures. Thus it was largely in the pre-Maoist government in China, carried over in 1950 to Taiwan by the evacuation from mainland China of the Kuomintang Forces under Chiang Kai-shek, that the resurgence of Confucianism was seeded. So it is in Taiwan that the Fundamentalist revival has borne the most fruit.

The contest between Maoist Marxism in China and Confucianism in Taiwan has been carried out primarily as an ideological contest. It has regularly degraded, though, into actual military conflict. Mainly, it has persisted in the form of political barrages, regularly exchanged. Over the last half century, however, with the modernization and capitalization of China, Confucianism has resurged within Maoist Marxism in China itself. Meanwhile, moderation of Taiwan policies and political rhetoric has the Fundamentalist Confucians in Taiwan increasingly forced into a defensive posture, marginalized, and isolated within their own society. This has increased their militancy and their calls for radical opposition to any rapprochement with China.

Thus, the potential for violent conflict between the Fundamentalist Confucians in Taiwan, and in a larger sense throughout industrialized East Asia and the forces in power there, is ideologically increased, while at the same time politically and militarily less likely of success. The Confucian resurgence has been, in part, a response to Westernizing influences everywhere in the world today, a quest for a more idealistic homegrown ethic and social code. It is an attempt to hold in check this Western type of modernization in the hopes of preserving more traditional or historic ideologies and codes, indigenous to East Asia itself. Moreover, the appeal for the Fundamentalist mindset of this Confucian revival lies in the general dissatisfaction with Western moral and ethical values, as well as with what is perceived to be trivial and trivializing Western philosophy and cultural models. It is not surprising that this is so, considering that so much of what is purveyed to the world in general as Western culture has taken the form of rather risqué Hollywood movies, rather cacophonous American music, rather violent videos from many sources but most surprisingly even from Disney productions, remarkably cynical Western philosophies, and weapons-oriented U.S. industrial products.

Tu Wei-ming reminds us of the 1958 manifesto that was prepared by a number of Chinese scholars as their proposal for Chinese understanding of how Confucian tradition may be made relevant to the future development of a holistic model of psychosocial idealism for their nation.[4]

A faith in the efficaciousness of the Confucian core curriculum and an assumption of the authentic transmission of the Confucian heritage throughout history are implicit in the manifesto, but the main thrust of the argument is to present a Confucian perspective on the human condition defined in terms of modern Western categories . . . a denunciation of the sterility of modern commercial culture and the New Confucians' reconstruction of the meaning of the human "life world." (773–774)

This Confucian revival is widespread and diverse in East Asia. It is a search for "cultural roots" as an "integral part of modern consciousness and . . . persistent universal human concern." Confucian Fundamentalism seems to have been the least violent form of Fundamentalism so far in history. That may be a derivative of a non-paranoid Chinese communal personality or the lack of need for violent aggression to achieve the goals of this conservative philosophical reawakening. It may be a characteristic inherent to Confucian principles themselves.

Conclusion

Fundamentalism was once thought to be merely a special type of rather obsessive and rigorist Protestant Christian heresy, championed by people who had a psychological need for high levels of spiritual and sociotheological control, who tended to be rather esoteric in their belief system, passionate in their certainty that they alone possessed God's truth, and aggressive in their compulsion to impose it and its implications upon others. Now we understand that Fundamentalism is a psychological pathology that can shape and take possession of the framework of thought and action in any arena of life, and particularly any ideology. This makes religion particularly vulnerable to the pathology of Fundamentalism, a dangerous heresy almost anywhere we find it.

The danger in Fundamentalism takes the shape of false Orthodoxies. They are dangerous in many ways, but especially in the ways in which they corrupt the truth, disrupt community, violate personal and communal prerogatives, and promote sociopolitical and physical-material strategies of destruction. We have been made profoundly aware in recent years of the intimate links between religious Fundamentalism and worldwide terrorism. This is associated in our minds at this time primarily with Islamic Fundamentalism. However, what we need to discern is the manner and degree to which every form of Fundamentalism has the potential for terroristic tactics to achieve its "divinely appointed" ends, and most Fundamentalisms have resorted to gross violence at some point in their histories.

It is imperative, therefore, that we identify Fundamentalism wherever it may be found, define and name it as the psychopathology that it is, engage it, contain its violent potentials, and reduce its influence as much as possible. As with countering all strategies of organized violence, the greatest challenge is to defeat it without resorting to its own tactics and thus being dragged down to its own subhuman moral level. In America's leadership strategies for the elimination of the Fundamentalist violence of worldwide terrorism today, it is crucial that we find our way without triumphalism or a resort to the arrogance of power. Power properly and humanely applied is one thing. Arrogant power is quite another. Ignorant arrogance is the worst of all.

The incredibly grace-filled late medieval or early modern philosopher Baruch Spinoza, in his tract on politics, said that in his quest for understanding the facts, foibles, and fruits of human life and thought he tried to be very careful not to laugh, cry, or denounce humans in their very human pilgrimage, but instead he always tried simply and gently to understand.[5] It reminded me of the noted acerbic cartoon editor of the *Kansas City Star*, who upon retirement was asked to say what he really thought of the human race, after his years of rather vicious caricatures of it. He rose and said, "I think we should be kind to it. It is the only one we've got." So, in the spirit of Spinoza and the cartoonist, I hope we can learn something crucial from the pathological experiments of the Fundamentalisms of the world and history, and shepherd ourselves to greater gracefulness and mutual goodwill.

Notes

1. *Jewish Zionist Fundamentalism: The Bloc of the Faithful in Israel (Gush Emunim)*, chapter 5 of *Fundamentalism Observed*, ed. by Martin E. Marty and R. Scott Appleby (Chicago: University of Chicago Press, 1991), 265ff.

2. T. N. Madan is the author of "Fundamentalism and the Sikh Religious Tradition," in *Fundamentalism Observed*, Martin E. Marty and R. Scott Appleby, eds. (Chicago: University of Chicago Press, 1991). He cites the work of Gopal Singh, *A History of the Sikh People* (New Delhi: World Book Centre, 1988), 177, as the source of his information about this story. He adds the note that according "to Sikh tradition, unsupported by historical evidence, the foundation stone of the Golden Temple was laid by a Muslim

Sufi, Mian Mir. It bears testimony to the traditional Sikh approach to religious differences that such a story should be believed" (623).

3. Marty and Appleby, Op. Cit.

4. Op. Cit., chapter 13, "The Search for Roots in Industrial East Asia: The Case of the Confucian Revival," 740–781.

5. I was reminded of this wonderful sentiment of Spinoza by Martin E. Marty's observation upon it in his chapter titled "Fundamentals of Fundamentalism," in *Fundamentalism in Comparative Perspective*, Lawrence Kaplan, ed. (Amherst: University of Massachusetts Press, 1992), 15.

CHAPTER 8

POSTURE AS A METAPHOR FOR BIBLICAL SPIRITUALITY

Edson T. Lewis

Disintegration

Spirituality's role in shaping and even determining human thought and action is not always recognized. Human beings may consult the insights of economics, physiology, psychology, politics, sociology, theology, and the like as they look for ways to avoid destroying themselves and the planet on which they live, but without giving much, if any, attention at all to spirituality as a determinative factor in human identity and conduct. Ignoring such an important feature of human beings exacts a severe price. Not only do we cripple efforts to understand others and ourselves, but also we avoid dialogue and accountability around an issue whose implications tend toward either the survival or the demise of the human race as we know it.

Attempts to include *spirituality* in the equation for the common good lead to an immediate and huge problem, however. No consensus exists as to the meaning of the term and its attendant issues. Therefore, any shared public discourse concerning spirituality and its implications becomes difficult, if not impossible. Furthermore, the swamp of meaninglessness into which *spirituality* has strayed shows no sign of relaxing its grip on a word that is bantered about freely in our conversations with one another. Retrieving it for more useful service in the public square will not be an easy task.

Neither the word nor its referents have caused this predicament. Nor is *spirituality* the only word so threatened. If Wendell Berry is right, the danger extends to language itself and is a sign of our times (Berry, 1983). He warns, "My impression is that we have seen, for perhaps a hundred and fifty years, a gradual increase in language that is either meaningless or destructive of meaning. And I believe that this increasing unreliability of language parallels the increasing disintegration, over the same period, of persons and communities" (24). The fortunes of the word *spiritual* and its cognates loudly declare the truth of Berry's suspicion.

That the disintegration of contemporary persons and communities has grown to dangerous proportions goes without saying. Erosion of traditional values throughout the world, coupled with new, and sometimes terrifying, political, social, economic, and religious alignments, magnifies the threats that these changes portend. That the magnitude of these problems is symbiotically related to the growing unreliability of language is not generally acknowledged. The assumed truth of that union provides much of the glue that holds this essay together. If the connection is real, as I think it is, then reclaiming language and its words for more useful service in human affairs is essential to the reconstitution of a disintegrating world.

Of course, the contributions that language makes to human community are ambiguous. They can be (1) beneficial, as in the promotion of empathetic understanding, consensual enterprises, and enduring fidelity. On the other hand, they may be (2) destructive, as in the case of calculated lies, prejudicial stereotyping, and vicious scapegoating. Ideally, this essay will weigh in its comments on behalf of the first alternative.

"Spirituality" at Risk

The trend toward trivializing language becomes particularly ominous when it threatens a word like *spirituality*. I shall argue that spirituality, as I understand it, of course, whether for better or worse, lies close to the center of every human being's identity. There it qualifies our fondest dreams, our largest fears, our deepest loyalties. It undergirds the sense that we make of the world, and how we behave in it. It shapes religious commitments in profound ways. If the term loses its substance, we cannot give an adequate account of who we are, either to others or to ourselves, or what we are to do in the world. "The failure of spirituality is the primary obstacle to an affective knowledge that, unlike mere intellectual apprehension, can move the whole personality" (*Encyclopedia Britannica*, 2003 CD edition). If *spir-*

ituality cannot be a shared concern in the public square, amenable to dialogue and accountability, then the threads of our social fabric loosen and start to unravel. Is it any wonder that willfully destructive survival strategies of avoidance, defense, or attack soon follow?

During the 1990s the word *spirituality* assumed status as one of the principal buzzwords of the decade. An educated guess indicates that its trajectory will maintain a prominent position on our cultural horizon for some time to come. *Buzzword* is an apt characterization. By their nature, buzzwords tend to merge into the background chatter of our public discourse, meaning most anything and therefore signifying very little. When one runs out of precision and discrimination, buzzwords furnish handy, though nonsensical, means by which to conclude a comment or clinch an argument, all the while proceeding under the mistaken assumption that the word means the same thing to everyone. Though pretense to profundity may be prominent, buzzwords cannot stand the rigors of dialogue and debate. Scratch beneath their surface and not much will be found.

The bewildered disciples of Jesus as portrayed in the musical *Jesus Christ Superstar* come to mind. In the party-induced fog of too much wine (the musical version), the buzz about Jesus was heard but not understood. The words were meaningless, signifying nothing. The buzz, all around them, was impenetrable. *Spirituality*, I think, is in danger of falling prey to the same predicament.

Consider, for instance, popular usage of the word. That it is used with haste and imprecision is everywhere evident. When, a few months ago, I commanded my computer to search for *spirituality* on the Web, it identified 333 sites. In vain I searched for the common thread running through all the associations it had found. Neurological synapses, environmental sustainability, annulments of marriage, tribal casinos . . . all were there claiming some connection to *spirituality*. It's obvious that common usage gives the term a great deal of latitude. Perhaps that's why Dr. Wayne Dyer can market his lectures under the title "There's a Spiritual Solution to Every Problem" (Dyer, 2001). The search of a library's catalog, as well as a visit to the bookshelves of most any bookstore, leads to the same conclusion. The sections on *spirituality* introduce a bewildering range of titles and resources, the contents of which may have little to do with each other.

Spirituality is one of the categories of books listed in the catalog of the Wm. B. Eerdmans Publishing Company, a well-known publisher of religious and theological literature. I asked the manager of its bookstore what sort of criteria qualified a book as *spiritual*. With a wry grin, he said there were no criteria other than the personal preferences of those who prepare the catalog. The publishing industry, reflecting a quandary of the larger culture, simply has not been able to settle on a universally acceptable definition of *spirituality*.

Though most of us do not have to adjudicate claims and counterclaims concerning the meaning of *spirituality*, judges and their courtrooms do not have that luxury. The community of Cassadaga, Florida, was founded in 1875 as a center for mediums, psychics, and other Spiritualists. When John Ferro tried to build a Christian church there, the town's first residents complained it would disrupt the town's *spiritual vibrations* and subject them to unwelcome evangelism. After filing a federal lawsuit in May 2001, the church was granted approval to go ahead in September of 2002 (*Christianity Today*, Nov. 18, 2002).

A story recited in the October 10, 2002, issue of a local newspaper may have summarized the current state of affairs as well as one might expect. According to the newspaper's report, a former employee sued a discount store chain in New England. She had refused to remove her eyebrow ring, and for that she was fired. The store claimed that she violated its employee dress code, which bans facial and tongue jewelry. The employee argued that the eyebrow ring is essential to the religion she practices as a member of the "Church of Body Modification" and cited a state law that says employers must allow workers to wear religious attire unless doing so causes undue hardship to the employer. The church's Web page describes itself as "an interfaith church whose members practice an assortment of ancient body modification rites, which we believe are essential to our spirituality" (*Columbus Dispatch*, Oct. 10, 2002). Then the newspaper summarized the matter: "Costco [the store] contends it's not breaking the law, although it doesn't want to get into an argument over what's essential to someone's spirituality. *In America these days, that's a losing argument*" (emphasis mine). When the term *spirituality* becomes virtually meaningless, it can validate most anything, which further implies that means for holding people accountable for their spirituality do not exist.

Two Concerns

To summarize, two concerns drive this essay from one paragraph to the next. First, it's true that arguments about what is essential to one's spirituality are a waste of time, but only so long as language continues its downward course toward disintegration, preventing, therefore, meaningful conversation and joint actions that are so essential to the common good. Language that displays little concern for fidelity between words and speakers and their thoughts and actions leads, as Wendell Berry argues, to "muteness and paralysis" (Berry, 1983, 29). Whether human beings and their social fabric can long endure a dysfunction that prevents dialogue and informed action from being linked to meaningful criteria for language and spirituality remains to be seen. Surely it is the case that our lives are patterned more than we realize by the sense invested in the words that we use. Violation and degradation of language are a violence done to the human psyche and to the psyche of the human community. It is a violation of our spirituality; and it can lead to violent modes of coping with life and with our need for life to be meaningful. Terrorists have moved beyond meaningful dialogue (employment of words, language) and attempt to satisfy the inner human spiritual need by creating new meaning for themselves through violent acts. Thus, the meaning of our words, or the lack thereof, is not a trivial matter. It is true that restoration of the word *spirituality* to a meaningful existence is only a small piece of the total cultural challenge. It is, however, a good place to begin.

Second, I do not wish to dispense with the word *spirituality*. Simply choosing another word to take its place will not solve our problem. Rather, we must, I think, do our best to invest the word with rich and substantial meaning. I wish to celebrate spirituality as an essential characteristic of every human being and acknowledge it as having fundamental importance for individual and collective human identity and behavior. The challenge is to invest the term with enough endurable substance as to enable it to remain standing in the public square in spite of the weight that dialogue and accountability expect it to bear.

Our culture's fondness for a vague notion of spirituality, stripped of any authority for public discourse, coincides with a major cultural shift that began to manifest itself in the late twentieth century (Schlumpf, 1999). Two features of that shift qualify any attempts made to enhance public discourse about spirituality: (1) the almost universal disenchantment with institutional religion; and (2) a growing reluctance to trust and therefore act on the Modern Paradigm. The concerns of this essay require that both receive the attention they deserve.

Spirituality Takes the Place of Religion

There may have been a time when *religion* and *spirituality* were, for all practical purposes, synonymous terms. If not that, then *spirituality* would likely have been defined as a *religious* category. That is no longer the case. Religion cannot command the authority and general respect that it once did. It does not have much credence in the public square. As a handy, more amorphous substitute, spirituality has taken its place. The implications of this must be understood by those who dare to engage in the public debate about the place of religion and spirituality in the world.

Younger folk seem to have caught the winds of this cultural shift more quickly than their elders. A Presbyterian college student responded to his denomination's survey of student opinion in the following words.

> What college students need, and what they're searching for is not religion, is not structure and rules. It is spirituality. A personal connection with God. A reason to believe that the temple to God in this New Testament is the individual. The national church should recognize this, learn about it, and incorporate [it] into their ministries. Locally and nationally. The church should be out in the environment and society doing good and being visible, changing the world through rallies, business, politics, statements, as opposed to bickering within its ranks about who's right and wrong. The national church should be an example of spirituality. (Presbyterian Church, 2001, 6)

Dismay and skepticism engendered by the perceived failures of institutional religion are pervasive. Religion (as ritual) is out. Spirituality (as experience) is in. Someone has suggested that all of the current books on spirituality are really about experience. They may be right. An advertisement for a women's spirituality center describes the labyrinth painted on the floor of its meeting room as an opportunity for "looking beyond the pulpit for spiritual experience and solace" (Schlumpf, 2000). Thomas Moore, author of a number of best sellers, is at the forefront of the current interest in spirituality. Though he lived for twelve years in a Roman Catholic religious community, he never made the final vows. He now has little use for religion, complaining that it has largely forgotten about the soul and is rather absorbed with all sorts of trivia (Moore, 1996).

Bill Hybels, senior pastor of the Willow Creek Community Church in Barrington, Illinois, described the purpose of the church as to build a church that would speak the language of our modern culture and encourage non-believers to investigate Christianity at their own pace, free from the traditional trappings of religion that tend to chase them away. (Noll, 18)

So as to preserve its interfaith posture, Alcoholics Anonymous, which Keith Miller calls "the greatest spiritual movement of the 20th century," describes its program as being spiritual, but not religious (Carr, 1995). The implication is clear. Organized religion may be helpful, but not necessarily so. It may even be harmful. However, for AA the foundation of spirituality is absolutely essential. Bill Wilson, its cofounder, is reported as having said, "We must find some spiritual basis for living, else we die" (Carr, 1995, 20–22).

Religion may be spiritual, but all spirituality is not necessarily religious. Thomas Clark, in *The Humanist* magazine, argues that one does not have to believe in God, or the supernatural, to be spiritual (Clark, 2002). He seems to be restricting religion to the ritual worship and service of God. Spirituality, whatever it is, may or may not include religion, and in any case is not restricted to the boundaries associated with institutionalized religion. Undoubtedly, Clark reflects the understanding of many.

Disenchantment with religion is illustrated in the story of the rabbi who went into the woods to pray.

He found a clearing in the woods and there he built an altar upon which he placed a sacrifice. When he prayed, fire plunged down from heaven to consume the sacrifice and God spoke to the rabbi. The rabbi returned many times to the holy place with the same results. This attracted many followers who venerated the rabbi and waited to hear what God said to him.

Eventually, the rabbi died. His followers continued to come to the clearing, built an altar, and placed their sacrifice upon it. However, being unable to remember the exact words of the rabbi's prayer, they approximated it as best they could. No fire leapt from heaven, and no word came from God. The next generation could not remember any words of the rabbi's prayer. So they sat before the altar in silence, and nothing happened. The next generation couldn't remember how to build the altar, so they waited in an empty clearing for something to happen. Nothing did!

We can anticipate the predicament of the next generation. They cannot remember the location of the clearing. Thus, without a holy place, without an altar, without appropriate words, they gather in their own places of worship week after week, and nothing happens. No fire! No word from heaven! (Conversation with a rabbi)

This is the problem that tends to afflict institutional religion: a loss of memory attended by a gradual drift into empty forms and lifeless rituals. So, folks can have their creeds, their theological traditions, and their institutional religious structures, but without fire, and without a word from God. It seems so empty and irrelevant, and it goes by the name *religion*. Then thoughtful young people, to say nothing of their elders, leave churches and systems of organized religion, because those institutions do not produce and nurture the hoped-for vital experiences for which their "spiritual selves" hunger and thirst. It is then that people, so Lenny Bruce is supposed to have said, leave the church so they can get back to God. This move may help to explain the response of a student who told me, when asked what his religion was, "I'm not very religious. I don't go to church, but I am working on my spirituality."

According to the Christian scriptures, religion was in a similar fix when Jesus came. Echoing the warnings of the prophets of Israel, he complained that the "tradition of men" (Mark 7:8) papered over an emptiness of inner darkness and death. The old wineskins of that tradition had become brittle and unable to accommodate the new wine of the Spirit. The temple, once a place of prayer, had turned into a den of thieves. Moses and Elijah were venerated, but folks could not, like them, look upon the face of God, or pray down fire from heaven. No wonder Jesus wept over the holy city with all of its forms of godliness, while lacking the power thereof.

Of course, not everyone has turned away from religion. Wade Clark Roof, who has been watching America's affair with religion and spirituality for several decades, suggests that we are in a time of transition. According to him, we now live in the context of a spiritual marketplace, which offers an ever-expanding array of products from which people may pick and choose to suit themselves (Weeks, 2000). A Christian woman may attend mass on Sunday and explore feminist writings on spirituality in a New Age group on Tuesday evenings. A young college student may attend a traditional Lutheran service on Sunday morning and then, to improve his prayer life, seek out a Zen Buddhist meditation group during the week. Looking for a more vital spiritual experience, those who have been in a mainline church's traditional worship service on Sunday morning may seek out a charismatic para-church healing service that same evening. All are attracted to a smorgasbord of offerings in the name of *spirituality*, which increasingly has become a handy, partial or total, substitute for *religion*. Whatever one may say, contemporary folk no longer expect religion to furnish the final word on spirituality.

Collapse of the Modern Paradigm

The substitution of *spirituality* for *religion* coincides with the collapse of the Modern Paradigm. For over two hundred years, coached by the Enlightenment of the seventeenth and eighteenth centuries, Moderns have been telling their story in terms of the triad of order, reason, and progress. Assuming (1) that creation is patterned by a dependable, and therefore predictable, built-in system of natural laws that (2) can be apprehended by the capable exercise of human reason, the Modern Paradigm (3) held out the promise of the certain progress of the human race toward a millennium of scientific and social perfection.

Kant, perhaps the prime philosopher of the Enlightenment, argued for a common structure of reason in all persons, which means that the knowledge of one person can be the same as that of another (Erickson, 2001, 65). *Foundationalism* was the "model for knowledge," all beliefs being "justified by their derivation from certain bedrock starting points or foundational beliefs," upon which an elaborate and coherent edifice might be constructed (73–74). The objective foundations were considered to be irreducible and timeless, safely beyond the reach of human subjectivity. Propositions encapsulated reality. Truth could be enshrined in enduring formulas of mathematics and the logical propositions of the philosophers. Scientific facts came out of laboratory test tubes, independent of the researcher. Academic enterprises presupposed the paradigm's veracity and practicality, for all disciplines. Implications that these assumptions have for language are obvious: the meaning of words is independent of the social reality of the persons using them. This leads to the proposition that definitions can be constructed apart from the willful prejudices of human beings and may, for example, be catalogued as such in dictionaries and encyclopedias.

The twentieth century dawned with the Modern Paradigm planted firmly in place. It did not survive. Millennial hopes were ground to bits in the appalling slaughter of the trench warfare of France during World War I. All dreams of reassembling those bits into some semblance of their former glory disappeared, probably for good, under

Immanuel Kant. Library of Congress.

the combined weight of World War II, the Holocaust, the assassinations of the 1960s, and the dwindling prospects for domestic tranquility and world peace as the century came to a close. Education (the majority of Hitler's SS forces were from the intellectual elite of Germany) and science (whose cutting edge is often in the hands of weapon makers) have not led the way to the promised land. At the beginning of a new century, the certainty that humans are contingent and fallible, and therefore able to destroy themselves and the world, goes unchallenged. One thing is clear. The Modern Paradigm can no longer convince us otherwise!

The Modern Paradigm, especially in the nineteenth century, made for some strange bedfellows. Conservative Christians, for instance, and secular modernists might work with basically similar epistemologies, each arguing for their respective positions on the basis of alleged objective facts and the reasonableness of their conclusions.

The comfort that this paradigm still offers to literalistic interpreters of the Scriptures is palpable. However, the comfort is an illusion. The clever parody of Calvinism's logic by Oliver Wendell Holmes, "The One-Hoss Shay" (Holmes, 1858), paints an unforgettable portrait of the risk that is to be run by religion when it adopts the rules of the Modern Paradigm. One weak link in the syllogism and the whole system collapses. When the paradigm itself collapses, mighty indeed is the crash of religious claims linked to it!

Popular notions of spirituality both encourage and reflect the cultural shift that has turned its back on the Modern Paradigm. If words are social constructs, then *spirituality* is one of them. It means what *I* want it to mean, on the basis of *my* experience. There is no predicting where this may lead. Nor is any arbitration possible for those who disagree with me since there are no standards for truth external to each of us. You have your truth, and I have mine, be they ever so different . . . especially when it comes to spirituality. That this has a familiar, and even convincing ring testifies to the distance we have traveled away from the Modern Paradigm.

Attempts to reassemble the scattered pieces of the Humpty-Dumpty Modern Paradigm will not work, though fundamentalists of all faiths, Muslim, Roman Catholic, Anglican Catholic, Orthodox Catholic, Jewish, and Protestant, doggedly pursue that end. Few academics would agree with them. Most argue that the Modern project is beyond repair. Though they may not embrace the more radical, sometimes nihilistic conclusions of their secular colleagues, many orthodox Christians have also turned their back on the Modern Paradigm. Signaling a shift away from Kant, Nicholas Wolterstorff, in his book *Reason Within the Bounds of Religion*, reports, to the dismay of not a few conservative Christians, that the alleged objectivity of Foundationalism turns out to be an untrustworthy prop for the Christian faith and that alternatives must be found (Wolterstorff, 1984). Wolterstorff is not alone in making this claim. Alvin Plantinga, who is writing a trilogy on the subject of warranted beliefs, certainly deserves to be mentioned. Clarence Walhout, professor emeritus of English at Calvin College, in a wonderful essay asserts that "texts and the language that composes them are never autonomous and context-free," and then steers his discussion toward narrative hermeneutics, hoping all along to avoid the charge of relativism with which narrative approaches are often branded (Lundin, 1999, 65).

Western civilization is engaged in a profound search for new paradigms, new narratives, new hermeneutics. Though we do not yet know what these may become, of this much we can be certain . . . they will not be Modern! For the moment we seem to have no choice but to label the emerging alternatives as *postmodern*, without being able to say exactly what that means. The new paradigms will acknowledge that both the topics and the content of knowledge are socially determined. They will admit that words come out of historical contexts and can mean different things to different people. Ideally, they will acknowledge that the far-reaching implications of the disintegration of human persons, their communities, and their languages must be addressed, and, mercifully, may they find a way to do all of that without straying into the sucking quicksand of a totally enervating relativism. An awesome challenge, to say the least, especially when it is the meaning of *spirituality* that cries out for clarification.

Definitions Won't Work

The collapse of the Modern Paradigm renders impossible foundational definitions of *spirituality*. It is usually assumed that dictionary definitions authoritatively decree the meaning of words. I have already suggested that this assumption reflects the Modern Paradigm's search for foundational certainties. As suggested earlier in this essay, the popular usage of the term *spirituality* amply demonstrates how illusive that target is. Dictionary definitions tend to propose something like *the quality of being spiritual*, and then may define *spiritual* as consisting of, or relating to, *spirit*, which in turn is defined in terms of the incorporeal or the supernatural. This circular course of reasoning gets us nowhere, because the foundation on which it hopes to settle does not exist.

Books and articles on spirituality, whose quantity is beyond numbering, display the same equivocation. One would be hard-pressed to extract a substantive definition of *spirituality* from any of them, and of course, none of their suggestions would enjoy universal acceptance. Howard L. Rice, in a fine book titled *Reformed Spirituality*, does not even attempt a definition (Rice, 1991). Since his book furnishes a detailed discussion of encounter and relationship with God, we can assume that is what he means by spirituality. Not everyone would agree. In a book titled *Christian Spirituality*, Rowan Williams expands the term so as to refer to the task of "each believer making his or her own that engagement with the questioning at the heart of faith which is so evident in the classical documents of Christian belief" (Williams, 1980, 1). Robert C. Solomon characterizes spirituality as "the thoughtful love of life" (Solomon, 2002). The authors of *For the Love of God* propose that spirituality has to do with love as the essence of our being (Shield & Carson, xii). Wolfart Pannenberg, in his *Christian Spirituality*, equates spirituality with piety, and then acknowledges that there are different types of piety (Pannenberg, 1981). Is it any wonder that folks in our culture wrap references to *spirituality* in clichés? Is it any wonder that we shrink away from holding one another accountable in public discourse for something as foggy as *spirituality?*

As far as the word *spirituality* is concerned, we probably should never have expected more from the Modern Paradigm in the first place. From the beginning it was not well prepared to deal with the immaterial realities of the spirit world unless they could be reduced, which they cannot, to the scientific categories of psychology, sociology, economics, history, and the like, which are so admired in the Modern Paradigm. To the extent that the Modern Paradigm has collapsed, conclusions based upon its hermeneutic will lack authority. That has provoked the search for new paradigms and opened the doors to alternative hermeneutics. One of those, the hermeneutics of narrative, offers some hope of sustaining humans in their quest for wholeness.

Narrative Hermeneutics

These days the inescapable significance of narrative is being acknowledged on several fronts. Its hermeneutical possibilities account for this attraction. This is certainly the case in biblical studies, which are paying more attention than ever before to the narrative, or "storied," character of the Bible. Before we attend specifically to its account of spirituality, some account of the nature of narrative must be given.

The term *narrative*, or *story*—I will use the terms interchangeably—can be used in various ways. We must mention two of them. First, narratives may be commandeered as vehicles whose purpose is entertainment or illustration. Toastmasters and preachers often resort to this form of story. In this case stories are used for purposes that can be distinguished from the stories themselves. I will refer to this as the *utilitarian* category of narrative. One might tell a story, as Aesop does, of the fox that talked a crow into opening her mouth and thereby dropping to him the bit of cheese she held in her beak. The story is told to illustrate the claim that flatterers are not to be trusted. Whether a fox has actually ever been able to do such a thing is not important. The truth being illustrated is the point, and it is separable from the story itself. The story is simply a vehicle to get to that point. Though some may disagree, I would be inclined to argue that myth and parable function in a somewhat similar fashion. The compelling story of a Samaritan who helped a wounded man lying alongside the road to Jericho could have happened just the way it was told, but that's not necessary to the point being made, as we all know. Whether the story actually happened is not of much concern and certainly should not become a matter of debate.

In contrast to the utilitarian use of narratives, a second use of the term can refer to those stories that give a narrative account of what happened. I shall call this the *witness* category of narrative since its aim is to give a faithful account of what occurred at a certain time and place. Perhaps it is a synoptic Gospel's account of Jesus. Perhaps it is O. J. Simpson's trial for murder. The concern is the same. Can someone tell us what really happened? Can a reliable, honest witness be found? This sort of story tells in sequential fashion what happened as one thing led to another. The connections in the story may, or may not, be logical ones. Parts of the story can be unexpected, out of character, or even ridiculous. This is why, as with any good story, the storyteller, as witness, has to keep on talking . . . because listeners keep on asking, "What happened next?" It is the genius of narratives that they can include anomalies, puzzling contradictions, and "nonessential" pieces, all of which might lack logical coherence but when taken together make "sense" the way a good novel does.

From the many things that can be said about narratives, I will mention several characteristics of those that attempt to give an account of what happened. First, let it be noted that everything and everyone have a story. Everything! Cats, dogs, houses, trees, people, institutions, nations, and even words like *spirituality;* all, without exception, have a story because their existence takes place in time. A full description of any person, place, or thing would take the shape of a narrative with a beginning, a middle, and an up-to-this-minute conclusion. John Dominic Crossan puts this nicely when he says that we live in story like fish live in the sea.

Second, though everyone and everything have a story, only human beings can formulate, preserve, and then tell them. Some of us are more reliable keepers (witnesses) of stories than others. This helps to explain why one telling of a story may not be as faithful to what really happened as another. To argue otherwise endangers the integrity of language itself. To settle for an absence of fidelity between words and speakers and their account of what happened leads, as Wendell Berry suggests, to "muteness and paralysis" (Berry, 1983, 29), a malady all too common in our time.

Third, we know God, ourselves, others, and the world in the context of narrative. The self-revelation of God in the Scriptures is framed more by story than it is by propositions, concepts, or doctrines. Most basically, what we have in the Bible is a narrative account of what happens as God creates, upholds, and redeems the world. It is this narrative that tells us *who God is*. Scholars tell us that the historically storied character of the Bible distinguishes it from most other sacred writings. Respective parts of that narrative qualify the sense of identity, obligation, *and spirituality* that Jews and Christians may have. Since to be human is to have a story, the extent to which we know our story measures the extent to which we know and can give an account of ourselves.

Fourth, community comes into being when stories are shared realities. Our stories can, and always do, overlap with those of others. Those links of shared stories bind people together into some sort of common experience, identity, and purpose. It could be found in a small group of Clinical Pastoral Education (CPE) students, a congregation, a whole town. Preaching, for instance, can be described as a communal effort to clarify the terms of overlapping stories, namely, God's and ours. The sense of community that comes out of shared stories can be deep and abiding, as ineradicable as one's ancestry, or as ephemeral as the superficial contacts one has at a cocktail party. In any case, the only way to really account for and explain the formation of a community is to tell what happened as folks encountered and related to one another. Contrariwise, community disappears when people no longer have a shared story. This goes far to explain the disintegration of people and their communities. A shared story is missing.

Fifth, narratives can be incomplete or false and still have great power and awesome influence. Psychotics tell false stories and insist on living by them. Ostensibly, psychotherapists are engaged in the enterprise of helping people discard false stories in favor of more true ones. The power of Hitler's false narrative of Aryan supremacy almost destroyed Western civilization. Individuals and their institutions, religious and secular, may have and live out incomplete or false stories with disastrous results. Agendas of terror, or war, by their nature demand the propagation of false or incomplete stories. We do well to be so warned when they come our way. Moral challenges often begin with the opportunity to tell the truth. Finding truth in politics has become more and more difficult because of the "spin" given to storytelling. Politicians are not alone in massaging stories! The temptation to place some spin on talk about spirituality seems to be a peculiar temptation of religious folk.

The first beneficiary of the false telling of a story may well be the storyteller! When the truthful telling of a story cannot be tolerated, false stories take the edge off reality, whether as white lies or as the full-blown delusions of a psychotic. Self-deception has positioned itself as a strong and persistent temptation in every human's life. Institutions, sacred and secular, succumbing to that temptation have lived and continue to live by false stories that spawn the sad commentaries of racism, sexism, and abuse, to name a few. *The Poisonwood Bible* gives a fictional account of the tragedy wreaked upon a missionary family because of the sustained self-deception of the father (Kingsolver, 1999). Surely a most needed skill is that of being able to recognize the lies in the stories by which we live.

Sixth, the meaning of every word is lodged in narrative. A story will explain what I mean. When teaching a course in metaethics at the Ohio State University College of Medicine, I sometimes called attention to the narrative-based nature of words by asking students what they meant by *care*, that being the alleged goal of their education at the college. Inevitably, the students responded with dictionary-type definitions, such as *to help sick people get well.* Then I would pick out the operative word in that definition, in this case *help*, and ask what that meant. Predictably, I would get another dictionary-like definition such as *to give assistance to someone in need.* Then I would ask what is meant by *give assistance*, and would get another definition. By this time most students usually began to catch on to what was happening. The series of progressions could go on indefinitely . . . as long as definitions were being cited. One definition always calls for another one.

How well I remember the day an exasperated student put an end to my endless chain of questions. "Don't you know what care is?" she fairly shouted. "That's what happened to me when I was three years old! I got a nasty scrape on my knee and my mother cradled me in her arms and helped me to stop crying. That's what care is! She cared for me!" Precisely! This student had come to one of the narrative sources for her acquaintance with the word, and there was neither need, nor possibility, of going further. All of our words are similarly imbedded in narratives. They are "storied" constructs.

Seventh, the very same words and phrases can be located in different, even contradictory stories. Since words gain their meaning from their narrative context, when the narrative changes, the meaning of the word changes—that is, as to their meaning words are equivocal, not univocal. Consider, for instance, the word *love*. We find the very same word in the Bible and in a titillating novel. Since the narrative context of the single word *love* changes from one story to the next, its meaning changes accordingly. How radical some of those changes have been . . . altering language and the course of history! *Indian* became *savage, Jew* became *vermin, African American* became *nigger, America* became *the great Satan,* and for some *Fundamentalist* became *terrorist.* The word *spirituality* is no different. Its meaning also mutates as it moves from one story to another. Like a chameleon it takes on the color of the story providing its context, be it charismatic, Eastern, secular Humanism, Fundamentalism, liberalism, patriotism . . . whatever.

One of those humorous stories that gets passed around on the Internet illustrates how radically the meaning of words can change when they are lifted from one narrative and placed in another. This one is worth retelling. It may help to erase any doubts that linger concerning the influence that narrative context has on the meaning of words.

After being nearly snowbound for two weeks last winter, a man departed from Seattle for his vacation in Miami Beach, where he was to meet his wife the next day after the conclusion of her business trip to Minneapolis. Both looked forward to pleasant weather and a nice time in Florida together.

Unfortunately, there was some sort of mix-up at the boarding gate in Seattle, and the man was told he would have to take a later flight. He tried to appeal to a supervisor but was told that the airline was not responsible for the problem and that it would do no good to complain. Upon arrival at the hotel in Miami the next day, he discovered that Miami was having a heat wave, and that its weather was almost as uncomfortably hot as Seattle's was cold.

The desk clerk gave him a message that his wife would arrive as planned. He could hardly wait to get to the pool area to cool off, and quickly sent his wife an e-mail message. Due to his haste, he made an error in the address. His message arrived at the home of an elderly preacher's wife whose even older husband had died only the day before. When the grieving widow opened her e-mail, she took one look at the screen, let out an anguished scream, and fainted dead away in front of her computer's monitor. Her family rushed into the room, where they saw this message on the monitor's screen:

Dearest wife,
   Departed yesterday as you know. Just now got checked in. Some
confusion at the gate. Appeal was denied. Received confirmation of
your arrival tomorrow. Can't wait for you to get here.
   Your loving husband.
   P.S. Things are not as we thought. You're going to be surprised at
how hot it is down here.

Eighth, as historical accounts, narratives are specific to, and therefore limited by, time and place. This particularity implies that as narrative accounts of what happened, one story cannot be arbitrarily
substituted for another one. Accounts of what happened may be very
similar, like the stories of some twins, but they cannot, like light
bulbs, be substituted the one for the other. Their stories may overlap
in many details, but the one cannot take the place of the other. As historically shaped individuals, the identities of the twins remain distinct, and so their stories are particular to each one of them. The
story of Harvard cannot be substituted for the story of Yale. The
story of the United States of America cannot take the place of
the story of Canada. Presbyterians cannot, willy-nilly, change the
story of their spirituality for a Lutheran one. This particularity is
true of all stories that attempt an account of what happened in some
historical context.
   The particularity of narratives poses troubling questions. From
time immemorial differences (or particularity) in personal and communal stories have been blamed for strife among people and nations.
It is tempting to suppose that the conflicts can be attributed to the
differences *themselves*, the conclusion being that peace will come when
we rid ourselves of those pesky differences, at least the more significant ones. An attractive strategy for many, in favor of an inclusive
perspective, is simply to deny that the differences exist. Universalistic
narratives of the human enterprise, as found, for instance, in New
Age visions, hold out that promise. These moves seem to be possible
only when the radical historicity of humans is either compromised or
denied.
   On the other hand, others argue that the historically conditioned
character and limits, including sinfulness, of all humans leave us with
no alternative. In 1989 Stanley Hauerwas and William Willimon
jointly authored a book, *Resident Aliens: Life in the Christian Colony*,
that stirred up a firestorm of criticism because it argued, as the title
suggests, for the particularity of the church. Critics accused it of

being "sectarian." Rodney Clapp has commended the work of Stanley Hauerwas for helping him to take seriously "the story-shaped faith of the church and its Bible and . . . why, on theo-philosophical grounds, their particularistic narrative should not be abandoned." (Roth, 2001, 140). In an article in *Tikkun*, Jose N. Ferrer cautions that the "Perennialist" position of inclusivism, though appealing, tends "to distort the essential message of various religious traditions, favoring certain spiritual paths over others and raising serious obstacles for spiritual dialogue and inquiry" (Ferrer, 60). Furthermore, universalistic visions ignore "the way spiritual reality itself is in a process of evolution." (Ferrer, 2002, 60). Process implies history, and history implies particularity.

The Dalai Lama clearly acknowledged the uniqueness of religious and spiritual traditions when he stated that only Buddhists can accomplish what their religion teaches (Ferrer, 2002, 60). Because of this particularity, Buddhism will not get you to the goal of Christian praxis. Perhaps you wish to follow the Advaitin path of Vedic study in the Hindu tradition. Sufi dancing will not get you there. The particularities of spiritual paths remain. The one cannot be exchanged for the other.

There is no necessary connection between differences and conflict. Differences can as easily be complementary, as in the case of differences between the sexes, or the wonderful variety built into creation. It is not the differences themselves that matter, but how humans tell the story of their differences. There are narratives that tell of peace between strangers, reconciliation between those who are very different, and a whole nation whose election to particularity was to benefit all peoples. The traditions of Anabaptists are more particular than most, but their differences from others have not led them to conflict and war. To the contrary, they are known for their peaceableness. Of course, narratives of particularity may serve agendas of self-righteous arrogance and triumphalism, but not necessarily so. Again, it depends on the way one's story is told. Why should folks aggrandize themselves if they are really certain of the story of God's goodness and providence?

No doubt the debates concerning particularity and its place in the human story will continue. Devoting more time to those issues would go beyond the boundaries of this essay. I will be satisfied if, for the time being, some of the edge has been taken off our worries about particularity. The charge of relativism may be a more worrisome matter.

The Truth of Narratives

The meanings of the words we use do depend upon the narratives in which they are placed. But in the case of differing or competing narratives, which one is true? That's fairly easy to determine in the story of the thunderstruck widow . . . unless one accepts the possibility that departed husbands can contact their grieving spouses by means of the Internet! It is not always that easy to pick out the true story from among false or partially true pretenders. Parents run into this sort of question most every day. If Susan tells a story of how brother Johnny knocked over the lamp in the den and Johnny says Susan did it, which story is true or mostly true? Without an appeal to some independent objective criteria, how does one decide to favor one story over another? Having rejected the foundational claims of the Modern Paradigm, does our turn toward narrative irresistibly lead to the spineless relativism so feared by Moderns?

Most of the thinking about the hermeneutics of narrative constitutes a debate over the issue of relativism (Lundin, 1999, 91). Critics call forth the epistemological dilemmas that relativism implies, whereas supporters try to mitigate its risks. If a narrative is the account a particular person or community gives of what happened, is not the story then relative to the social reality and worldview from which these people come? Then is not the meaning invested in words such as *spirituality* linked to subjective criteria that cannot be judged in terms of true and false? Who is to say that Hitler's telling of the story of Germany was false? It was true for him, and for many of his contemporaries. It was false for others. What more can be said? You have your story (worldview, spirituality, religion). It is true for you. I have my story (worldview, spirituality, religion). It is true for me. Isn't that the end of the matter?

Obviously, capitulation to an absolute relativism would reconstitute the "law of the jungle" and accelerate the disintegration of persons and communities against which potential tragedy this chapter is directed. On the other hand, passageways back to the certainties of the Modern Paradigm seem to be closed. It is instructive to pay attention to Stanley Hauerwas' rejoinder to this dilemma. His most detailed response may be found in the book *A Community of Character*, in which an earlier essay, "The Church in a Divided World," is reprinted. In that essay the accusation of relativism is discussed under four headings.

In the first place, Hauerwas reminds us that being human neces-sarily entails a certain measure of relativism. To be human is to be finite, to know in part, to be contingent, to say nothing of being sin-ful! Our insights are always partial. We do not get beyond having to see more clearly, having to change our minds, having to beg forgive-ness for ignorance and error. This sort of relativism is unavoidable. It infects everyone, including the critics of relativism. The narrative approach to hermeneutics takes seriously these limitations.

In the second place, Hauerwas takes issue with the positivistic assumptions that so often undergird the complaints hurled against narrative hermeneutics. The complaints define relativism in terms of rational criteria, which themselves are relative to some theory of rationality. However, even Kant seemed to realize that human reason itself has limitations when he said that "reason has the ability to raise questions to which it cannot give answers" (Erickson, 2001, 109). Rational objections to relativism are not as objective as the critics suppose. The critics might at least admit to the relativism of their criticism!

Third, the claims of narrative hermeneutics are not absolutely rel-ative. The communal dimension of stories, among other things, reminds us that narratives are never simply personal ones. There is no such thing as a narrative of a solitary *I*. Narratives, even the ones we know of God, are always an account of the *I* in relationship to the stories of others. Radical subjectivism does not seem to be possible either for humans . . . or even for God, after the Creation! In some measure we are always disciplined and held accountable by the stories of others. I cannot make my story, my behavior, my words mean just anything I want them to mean. I learned this soon enough from my mother. I would tell my story, and she would say, "That is not exactly right. This is what happened." I had to deal not only with the way I told my story, but the way she told it as well.

Fourth, Hauerwas argues that the essential task of the church is witness rather than apology—that is to say, the church is not, in the first place, called to argue about foundations so as to prove others wrong. Rather, it is called, in its own tragic existence, to live faith-fully in accord with the story of God in Jesus Christ without trying to convince or change others. The church best serves others by being true to its own story. Therefore, those living by the biblical story should not be so concerned about the charge of relativism, and the possibility that their knowledge may be both partial and unconvinc-ing to others. The calling of Christians is to attend faithfully to the biblical story and nurture an individual and communal spirituality that postures them for service to God and others. Faithful living of the story is the thing.

As creatures of history, human beings cannot help but engage the question "What *really* happened?" In common parlance the question often becomes "What is the truth?" The answer to the question matters. Ask any prison inmate whether it matters that the jury got its hands on the *real* truth. It matters to me whether my parents were *really* my parents. It matters whether my great-great grandfather was *really* a full-blooded Cherokee. As a Christian, it matters to me whether the historical claims of the Gospel are *really* true. One might expect accounts of what *really* happened to place more weight upon the considerations of historical creatures than imaginary ones. A story from the Christmas of 1990 comes to mind. This is the way it *really* happened.

> As a Christmas gift, Jill, our daughter, who is a teacher, gave a copy of *The Lorax*, by Dr. Seuss, to one of our grandchildren. The book contains a fictional account of the willful destruction of imaginary truffla trees for the sake of their tufts (from which marvelous fabrics can be woven). In spite of the fact that truffla trees provided food and habitat for all sorts of animals, a thriving industry cut them all down so as to harvest their tufts. Finally, all the truffla trees are gone; the businesses collapse and leave behind a polluted wasteland and associated ecological disasters. However, one truffla seed has been saved by the Lorax (an imaginary creature) who intends to plant and care for it in the hope that the truffla trees will come back to save the animals and the world.
>
> After reading the story our teacher daughter tried to make her point. "What," she asked our four-year-old granddaughter, "would you do with the *last* truffla seed?" Quick as a flash, without a pause, without having to think about it, came the reply. "But trufflas are not real."

Apparently, our granddaughter couldn't be persuaded to make a moral decision on the basis of something that did not *really* happen. As a child she was engaged in the business of apprehending and responding to the *real* world. In time she would learn that imaginary stories can assist us in doing that, but for the present, not yet "educated" well enough so as to betray the wisdom she had been given as a child, she seemed to say, "If you want me to do something, tell me what is *real*."

Is it not strange? The same people who cannot tolerate historical ambiguity in the mundane dimensions of their lives may embrace it without a moment's hesitation in matters of faith and spirituality. A classroom curriculum would never be allowed to proceed in terms of "What's true for you is true for you, and what's true for me is true for me." Nonetheless, with reference to religion and spirituality, that notion is fairly common. To *believe* is to have a firm conviction as to the reality of something. To talk about *believing* what *did not really happen* is an oxymoron, a nonsensical combination of words. Yet the notion seems to be well established, especially among the educated. This may be a good example of the disintegration of language that Wendell Berry fears (Berry, 1983, 24). I can tolerate a certain amount of uncertainty as to the historical veracity of Christian claims, but not the notion that the issue of historical veracity itself is unimportant.

This leads to questions concerning the relative values of myth, fable, and parable. All claim to offer accounts of what happened, but, as most would agree, not what *really* happened. Nevertheless, they are an important genre of human discourse, often furnishing profound insights into the human condition. Their narratives may be imaginary, but they do allude to things that are *real*. The ability to imagine the unseen and to live into a fictional narrative are singular blessings, but they do not take the place of accounts of what *really* happened. We cannot that easily escape the historical matrix of our lives.

Following the lead of Stanley Hauerwas, I am persuaded that our convictions about what is *real*, if acknowledged, take their form from *particular*, historically conditioned narratives. On the anvil of those narratives we hammer out the sense we make of ourselves, others, the world, God, and spirituality. There are, of course, many particular, and therefore distinct, narratives from which notions of spirituality are being forged in our time. The narrative of the Bible is only one of them. Some of them are in violent conflict with one another. All along it has been the purpose of this chapter to work toward some means by which meaningful dialogue and accountability may take place in spite of these differences.

The Biblical Narrative of Spirituality

The Bible has a lot to say about spirituality. It does not anchor that information in a definition of *spirituality*. Rather, *spirituality*, like a thread, runs through a particular narrative account of God's way with creation. I will not review the story in great detail. Resources for doing that are numerous and readily available. For our purposes reference to its principal features will suffice. I hope the preceding discussion has explained how I can, without apology, now spell out the outlines of a very particular reading of the biblical narrative. That is the only kind of reading there is! This one is shaped by a lifetime in the communal embrace of the Reformed theological tradition.

The biblical narrative begins with an account of Creation. In short compass the recitation of those beginnings touches on the nature of humans and their assigned place in the cosmos. According to the story, humans were created in the "image of God," compromised in the Fall, and promised a future restoration by a covenant-keeping God. All three make their contribution to the biblical notion of *spirituality*, especially the first.

The designation of "image" suggests that human beings have no independent existence apart from their Source, or Maker. Take away the Source, and the image, like that in a mirror, disappears. The intimate relationship between Source and image suggests all sorts of fascinating, yet puzzling implications. One is that humans are the only creatures, in all of creation, equipped to sustain the role required of an "image" of God. The term *spirituality* refers to that capability. Humans, though we are not God, are enough like God as to be able to participate in that relationship. That is what the biblical story intends by its references to *human spirituality*.

In spite of the Fall into sin, humans have not been totally abandoned by God. We can still, though with considerable distortion, reflect and therefore "image" God. Some have compared the effect to that of shattering the smooth face of a mirror into shards that still reflect, though imperfectly, their Source. The initial constraints placed upon human spirituality at Creation (we are not God) are compounded by the additional restrictions of sin and issue loud warnings against human arrogance and triumphalism.

Humans therefore live a tragic existence: attracted by visions of perfection they inevitably stumble into the ditches of ignorance, deception, violence, and ultimately death. The biblical narrative underwrites the "good news" that prodigals, in spite of distant wanderings, still robed in the rags of their failures, are nevertheless invited to a spirituality of hopefulness and encouraged to head for home.

Since humans are an "image," like a mirror we inevitably stand over against someone or something, which we reflect from deep within ourselves. Christian theologians have referred to this trait under a variety of terms. In his *Confessions* Augustine pointed to the heart that is "restless" until its rests in God. John Calvin referred to the "seed of religion" that lies in every human heart. Paul Tillich became well-known for attributing to every human an "ultimate concern." Since humans are contingent spiritual beings, from deep within every human there is a yearning for something that we cannot be by ourselves.

Accounts of those who stood over against God, the Source of the "image" they were, fill the pages of the Bible: Abraham, Moses, Job, David, Isaiah, Mary the mother of Jesus, Jesus himself, Saint Paul, to name just a few. Most of what we know about biblical spirituality comes from their stories along with those of a "cloud of witnesses" who help us to know what happens when we stand before our Maker. One will probably find a reference to one or more of them in most every Sunday sermon as we too are invited to stand over against the same source.

An image's need for connection with a source does not necessarily lead to its Maker. Humans are well-known for substituting false gods for the True One. The "seed of religion" demands that we stand over against somebody, even if it be a projection of ourselves. It seems that Adolf Hitler bowed down to Aryan supremacy. Some, having sold themselves to the custodians of satanic ritual, come close to exhibiting the spirituality of the demons themselves, wreaking terror and destruction upon themselves and others. Others may come so thoroughly under the spell of a charismatic or cultic leader as to lose touch with themselves. All humans are spiritual creatures. That gives no guarantee of a trustworthy relationship with God.

The biblical narrative makes it abundantly clear that imaging our Maker entails imitation of God in our relationships with others, and for that matter, with all of creation. Since God loves the world, faithful images are to do the same. Jesus, the image of God par excellence (Col. 1:15, 2:9), has demonstrated best of all what that entails. No wonder, then, that the biblical narrative recommends that Christians follow him (1 Pet. 2:21) . . . which amounts to becoming images of him. The Christological assertions of Christians make it clear that this can be done without infringing on the prerogatives of God in any way. This helps to explain why, for Christians, biblical spirituality is profoundly shaped by the life, teachings, death, and resurrection of Jesus. His focused attentiveness on the will of God provides the model for the very core of Christian spirituality. What we need now is a metaphor to draw these various threads together.

A Metaphor for Biblical Spirituality

Webster's dictionary defines *metaphor* as a "figure of speech in which a word or phrase denoting one kind of object or idea is used in

place of another to suggest a likeness or analogy between them"
(*Webster's Seventh New Collegiate Dictionary*, 1965). Then it offers an
example: *the ship plows the sea.* The word *plows* is the metaphor. It con-
jures up the image of the arduous task of breaking up the sod of a
reluctant field so as to turn furrows of soil in preparation for plant-
ing. How that is done with a team of horses, or a John Deere tractor,
could be narrated. The telling of that story would require several
sentences. *Plow* puts the story into one word, and then, as a
metaphor, links that with the story of a ship making its way through
the heavy seas.

If I have belabored the way a dictionary defines the word *metaphor,*
it is to make the point that a more complete understanding of
metaphors would accept them as *compressed stories.* The dictionary definition itself points in that direction. Metaphors are really very handy
ways of summarizing the narrative implicit in a word or phrase. They
sprinkle speech and writings with pictures that color and expand our
language in unforgettable ways. I began to look for a metaphor that
might hold together the various themes that the biblical narrative of
spirituality contains.

Quite by accident I came upon the metaphor in the tae kwon do
class of our six-year-old grandson, Noah. That is his real name. He
will not mind my using it. Noah has earned his fourth belt (blue) in
tae kwon do. It's been my privilege to take him to some of his classes
and watch him practice this art. On one such occasion I paid more
attention to him than usual. His alertness and focused concentration
caught my attention. His mind and body were taut like a bowstring.
Every fiber in his body and mind were unequivocally focused on his
instructor or partner. Tae kwon do requires the exact duplication of
a sequence of stylized postures called "forms," of which Noah already
knows several. The imitation of the instructor had to be exact, with
arms, legs, and body held just so. I was amazed that Noah could
remember all of the movements, that he knew the meaning of the
Korean words the instructor shouted out, and that his attention never
wavered. Sometimes Noah was absolutely motionless. With wrists
cocked, with knife-edged hands, knees bent, eyes not moving, he was
an image of total absorption. Then he was paired up with another
student and together they went through a series of exercises that
required careful, sustained attention, anticipation, and patterned
response to the other's movements. It was all about using the postures of the forms, all about getting one's body in the right position
and the right place at the right time.

That's when I saw the biblical metaphor for spirituality! It has taken a rather long paragraph to introduce the bare outlines of the dynamic demands that tae kwon do makes on Noah's posture. It became clear to me that I could transfer that narrative, compressed into the word *postures*, as an analogy to the essential outlines of biblical spirituality. It is important that *postures* be understood in dynamic, not static terms. That is why I will insist on using the plural rather than the singular form of the word. This is exactly what biblical spirituality is about: focusing the attention of one's whole self, body, mind, and spirit, on the will of God, all articulated in the dynamic postures of a series of cheerfully obedient responses to God. The gift of a six-year-old to his grandfather . . . and he was not even aware of it!

In *postures* we have a metaphor that may endure the rigors of the public square. It has enough formal integrity so as to secure its relevance for a variety of spiritual traditions. Regardless of their nature, we ought to be able to talk with each other across the boundaries of those traditions in terms of the *postures* we adopt with respect to our ultimate concerns. I will admit that whether this approach promotes understanding and accountability in the public square remains to be seen. I think it is worth a try.

No single metaphor is large enough to comprehend all that it means to mirror God. Other metaphors for *spirituality* have been proposed and explored: runner, soldier, and pilgrim, to mention only three. Each one has served Christians well for centuries. Each one identifies important features of the image that Christians are called to be. In time, perhaps *postures* will be added to the list.

Spirituality, as Postures, in Action

The metaphor of *postures* suggests that many skills are required of those who practice biblical spirituality. Just as Noah's proficiency in tae kwon do is grounded in his mastery of many moves from one posture to the next, so must an "image" of God learn the "moves" that can be associated with the nurture of biblical spirituality. The partial listing of some of those skills, which follows, is designed to encourage attention to the fact that the development of one's spirituality requires time, attention, and effort. It does not come automatically. Nor can its associated skills be summoned full-blown, as if by magic, on the spur of dangerous or tragic moments. As the student mentioned earlier in this chapter suggested, one has to work at spirituality. We are made to "image" God, but the actual doing of that is not congenial to a sinful nature. It takes patience and practice.

The listing, and expansion of it, may serve an additional purpose. When the time comes to give an account of one's spirituality in the public square, listings like this one can suggest items for that conversation's agenda. So, let's list some of the skills that are associated with the practice of biblical spirituality.

1. The one to whom attention is given has a *name*. Biblical spirituality is tethered to a person, not a vague idea or theme of *spirituality*. The biblical narrative insists on the importance of being able to name God. One can imagine how impossible it would be to learn the skills of tae kwon do by means of giving general assent to the idea of "forms" without having concerns for more than that. One must learn the forms by practicing them in the presence of an instructor who is particular, specific, present, and enough alive to have a name.

2. It is important to know *where* to find the one to whom attention is to be given. Biblical spirituality requires that the "image" be in the right place and facing in the right direction at the right time. For instance, one cannot expect to image the will of God if the Bible is a closed or misused book. Nor can God's concern for the poor be imaged if one does not know the poor and know them by name, as God does. Images cannot do their work by proxy. Knowing where the Kingdom of God is coming in the affairs of the world, and being there, is essential to the nurture of biblical spirituality. Again, the analogies to tae kwon do are provocative.

3. Imaging God is hard work. The practice of biblical spirituality in a troubled world entails living by an agenda that is set by someone else . . . like God, or an injured man on the road to Jericho, or a stranger needing a cup of water. Paying attention to God, others, the world, and even ourselves leads to bothersome, unexpected encounters and the demands they can make on one's time and resources. It's akin to dying . . . to oneself! Active listening, as anyone who has done it can tell you, is hard work. I saw that in Noah. It is likewise true for the "image" that heeds the call to grateful discipleship.

4. Developing the skill of biblical spirituality takes practice. The exercise of biblical spirituality is akin to tae kwon do in that hitherto unused and underdeveloped muscles will be called upon to do their part. Development of their strength and flexibility requires endless exercise and the time that entails. I remember the time Noah grew tired of attending the endless classes of tae kwon do and considered dropping out. Somehow, his mother was able to transfer his focus

back to the more distant objective of the black belt. That brought him back to class. No doubt many Christians remain spiritual weaklings because they have given up too early. Biblical spirituality entails a process that takes time! Someone has said that spiritual formation is 90 percent routine. That may be an overstatement, but the importance of repetition for perfecting the *postures* cannot be overstated.

5. Images of God can expect many *posture* adjustments. In our attempt to mirror God we make mistakes, perhaps many of them before we get it right. The lives of the saints are filled with stories of changes, conversions, and false starts. Broken, wounded, and sinful images cannot expect it to be otherwise. The biblical claim that our *postures* are too often unacceptable, need changing, and will continue to need adjustments may be discouraging. The editors of *Children's Letters to God* have compiled a touching, sometimes heart-rending, collection of letters that children of various ages sent to God. In most every one, a child is struggling to adjust his or her posture before God. One wrote, "Dear God. Thank you for the baby brother but what I prayed for was a puppy. Joyce" (Hample & Marshall, 1991). Most of us can relate to the challenge of that sort of adjustment! Maybe Noah's experience can lend some encouragement. His innumerable adjustments have led to a gradual improvement in "forms." The same thing seems to be true of spiritual formation.

6. We can never learn the *postures* of biblical spirituality without denying ourselves, taking up our cross, and following Jesus (Mark 8:34). The doing of that requires the exercise of humility . . . lots of it! If *pride* is the chief of sins, then learning the postures of genuine humility are close to the center of biblical spirituality. Human contingencies and sinful limitations, if nothing else, cancel out all claims of self-sufficiency, authority, and power that we may be tempted to entertain. No one better displays the terms of that than Jesus, and those saints who have learned well the lessons of humility. Noah's lessons are begun and ended with the students on their knees! A model for the practice of biblical spirituality?

Conclusion

Acknowledging the claims that narrative hermeneutics have had on this essay, it is only fitting that it should be concluded with a true story. It displays the *postures* of a biblical spirituality in action.[1] In the summer of 1964 it was clear that President Lyndon Johnson would receive the presidential nomination at the coming convention of the Democratic Party. However, a controversy brewing in the state of

Mississippi threatened to derail his hopes for a controversy-free celebration of his nomination.

The all-white Mississippi Democratic Party had commissioned an all-white delegation to represent Mississippi's interests at the convention. Excluded from the process that chose those delegates, Fannie Lou Hamer, a black woman, with others organized the Mississippi Freedom Democratic Party and promised to be at the convention with an integrated slate of delegates who would challenge the credentials of the all-white delegation. Fannie Lou Hamer was no stranger to the civil rights struggle. She, and other African Americans, had been punished for even daring to register to vote in Mississippi.

President Johnson knew that a challenge spelled out along racial lines could wreck the party's hoped-for image of racial harmony. He therefore sent his vice president-in-waiting, Hubert Humphrey, to visit Mrs. Hamer, with orders to persuade her to remove the potential challenge. Humphrey did not succeed.

Fannie Lou Hamer, a devout evangelical Christian, began the conversation by making clear she had more than the success of the Democratic Party in mind. Her objective, she said, was "the beginning of a New Kingdom right here on earth." Humphrey tried to explain that the challenge could threaten not only the political future of himself and President Johnson, but the momentum for racial equality that they represented as well. Senator Humphrey, in particular, had fought for civil rights long before it became fashionable in the Democratic Party. His speech on the subject of civil rights at the 1948 convention has been characterized as one of the most important discourses in twentieth-century political history. Didn't Mrs. Hamer realize to whom she was speaking?

Having survived beatings and torture in a Mississippi jail for insisting on her constitutional rights, Mrs. Hamer was unimpressed. Profoundly aware that she *postured* herself before a Higher Authority, this, in part, was her reply:

> Senator Humphrey, I know lots of people in Mississippi who have lost their jobs for trying to register to vote. I had to leave the plantation where I worked in Sunflower County. Now if you lose this job of Vice President because you do what is right, because you help the Mississippi Freedom Democratic Party, everything will be all right. God will take care of you. But if you take the nomination this way, why, you will never be able to do any good for civil rights, for poor people, for peace or any of those things you talk about. Senator Humphrey, I'm gonna pray to Jesus for you.[2]

According to the story, that was the end of the Johnson administration's attempted negotiations with Mrs. Hamer.

Notes

1. The story is cited in the essay "Liberalism's Religion Problem," by Stephen L. Carter, published in *First Things*, No. 121, March 2002 (21). (Carter himself found the story in the book *God's Long Summer* by Charles Marsh.)
2. Ibid.

References

Berry, W. (1983). *Standing by words*. San Francisco: North Point Press.

Carr, N. J. (1995, June 17–24). Liberation spirituality: 60 years of A.A. *America*, 172.

Carter, S. L. (2002, March). Liberalism's religion problem. *First Things*, no. 121, 21.

Clark, T. (2002, January/February). Spirituality without faith. *The Humanist*, 62, (1), 30–35.

Columbus [Ohio] Dispatch. (2002, October 10). Editorial page.

Dyer, W. (2001). *There's a spiritual solution to every problem* [Videocassette].

Erickson, M. J. (2001). *Truth or consequences: The promise and perils of postmodernism*. Downers Grove: InterVarsity.

Ferrer, J. N. (2002, September/October). Spirituality: An ocean with many shores. *Tikkun*, 17 (5), 65.

Hample, S. & Marshall, E. (Eds.). (1991). *Children's letters to God*. New York: Workman.

Holmes, O. W. (1848/1985). The deacon's masterpiece, or the wonderful 'One-Hoss Shay.' Quoted in G. McMichael (Ed.), *Anthology of American literature* (1712). New York: Macmillan.

John Calvin: Spirituality. (2003). In *Encyclopedia Britannica*. CD edition.

Kingsolver, B. (1999). *The poisonwood Bible*. San Francisco: HarperCollins.

Lundin, R., et. al. (1999). *The promise of hermeneutics*. Grand Rapids: Eerdmans.

Moore, T. (1996, September/October). Does America have a soul? *Mother Jones*, 21, 26–33.

Noll, M. (2002). *The old religion in a new world*. Grand Rapids: Eerdmans.

Pannenberg, W. (1981). *Christian spirituality*. Philadelphia: Westminster.

Presbyterian Church USA. (2001). *Renewing the commitment: A church-wide mission strategy for ministry in higher education*. Philadelphia: PCUSA.

Rice, H. L. (1991). *Reformed spirituality: An introduction for believers*. Louisville: Westminster/John Knox.

Roth, J. D. (Ed.). (2001). *Engaging Anabaptism: Conversations with a radical tradition.* Scottdale: Herald Press.

Schlumpf, H. (1999, August 30). Religion vs. spirituality. *Publishers Weekly, 246* (35).

Schlumpf, H. (2000, September). Walk this way. *U.S. Catholic, 65* (9), 49.

Shield, B. & Carlson, R. (Eds.). (1990). *For the love of God.* San Rafael: New World Library.

Solomon, R. C. (2002). *Spirituality for the skeptic: The thoughtful love of life.* New York: Oxford.

Webster's seventh new collegiate dictionary. (1965). Springfield: G. & C. Merriam.

Weeks, L. B. (2000, February 23). At home in the spiritual marketplace. *Christian Century, 117,* (6), 210–213. [Review of *Spiritual marketplace: Baby boomers and the remaking of American religion* by Wade Clark Roof.]

Williams, R. (1980). *Christian spirituality: A theological history from the New Testament to Luther and St. John of the Cross.* Atlanta: John Knox.

Wolterstorff, N. (1984). *Reason within the bounds of religion* (2nd ed.). Grand Rapids: Eerdmans.

CHAPTER 9

THE MYTH OF REDEMPTIVE VIOLENCE OR THE MYTH OF REDEMPTIVE LOVE

Wayne G. Rollins

Where love stops, power begins, and terror and violence.

—C. G. Jung

Introduction

Analytical psychologist Carl Jung once commented that when a scholar in white shirt and tie, with degrees from the best of universities, contributes to a technology to create a weapon of mass destruction, his unconscious is up to more than scientific advance. Violence has its finger in the pie (Jung, 99–100). When President George W. Bush, recent born-again Christian , tells us on the one hand that Jesus is his favorite philosopher, but on the other that a bullet is faster than a war in dealing with Saddam Hussein, you know that violence, rightly or wrongly, is at least an option and perhaps an imperative for the White House.

Violence holds archetypal attraction for the human soul and is readily activated whenever the scent of threat or conflict is at hand. It is ready for action in everyday experience from domestic conflicts to tribal, national, religious, and social class wars. It clearly has its advocates and practitioners in the pages of the Bible.

The dividing line in the Bible between violence and nonviolence is not to be found, as commonly thought, between the Old and New Testaments. The fault line does not lie between two documents, but between two psychic attitudes that run longitudinally through both Testaments, and by inference through every stratum of the history of the human race. In the Old Testament (Hebrew Bible), for example, we find Samuel slaying Agag, King of the Amalekites, before the Lord (1 Sam. 15:33), and we read of Joshua slaughtering sheep, oxen, asses, men, women, and children to deliver Israel from Canaanite religion (Josh. 6:21). But we also find the poet Isaiah envisioning swords being turned into ploughshares and spears into pruning hooks (Isa. 2:4), and Hosea preaching to Judah that deliverance does not lie in bow, sword, horse, horseman, or war (Hos. 1:7).

The antithesis persists in the New Testament. On the one hand, we find the command to love our enemies (Matt. 5:44) and to forgive until it hurts (Matt 18:22), and on the other, the story of Ananaias and Sapphira struck dead by God for failing to pay their full tithe of goods to the nascent Christian community (Acts 5:1–11). Also, in the Book of Revelation we find Christ portrayed as the innocent lamb who was slain (5:6) but at the same time, as the one presiding over the machinery of heaven bent on the violent destruction of the enemy (6:1ff.). At one point, Christ sits astride a white battle steed, leading a heavenly army "to tread the wine press of the fury of the wrath of God" (19:11–16).

Within the later religious traditions that spin off from both Testaments, Judaism and Christianity, we find the same contradictory leitmotifs: acts of mercy, benevolence, and healing, profound spirituality, and lofty moral standards, combined with the crusades and inquisitions, the systematic and often violent oppression of Palestinians by Zionist zealots, and the black irony of the cross-burning Ku Klux Klan. Violence is a frightful but predictable aspect of human behavior in the best of company, as native to the human scene as the white-steepled church to the New England village green.

Exposition

Whence the resort to violence? The answer is a family secret of the human race with profound and complex psychological, biological, sociopolitical, economic, demographic, and possibly genetic roots. But the more profound question may be, "Whence the justification of violence among a people who think of themselves as decent, law-abiding, respectably religious and moral people? Whence the defense of violence within a tradition that values the prophetic warning against reliance on tanks and missiles, while trying to take seriously the command to love one's enemies? Why the tolerance of violence in families of nations that regard themselves as civilized, high-minded, and fundamentally on the right track?"

One answer comes from biblical scholar Walter Wink in a brilliant exposition of the history and amplification of the myth of redemptive violence in biblical and Western culture. Wink advances this thesis in a superb one-volume summary of his trilogy on the biblical image of the principalities and powers titled *The Powers That Be: A Theology for the New Millennium* (Wink, 1998). Wink is not ignorant of the psychodynamic factors that contribute to the violent programs of "good people," such as repression, denial, projection, displacement, and rationalization. But his primary emphasis is on a mythic construct he has discovered operative in the collective consciousness of the West for over three thousand years that has been able for centuries to put a virtuous mask on the face of violence. His detection of this construct began with his preoccupation with the biblical image of the "powers," a first-century metaphor for a perennial phenomenon, namely, systems of domination and the violence they breed.

The "Powers" and Violence

Wink tells us that he has been poring over the mystery of systems of domination and violence for three decades, beginning with his research on the New Testament metaphor of the "powers," or "principalities and powers" (Rom. 8:38; Eph. 1:21, 3:10, 6:12; Col. 1:16, 2:10, 2:15; Titus 3:1). Even though the New Testament tradition portrayed these powers as celestial, angelic, or demonic forces, Wink found behind their "gross [heavenly] literalism . . . the clear perception that spiritual forces impinge on and determine our [earthly] lives" (3). This led him to suspect that this biblical metaphor represented something true about ourselves and our society, an idea that Wink elaborated in three volumes over the course of eight years. Their titles virtually tell the story of his gradual discovery: *Naming the Powers: The Language of Power in the New Testament* (1984), *Unmasking the Powers: The Invisible Forces that Determine Human Existence* (1986), and *Engaging the Powers: Discernment and Resistance in a World of Domination* (1992).

What are the powers? One of the first facts about the powers is that they are trans-individual. Individuals participate in the powers and exercise their authority, but individuals do not comprise the powers. The powers are rather "the systems themselves, the institutions and structures that weave society into an intricate fabric of power and relationships" (Wink, 1998, 1). They have the capacity for "unmiti-gated evil" but also for surprising good, though Wink's immediate goal is to explore the former.

Wink found himself fascinated also with the New Testament sug-gestion that the powers are invisible, which seemed to imply meta-physical as well as physical aspects. Wink noticed, for example, that "the letters to the seven churches" in the Book of Revelation are addressed to the "angels" of those churches. What does "angel" mean? Wink speculates that it refers to the idiosyncratic inner spirit, character, or disposition of each of the churches. Powers are not "sim-ply people and their institutions . . . ; they also include the spiritual-ity at the core of those institutions" (Wink, 1998, 4). Changing these systems, accordingly, requires dealing not only with outer forms but also with the inner core, whether with a corporation, the federal gov-ernment, a political party, or an ecclesiastical institution.

Out of a desire to better understand the dark side of the powers, Wink traveled with his wife, June, on a sabbatical leave to Chile in 1982 to experience firsthand the military dictatorship of General Augusto Pinochet in Chile. He visited other parts of South and Central America as well, to see the *barrios*, the notorious *favelas*, and to speak with nuns and priests who were working for human rights and with defense lawyers searching for the "disappeared ones."

Wink's reaction was one of devastation. He found himself over-whelmed with despair, even physically ill. "The evils we encountered were so monstrous, so massively supported by our own govern-ment . . . that it seemed nothing could make a difference" (6–7). He began to wonder "how the writers of the New Testament could insist that Christ is somehow, even in the midst of evil, sovereign over the Powers." Only in time was he able to find any hope in it all, and then only by holding tenaciously to Paul's pronouncement in Romans 8:38–39 that "neither death, nor life, . . . nor principalities . . . nor powers . . . will be able to separate us from the love of God in Christ Jesus," in the hope of excavating the truth that might be anchored in those words.

A question Wink wrestled with throughout was how to combat the institutionalized violence by which "unjust systems perpetuate them-selves" (7); by violent or nonviolent means. Wink began as an advocate of qualified nonviolence: "Try nonviolence, but if it fails, try violence." But, he writes, "I began to realize that if violence was my last resort, then I was still enmeshed in the belief that violence saves" (8).

Former Chilean dictator General Augusto Pinochet is shown in this March 10, 1998, photo. AP/Wide World Photos.

To test the waters of nonviolence Wink spent a second sabbatical in 1986 in South Africa. Taking exception to antiapartheid allies who denounced nonviolence as ineffectual, Wink "discovered a remarkable variety of effective nonviolent actions that many people there were employing in perhaps the largest grass roots eruption of diverse nonviolent strategies in a single struggle in human history" (8). The outcome was a new book by Wink, *Violence and Nonviolence in South Africa* (1987), later published as a modestly bound South African version under the title *Jesus' Third Way*, mailed out to 3,200 black and white clergy in South Africa and 800 Roman Catholic priests and pastoral workers.

Out of the encouragement that came from seeing the contribution of nonviolent strategies to the "fall of the Berlin Wall, the collapse of Communism in the Soviet Union and Eastern block, and the transformation of South Africa" (1987, 10), Wink was motivated to examine further the psychocultural roots of violence. This route of inquiry led him to the realization that a mythos operative for 5,000 years in

Western culture has provided the rationale for "good people" to allow themselves and their cultures to be violent in the service of a higher cause: the myth of redemptive violence.

The Myth of Redemptive Violence

Wink tells us that he first became aware of the myth of redemptive violence while reflecting on children's TV shows, pondering the "mythic structure of cartoons" and the ingenuous and gratuitous violence that plays across the screen, from the Teenage Mutant Ninja Turtles to Captain America, Batman and Robin, Tom and Jerry, cowboy-and-Indian westerns, and even the demolition of the monster Bluto by a spinach-eating Popeye. Wink tells us "the format never varies" (1987, 44). The hero brings the world back into order with violent exhibitions of power.

These shows for the young are reprises of an old, old story, native to systems of domination, where, as in the case of Mesopotamian culture of 3000 B.C.E., the perennial challenge was to maintain the power of the dominant patriarchy over the enemy, and over the women, children, slaves, and hired workers as well. The law declared, "If a woman speaks . . . disrespectfully to a man, that woman's mouth is crushed with a fire brick" (40). "It is one of the oldest continuously repeated stories in the world." The story "enshrines the belief that violence saves and that war makes peace" (42). As Havelock Ellis observes, it is that "insidious delusion" whispered in the ears of mankind for centuries: *Si vis pacem para bellum* (Seldes, 1972, 958). It does not appear in the least as mythic to those who hold it as true. It is simply "the nature of things. It's what works. It seems inevitable, the last and, often, the first resort in conflicts" (Wink, 1987, 42).

Wink reports that the mythic scenario he found playing out in children's movies, cartoons, and Nintendo games suddenly "rang familiar" (44). It dawned on him that the same mythos was rehearsed in a story dating from 1250 B.C.E. in the *Enuma Elish*, the Babylonian Creation story. It could have been produced in Hollywood, yet it comes from a pre-biblical era, and like the biblical myths, it has been rehearsed for generations, reinforcing the same values of the system of domination that engendered its promulgation.

The Babylonian Creation story opens with Apsu, the father god, and Tiamat, the mother god, dragon of chaos, giving birth to a host of younger gods. The plot immediately thickens when the younger gods proceed to generate so much noise in the heavens that the older gods plot to liquidate them. When the fledgling gods catch wind of the plan, they murder their father, Apsu. Tiamat, outraged, pledges vengeance against them. Terrified, they turn to the youngest among them, Marduk, and promise him unqualified power over them if he will protect them from the wrath of Tiamat.

Marduk accepts. He catches Tiamat in a net, driving an "evil wind" down her throat. He bursts her belly with an arrow and pierces her heart. Her skull is split with a club and her blood scattered. He then stretches out the corpse, dismembers it, and from the pieces creates the world. Simultaneously, with the aid of Ea, Marduk imprisons the older assembly of gods associated with Apsu. He executes one of them, and from his blood Ea creates the human race as servants of God.

What are the truths conveyed by this myth? The human race and the whole creation are the progeny of violence and have violence written in their bones; the gods, that is, the "voices" at the heart of the universe, are violent; women are the mythic embodiment of chaos and are to be controlled, if need be, violently. Over against the Creation myth in Genesis 1, which holds that men and women are equally enjoined to be fruitful and multiply and are made in the image of a beneficent creator God, we hear another story:

> The Myth of Redemptive violence is the story of the victory of order over chaos by means of violence. It is the ideology of conquest . . . The gods favor those who conquer. Conversely, those who conquer must have the favor of the gods . . . the king, the aristocracy, and the priesthood. Religion exists to legitimate power and privilege. (Wink, 1987, 48)

This same mythic taste for violence permeates the Bible. Wink cites (1998, 84) biblical scholar Raymund Schwager, who points out 600 passages of violence in the Hebrew Bible, 1,000 instances of God meting out violent punishment, 100 passages where Yahweh orders to kill, and several stories of God's inexplicable desire to kill someone, such as his attempt at Moses' life in Exodus 4:24–26. "Violence," Schwager concludes, "is easily the most often mentioned activity in the Hebrew Bible" (1987, 209).

Wink finds this mind-set duplicated in a contemporary admonition from a member of the religious right:

> That it is a privilege to engage in God's wars is clearly seen in the Psalms, perhaps nowhere better than in Ps. 149:5–7, where the saints sing for joy on their beds while they contemplate warring against God's enemies, or Ps. 58:10. "The righteous will rejoice when he sees

the vengeance; he will wash his feet in the blood of the wicked." Those who cannot say "Amen" to such sentiments have not yet learned to think God's thoughts after him . . . The righteous . . . are called by God's law to exercise a holy "violence" against certain of the wicked, thereby manifesting God's wrath. (1987, 59)

Wink finds the Babylonian myth alive and well also in contemporary culture in general—in the media; in foreign policy; in the Super Bowl; in *Rambo* movies; in vigilantism; and in spy thrillers where murder, lying, stealing, illegal entry, and seduction are justified in the service of "national security" (48–51). He cites an astonishing parallel to the Apsu–Tiamat tale resurrected in the movie *Jaws*. The police chief encounters a gigantic shark, read by critics as a symbol of consummate evil, and "kicks an oxygen tank into the attacking shark's throat, then fires a bullet that explodes the tank, thus forcing into the shark's body a wind that bursts it open." Though there is no procreation of a universe or of human beings from the shark's corpse, Brody, the police chief, becomes a superhero. "Chaos is subdued, and the island is restored to a tourist's paradise" (51).

The Myth of Redemptive Love

"I believe that Jesus' gospel is the most powerful antidote to the myth of redemptive violence that the world has ever known" (62). With these words, Walter Wink voices the conviction that appears across his writing, that the "third way" that Jesus teaches and walks is the model for sane human behavior on the planet. It is also the cure for the spiral of domination and violence dramatized in the Apsu–Tiamat myth that is replayed literally millions of times in the stories that twenty-first-century American culture and much of world culture tell themselves and their young. The antidote to the myth of redemptive violence is another story, the myth of redemptive love. The life and death of Jesus pen this mythos on the consciousness of those who hear and follow him.

Were we to locate any single word from the library of Jesus' utterances that provides the fulcrum on which his attitude toward violence and domination turns, it would be the stunning challenge in the Sermon on the Mount that we are to love our enemies and pray for those who persecute us (Matt. 5:44), matched by the contrapuntal echo in Paul's spiritual arsenal, "Do not be overcome by evil, but overcome evil with good" (Rom. 12:21). Nowhere in religious or political history have these enjoinders been advanced as the foundation stones for a way of living in a world marked by domination and violence.

With his unique angle of vision, Wink sees that these words and every piece of Jesus' life and teaching are dedicated to undermining systems of domination and the violence that germinates within them. "The kings of the Gentiles lord it over them, . . . but not so with you; rather the greatest among you must become like the youngest, and the leader like one who serves" (Luke 22:24–27). Jesus subverts every system and structure of domination—economic domination, the domination and repression of women, religious and cultic domination with exclusivizing codes of purity and holiness, the domination of ethnicity and racial identity, and the domination of family that can so insidiously thwart change and new possibilities. Jesus in fact announces his identity with a new family: "Whoever does the will of God is my brother and sister and mother" (Mark 3:35). Jesus' death, as well as his life, succeeds further in unmasking the violence at the heart of the religious and political systems of domination that put him to death.

"Jesus' Third Way" is the title of a chapter in *The Powers That Be*, and also the popular title, as mentioned earlier, of Wink's book *Violence and Nonviolence in South Africa*. The "third way" is a third option to the two standard, competing approaches to the question of violence. The first is the acceptance of the inevitability of and need for violence to secure the peace, the myth of redemptive violence. The second is a nonviolent route that is passive and nonresistant and refuses to coerce or resist in any form. The third way of Jesus, as Wink discerns it, is a resistant nonviolence, one that is confrontational and coercive without being lethal. It is the nonviolence of Gandhi, Dorothy Day, Leo Tolstoy, Martin Luther King Jr., and Cesar Chavez. It is the resistant nonviolence that Witness for Peace initiated in the warring environments of Nicaragua, El Salvador, Guatemala, and Haiti (1987, 117). It is the resistant nonviolence forged by the collaboration of Catholics and Protestants that challenged the Marcos dictatorship in the Philippines (121ff.); that brought an end to the genocide inaugurated by the Soviets in Lithuania (151); and that resisted the Nazi pogroms in Finland, Norway, Denmark, Holland, and Bulgaria (152ff.). It is the resistant nonviolence that is imagined in the enjoinders to turn the other cheek and walk the extra mile, designed to confront, disarm, and raise the consciousness of the oppressor and demean his power and authority (98–111).

At the heart of the command to love one's enemy and pray for one's persecutor is the conviction that the Holy is all-inclusive and at work in every individual. This means that no one is beyond the pale of regeneration and transformation. As Wink puts it, "Loving enemies is a way of living in expectation of miracles" (178). I recall Cesar Chavez once telling a group of theological students that on the mornings of those days on which he would be meeting about workers' rights with the owners of the huge grape farms, he would rise at 4 A.M. to meditate and pray, preparing to love everyone in the room that he would enter that day: "It changed me and changed them."

Wink adds a series of stories that demonstrate the real possibility of the aggressive, resistant nonviolent approach to enemies (145–179). The stories demonstrate the imagination, the daring, the originality, and the hope that informs the Promethean will to love one's enemies and to resist the myth of redemptive violence.

The most astonishing of these stories takes place at the home of Cantor and Mrs. Michael Weisser in Lincoln, Nebraska, in 1991. No sooner had they moved into their new home on a new assignment than the Weissers received a phone call. The voice said, "You will be sorry you ever moved into 5810 Randolph Street, Jew boy." The call was followed by a mailing that included the message "The KKK is watching you, scum." The envelope included pictures of Hitler and caricatures of Jews and blacks.

The police told Cantor Weisser that they knew the culprit—Larry Trapp, the state head of the KKK who had terrorized Jews, Asians, and blacks in Iowa and Nebraska. They regarded him as dangerous: "We know he makes explosives." An irony is that Trapp, 44 years old, was physically ill, in the late stages of diabetes, confined to a wheelchair. He lived in a small apartment festooned with Nazi artifacts, pistols, and shotguns.

Weisser followed Trapp's activities on television as a white supremacist TV showman. After one particularly odious show, Weisser left a message on Trapp's KKK hotline: "Larry," he said, "do you know that the very first laws that Hitler's Nazis passed were against people like yourself who had no legs or who had physical deformities or physical handicaps? Do you realize you would have been among the first to die under Hitler? Why do you love the Nazis so much?"

Weisser continued the calls until Trapp finally picked up personally and bellowed, "What the f___ do you want?" "I just want to talk to you," said Weisser. "You black?" Trapp demanded. "Jewish," Weisser answered. "Stop harassing me," said Trapp, who asked him why he was calling. Weisser remembered a suggestion of his wife's. "Well, I was thinking you might need a hand with something, and I wondered if I could help," Weisser extemporized. " I know you're in a wheelchair and I thought maybe I could take you to the grocery store or something."

Trapp was speechless, mumbled something about Weisser's "niceness" but refused help. Weisser ignored his rebuff and called again, several times. At one point Trapp suggested he was rethinking a few things, but in his next show reverted to the same old hatreds. Weisser called again, furious, denouncing him as a liar and hypocrite.

To Weisser's surprise, Trapp began to backtrack. "I'm sorry I did that. I've been talking like that all of my life . . . I can't help it. . . . I'll apologize!" That evening with his congregation the cantor offered prayers for the grand dragon.

The next night Cantor Weisser answered his phone. It was Trapp. "I want to get out," he said, "but I don't know how." When the Weissers offered to go over to Trapp's home to bring him some food, he hesitated, but then told them to come. When they walked into Trapp's small apartment, Trapp began to cry and threw his two rings with swastika symbols to the ground. All three cried, laughed . . . and hugged for the first time.

Trapp soon after renounced his racist activities and penned apologies to those he had threatened over the years. Weeks later, when his physicians gave him only a month to live, he accepted an invitation from the Weissers to move into their home. It had two bedrooms. They had three children. As Trapp's physical state worsened, Weisser's wife, Julie, gave up her nursing job to care for Trapp, for a period of over nine months. Three months before he died he converted to Judaism (1998, 172–175).

Wink interjects, "Most people who are violent have themselves been the victims of violence. It should come as no surprise, then, to learn that Larry Trapp had been brutalized by his father and was an alcoholic by the fourth grade." And he adds, "Loving our enemies may seem impossible, yet it can be done. . . . No miracle is so awesome" (175).

References

Jung, C. G. (1958). *The undiscovered self.* Boston: Little, Brown.
Schwager, R. (1987). *Must these be scapegoats?* San Francisco: HarperSanFrancisco.

Seldes, G. (ed.). (1972). *The great quotations*. New York: Penguin Pocket Books.

Wink, W. (1984). *Naming the powers: The language of power in the New Testament*. Philadelphia: Fortress.

Wink, W. (1986). *Unmasking the powers: The invisible forces that determine human existence*. Philadelphia: Fortress.

Wink, W. (1987). *Violence and nonviolence in South Africa*. Philadelphia: New Society.

Wink, W. (1992). *Engaging the powers: Discernment and resistance in a world of domination*. Minneapolis: Fortress.

Wink, W. (1998). *The powers that be: Theology for a new millennium*. New York: Doubleday.

CHAPTER 10

VIOLENCE AND CHRIST: GOD'S CRISIS AND OURS

J. Harold Ellens

Introduction

During the last seven years it has been the privilege and challenge of the biblical studies and pastoral theology communities to wrestle with the literary work of Jack Miles. He has written two books on the Bible, treating it from the point of view of a unitary literary text that can be read from beginning to end. He has done exactly that, with delightful skill, setting forth a literary picture of God in creation, in providence through history, and in Christ. His work must be addressed. It constitutes something of the magnitude of an earthquake in the field of biblical studies and Christian thought.

Miles' more recent of the two publications will be a particularly urgent read for those of us in the Christian community of faith. It is titled *Christ, a Crisis in the Life of God*.[1] This constitutes his study of the New Testament as literary narrative. It follows appropriately upon his 1995 publication, *God, a Biography*.[2] That volume, a Pulitzer Prize winner, addressed the Old Testament, or Hebrew Bible, as a unified literary narrative about God's personal development. Both volumes intend to take the canonical story seriously as literature and divine biography. Together these volumes are a crucially important study for anyone who is serious about any form of religion and any sacred scriptures. Some readers will have noticed that Miles has given us, to savor the flavor of his work a substantive chapter in volume 1 of this series, *The Destructive Power of Religion*. That volume is titled *Sacred Scriptures, Ideology, and Violence.*

Stanley Hauerwas urges that we can know no truth but story. Only in telling stories to each other do we distill what is operationally true for us. I would add that what is only abstractly or theoretically true is not true insofar as it is not operational. Thus Hauerwas argues that it is utterly crucial that we take story with the utmost seriousness. As our stories intersect with those of others, both are illumined, and meaning is enlarged. When that other is God, whose story we intersect or whose story may be riding on another person's story, our stories are enlarged supracosmically. When we intersect God's story while realizing our own stories, the enlargement of meaning and illumination has the potential of achieving a transcendental dimension.

Miles has undertaken to listen seriously to the Lord God's story about himself and to retell it as a tragicomedy, or as a comic-tragedy. Some years ago I proposed to write a book called *Bringing Up God,* addressing the psychosocial and educational-cultural experiences a child would encounter in first-century Galilee; thus describing Jesus' developmental years. The subtitle would probably have been *Jesus and How He Got That Way.* That project is still awaiting its moment. Miles' tour de force has made my proposed work decidedly less necessary—and much wiser when and if I ever get to it.

Exposition

Christ, a Crisis in the Life of God reached me at an overwhelmingly critical moment in my life and that of my family. Four days after the tragic terrorist assault upon the World Trade Center in New York City and the Pentagon in Washington, D.C., my young brother, Gordon, fell severely ill from an antibiotic given him by his dentist. Ten days later, on September 26, 2001, Gordon died a horrid death from fulminating sepsis. He was more a son to me than a brother. He was in the full stride of a very valuable and productive life, esteemed as a towering and heroic figure in the state of Michigan. His death was unnecessary, too quick, too soon, and too deadly for us all.

While we sat as a family at his deathbed on Tuesday afternoon at 3:00 P.M., my brother-in-law, Orville, stood up to say that he needed to do an errand for a friend. At 6:00 P.M. he was brought back on a stretcher, into the same ICU in the same hospital and into the bed next to Gordon's, his brain destroyed by a fall from his friend's roof. Gordon died the next day at 8:00 A.M., Orville at 8:20. It was in that context that Jack's book came to me. It reached me in the nick of time, you might say, if you permit time to mean *chairos*, not just *chronos*. *Chairos* is that Greek word for time that means more the timeliness of something in the long stretch of God's business with us in the world; whereas *chronos* means the hour indicated by your wristwatch. So it is in that context that I wish to address *God, a Biography*, and particularly *Christ, a Crisis in the Life of God*. I am using Miles' work as a foil in terms of which I can play out my own struggle with the violence of God, or rather the violation of humankind in God's world.

Miles' work is a sensitive and sensible retelling of the biblical story, as though it were a lens upon God's continuing personal development, from his act of creation through the impasse and failure to fulfill his promises to his people in the Hebrew Bible, and on into the New Testament and the meaning of the historical crisis of the crucifixion. Miles points out that at the close of the Hebrew Bible God ended his story in abject silence, having cursed his lovely creation, having overreacted to human inadequacy to the responsibilities of life and challenges of godliness, and having failed disastrously to keep his triumphalistic promises to his people. Miles sees the New Testament narrative as that of a thoroughly chastened God who endeavors to rectify what he has so senselessly demeaned. He does it by recognizing his own guilt and determining to die for it, interjecting into history, thereby, a new mode in which error and evil are ruled out of the cosmic equation and in which only grace and love count—indeed, in which nothing else works.

Miles has set himself an awesome undertaking here, to do for the twenty-first century what John Milton did with his literary tour de force for the seventeenth century. In his prologue to *Christ, a Crisis in the Life of God*, Miles articulately summarizes his own proposal that someone ought to do just such a thing.

> *Paradise Lost, Paradise Regained:* The English language may never surpass John Milton's four-word summary of the Bible. But there is another way to "justify the ways of God to man," as Milton aspired to do, than by granting God blanket immunity and then bowdlerizing his testimony lest he incriminate himself. An interpretation of the Bible in which God is allowed to be more hero than saint and in which it is taken for granted that no hero is without his flaw, not even the hero of a divine comedy, is the kind that, if a new Milton ever arose, could yield a new biblical epic.[3]

Jack is the new Milton. He has done it himself.

John Milton. Library of Congress.

Marcus Borg has developed the notion that for most believers Jesus Christ is just another name for God, the Father, another name by which we refer to the God of the Hebrew Bible.[4] *Christ, a Crisis in the Life of God* assumes and demonstrates that for Miles Jesus Christ is another name for Yahweh. The story of this person whose name is a new name for God, the God in history, is a story that ends as the tragicomedy of the "great reversals." It reaches its climax in a joyful marriage feast, a Roman triumph, a peaceable kingdom, and a grand liturgical wedding drama, as we see it in the Revelation or Apocalypse of St. John, the last book of the Bible.

However, while the literary narrative of the Hebrew Bible ends in a silenced God, who cannot, will not, at least does not, keep his promises to rescue his people and give them the peaceable kingdom; the New Testament literary narrative may prove to set that old narrative back to a minor key. What about this grand triumph of the God of remorse, of self-acknowledged responsibility for pain and suffering and evil, of self-imposed guilt, of self-inflicted death? What about this suicide God who thereby triumphs so gloriously in the New Testament story?

Is this triumphalism not more obscene than that of the Hebrew Bible's story, eclipsed by ultimate silence of God? Does the New Testament literary narrative, taken seriously as Miles takes it, not prove to be a more monstrous betrayal of humanity and subterfuge of creation and history than the strange God-story of the Old Testament? This new story substitutes a loud and grand divine triumph for the former divine silence. Is not the triumph real only on the fictional stage of words, with no operational alteration of the human experience that "The world is a great crime and someone must be made to pay. . . ."?[5] To quote Nietzsche, as Miles does, "God on a cross—are the horrible secret thoughts behind this symbol not understood yet . . . Christianity was a victory; a nobler outlook of it perished—Christianity has been the greatest misfortune of mankind so far."[6]

Miles has written a play or a film script on a novel called the New Testament. The question is, does the script work? Does it come out at a satisfying place? Does it carry the story line authentically? Does it build the characters with integrity, in keeping with the novel, and does it develop them and the plot with adequate theatrical dynamism? Does it produce a believable denouement? Will it draw us beyond the margin of poetic distance and the boundary of disbelief, carrying us gratifyingly into the triumphant story itself? Does the script work?

Of course the script works, and very well, indeed—as a theatrical script! *Christ, a Crisis in the Life of God* becomes a phenomenally engaging stage drama. It works so well that I want to be in it. I want to sign up for that play-full world. I want to get onstage. I want that to be my drama, mercifully our drama. I have wanted that play more than I have wanted life, since September 26, 2001. Miles' script works exactly where and as he wanted it to work. It works on the literary stage.

Of course, "Does the script work?" is a question that forces itself to be asked on three levels, not just one. On the literary level Miles' "screenplay" works very well, even if the denouement seems forced and fantastic. In this work the triumph seems much less forced and fantastic than it does in the book of the Revelation of St. John. When we leave Miles' theater we are full of the excitement and expectation of the grand triumph. We want the wedding liturgy to go on forever and the marriage feast to embrace the whole community of unsuspecting humankind. We want to go home to that world. Can we make the story our story? Can we take it home with us? Will it move from the stage to life? Will it work in the ICU?

That is the second level of the question. That takes us away from the script and the stage, but we cannot avoid the question. Miles' script does not need to answer this question because it is written for the stage, but everyone who sees the play cannot get the psychological question out of the human heart. The tearing and wrenching as we leave the theater and start down the grand marble steps to the streets and curbs and gutters of our existence intensify as we feel the sharp wind in our faces and the winter chill searing us. At this psychological level the script feels at once too idealized and too offensive to entice belief or produce therapeutic resolution. The intensely consoling drama, while it lasts, serves in the end to tease out the terrorizing question of meaning. "There's the rub that makes life of so long last."

But, of course, that is a problem not with the script, but with the ultimate story behind the script. That is not Miles' problem. That is the problem of God!

That problem throws us headlong into the spiritual level of the question. If indeed Miles had written a screenplay and the Bible were a novel about this main character, the Lord God, Miles' take on it would be wildly acclaimed to be lucid, compelling, and transcendentally appealing. But will it bury a child? Can it help me when I stand at the edge of that open grave? Will it facilitate the burial of my beautiful, blond, blue-eyed boy? That is always and only the bottom line for everyone, everywhere, is it not? Does the script work—not at the level at which Miles wrote it, but at the level of the inner brokenness of the shattered spirit, when the monstrous has happened, when helplessness reigns, and hope is gone? Will the script work—not Miles', God's?

In the end, the story does not work. That, of course, is the Bible's problem, not Jack Miles'; in exactly the way in which the Book of Job finally says that for all of Job's problems, *that* problem is God's problem, not Job's—indeed it is a problem *in* God and not in Job. The Bible's problem, which is God's problem, is that he made grandiose promises to humanity in the Hebrew Bible, then fell silent, and could not perform. He betrayed their hope and failed their faith.

In the New Testament, greater, more profound, and heavenly—indeed, millennial and magical—promises were made, neglected, betrayed, failed of their redemptive proposals. Only through massive reframing by heroic grieving hearts of true believers throughout our pathetic history has anything redemptive been able to be fashioned from God's history by grace-filled revisionist historians. God sanitized, revised, Christianized! God redeemed, postbiblically, theologically.

Even so, that "the last shall be first" still does not cut it! Honest human hearts naïvely long for all to be first and redeemed and healed—all persons, relationships, and institutions. Apparently, we can imagine a more ideal world than God can create or produce. The shortfall between what we can envision and what God can do is what we call evil, and we blame ourselves for it, as children who always internalize pain as guilt; and as children always prefer to afflict themselves than indict the parent. But is it not God's evil and is he not to blame? Nonetheless, his taking the blame in Miles' script affords us neither relief nor satisfaction. "It is finished?" "I am finished?" "I have finished myself off?" In the end, these are no different and make no difference.

Spiritually the script does not work! The world is still a great crime. I do not care if nobody pays for it. I want it healed. Merely writing poetry about that possibility, through the pathos of the prophets and apostles, is an obscenity. "He shall wipe away every tear from their eyes—and death shall be no more"? Where the hell has God been for 2,000 years—in his new siege of silence and impotence: 2,000 years of abuse and grief, mostly caused from intentions driven by various forms of God's story—religious "revelatory texts" everywhere. What about the 3,500 of 9/11, and their 350,000 grieving?

Conclusion

The Hebrew Bible's Deuteronomistic principle of justice has remained dysfunctional. The principle of divine mercy as a world changer remains largely incredible. Even the grace theme of Micah 7:18–20 and Romans 8 is only psychologically enticing, but is it really spiritually operational? Does it not remain theoretical and psychological rather than phenomenologically experienced or heuristically demonstrable? Is not God actually silent and absent? The Bible connects God with suffering and its explanation in such a way as to leave space between the two to speak. But does it really offer there a place to stand?

The only approach that has any possibilities in it seems to be the revisionism of Rabbi Harold Kushner.[7] In his work God is not in control because his gift of freedom to his universe precludes his intervention. God has tied his own hands. But does not removing God from direct responsibility, glorifying his distant silence with the chimera of cosmic "freedom," projecting divine resolution to the infinite and intangible future, and removing it to an inaccessible transcendent plane simply become another dysfunctional theodicy? Moreover, does that not make the cruciform Christology all the more obscene, unhelpful, and pathogenic? A psychiatrist friend of mine spoke for the hurting human heart. She said, "I like a little less freedom and a little more nurture."

What if a radical form of grace could be a human thing between us, perhaps an analogy of a truly ultimate and finally satisfying analogue in God? Then why does he need to be so subtle? Is it just to save us from the idolatry of enshrining his appearances instead of waiting for his *chairos?*

Notes

1. Jack Miles, *Christ, a Crisis in the Life of God* (New York: Knopf, 2001).

2. Jack Miles, *God, a Biography* (New York: Knopf, 1995).

3. Miles, *Christ*, 11.

4. Marcus Borg, from a lecture delivered at the First Presbyterian Church in Ann Arbor, Michigan, in spring 2000.

5. Miles, *Christ*, 12.

6. Ibid., 6.

7. Harold Kushner, *When Bad Things Happen to Good People* (New York: Little, Brown, 1981).

References

Ellens, J. H. (ed.) (2004). *The destructive power of religion* (Vols. 1–4). Westport: Praeger.

Kushner, H. (1981). *When bad things happen to good people.* New York: Little, Brown.

Miles, J. (1995). *God, a biography.* New York: Knopf.

Miles, J. (2001). *Christ, a crisis in the life of God.* New York: Knopf.

CHAPTER 11

PSYCHORELIGIOUS ROOTS OF VIOLENCE: THE SEARCH FOR THE CONCRETE IN A WORLD OF ABSTRACTIONS

Ronald Johnson

Introduction

Psychology has been undergoing a dramatic shift at the beginning of this new century not unlike the shift in thinking brought about by Sigmund Freud at the turn of the last century. Freud debated his colleagues regarding the existence and influence of the unconscious and essentially won that debate. Psychoanalysis prevailed in the field of psychology for the following half century only to be largely supplanted by behavioral psychology and to some degree by humanistic psychology at midcentury. The spectacle we are now seeing in psychology is the increasing influence of the field of neuropsychology and the effect that genetic predisposition has on personality. Behavioral, humanistic, and dynamic psychological theories of personality now take a backseat to this new biological view of why people do what they do. For the time being, however, a truce of sorts has occurred between those who militate for nurture as compared to nature in personality and behavior, a truce that suggests that each of these elements contributes a 50-percent influence on personality development.

A psychologist who seeks to conduct a thorough psychological evaluation of a patient now must be fluent in several areas formerly outside of his or her realm of expertise. Specifically, an assessment of personality must now include neuropsychological assessment, personality assessment, intellectual assessment, interpersonal relations ability, cultural and family background, and perhaps spiritual assessment. From this broadly based assessment, the clinician can then approach the understanding of the difficulties confronting the patient, whether they are vocational, interpersonal, intrapsychic, or even physical or spiritual. Similarly, an assessment of violence, especially when it is seemingly grounded in a religious framework, needs to be examined within and from the various perspectives of this broad spectrum. Our intent in such an inquiry should be to understand how such violence *makes sense*, however heinous we might find the actions of persons who would perpetrate such offense.

In the discussion that follows we shall examine but one of the elements that contribute, in the minds of some, to the apparent legitimation of violence on religious grounds. This element originates deep in souls and personalities as well as in the culture, as suggested by psychologist Carl Jung (1959), his predecessors, and his followers.

The Theory of Personality Types Developed by Carl Jung

Carl Jung, along with Alfred Adler and Karen Horney, was one of the principal students of Freud at the turn of the century, although he broke with his mentor along theoretical lines. Jung believed that while attending to the pathological elements of personality Freud had neglected a deeper understanding of certain personality characteristics that were shared by all people. In his *Psychological Types* (1923/1971) Jung proposed that at least three basic dimensions together fashioned the human personality in their various combinations: energy, perception, and judgment. The energy dimension ran from external to internal, or, in Jungian terms, *extroverted* to *introverted*. External (extroverted) persons gain energy by "coming out" and giving to the world, whether with their words or actions, whereas internal (introverted) individuals gain energy by "taking in" and receiving from the world.

The second and third Jungian dimensions relate to objectivity and subjectivity. Jung called the second, the *perceptive dimension*, irrational because it "is not based on rational judgment but on sheer intensity of perception" (370). Jung suggested that the perceptive dimension of personality is constructed with objective and subjective elements. He called the objective function of perception *sensation* and the subjective form of perception *intuition*. Hence, people who perceive objectively use their five senses whereas those who perceive the world subjec-

Anonymous portrait of Carl Jung. Snark/Art Resource, New York.

tively might be said to use their sixth sense, or intuition. The third dimension of Jungian personality type construction, that of *judgment*, is made up of objective decision making that Jung called *thinking*, and subjective decision making he called *feeling*. Jung referred to the thinking and feeling elements of judgment as rational because a rational process of judgment appeared to be going on, compared to the irrational process of perception. For the purposes of the present discussion we are primarily interested in the perceptive dimension proposed by Jung. But before we enter that dialogue, we must first elaborate on Jung's theories and those of his students.

Isabel Briggs Myers began working with Jungian typology in the 1930s and made two important additions to the theory. First, she discovered another dimension, now referred to as a dimension of *boundary*, that was implicit in Jung's work. Myers (1980) suggested that people are either low boundaried, preferring the function of perception, gathering information, and hence spontaneous; or high boundaried, preferring the function of judgment and hence planfulness.

Second, she developed, together with her daughter, the Myers-Briggs Type Indicator (MBTI) (Myers & McCaulley, 1985) as a means of testing one's personality type. Furthermore, the MBTI suggested an abbreviated means of referring to one's personality type with the use of letters to represent the four dimensions.

The original MBTI and its subsequent upgrades have become very popular in educational and business settings but have not found much favor in the more exact psychological community because of the preference for personality *type* over personality *characteristics*, the latter having been the primary domain employed by psychologists. Costa and McCrae (1992) developed a model and a psychological test utilizing the same Jungian model of personality but without the idea of type, preferring personality characteristics. The MBTI was popularized by David Kiersey (Kiersey & Bates, 1978), who attempted to utilize the MBTI personality type system in reestablishing a personality *temperament* system. Despite the differences among these approaches to Jung's work, the idea of understanding personality along these four dimensions has continued to gain popularity, seemingly because of its positive orientation as opposed to a pathology-based system of personality assessment.

Kierkegaard's Assessment of Personality

In the most popular of his works, *The Sickness Unto Death*, Soren Kierkegaard (1843/1969) puts forth an amazingly early proposal of differences in personality. The theme of this work is that *despair* is this "sickness unto death," or the despair of surviving life alone, without having faith in God. Kierkegaard goes on to make one of the simplest, yet most profound definitions of sin, namely, that sin is faithlessness, which equates to this "sickness unto death" and despair. The idea that sin is nothing more than faithlessness succinctly takes sin out of the realm of being something bad or something behavioral and simultaneously broadens the concept of sin to every aspect of life. Specifically, one is faithful when one trusts God, and one is sinful when one fails to trust God. Thus, sin and faith alternate from minute to minute as well as from day to day. Furthermore, when one finds oneself in sin, or lacking faith, the only way back to faith is to come to God not believing in God and asking for faith.

The balance of Kierkegaard's work examines the various ways that people despair and become "sick unto death." His descriptions of the different personality patterns are so similar to Jung's that one is tempted to conclude that Jung only rediscovered personality types. Kierkegaard begins his personality treatise by suggesting that a number of dimensions of personality lead to an equal number of ways of sinning, that is, despairing. One dimension is that of "finitude/infinitude" (162): "The despair of infinitude is due to the lack of finitude" (164) and "the despair of finitude is due to the lack of infinitude." So, regardless of whether one is a person of "infinitude" or "finitude," one will despair of God's love. This infinitude/finitude dimension constructed by Kierkegaard is remarkably similar to the boundary dimension implied in Jung's work and clarified by Myers. People whom Kierkegaard calls those of infinitude correlate to people of low boundary in the Jung-Myers system, namely, people who think of the infinite and are spontaneous in their daily lives. Comparatively, finitude people are similar to high-boundary individuals who are planful and prefer closure. Other dimensions suggested by Kierkegaard include weakness/defiance, conscious/unconscious, and possibility/necessity.

The dimension of possibility/necessity most interests us in this discussion because of its similarity to the dimension of sensation/abstraction suggested by Jung. Kierkegaard suggests that "the despair of possibility is due to the lack of necessity" (168) and "the despair of necessity is due to the lack of possibility" (170). More specifically, Kierkegaard suggests that a person who is inclined to possibility gets lost in possibilities: "possibility then appears to the self ever greater and greater, more and more things become possible, because nothing becomes actual" (169). Kierkegaard states the (despair) problem with a possibility person, "What really is lacking is the power to obey, to submit to the necessary in oneself, to what may be called one's limit" (169). In contrast to the possibility way of life is that of necessity, in which an individual prefers the concrete, the absolute, and the visible. Despair in such a person occurs because he or she does not believe that all things are possible with God. Such a person becomes deterministic, believing that all things are predictable, and in so believing feels a loss of himself. Kierkegaard concludes this discussion by stating that "personality is a synthesis of possibility and necessity" (173), suggesting that the mature believer realizes that truth lies not with possibility or with necessity but alternately with both. Without knowing it, Kierkegaard suggested the metaphor of alternating electrical current, in which the truth of life alternates constantly between what is necessary and what is possible, or, in Jungian terms, what is concrete and what is abstract.

Concrete and Abstract as Hallmarks of Personality and Success

Let us now return to the more basic Jungian theory of personality construction, recalling that Jung (1959) suggested that anything that occurs naturally in personality also occurs naturally in society and is reflected in various archetypes: symbols and actions. The element of Jung's personality type theory that most concerns us in the present study is the dimension of perception. Recall that Jung suggested that one of the elements of personality is that of perception, and that people tend to perceive, either concretely or abstractly, a notion that is quite similar to Kierkegaard's understanding of necessity and possibility. Jung (1923/1971) suggests that concreteness, or sensation, as he calls it, is dependent on objects. Hence concrete people perceive the objective, the visible, and the objectively identifiable. Furthermore, "Objects are valued in so far as they excite sensations . . . and are fully accepted into consciousness whether they are compatible with rational judgments or not" (362). Jung goes on to describe different combinations of other personality characteristics with perception, such as introverted sensation and extroverted sensation. People who combine the elements of extroversion (of energy) and sensation (in perception) tend to be very "dependent" on visible objects, whereas people who are introverted and intuitive tend to be a bit more removed from objective things but still subtly and unconsciously dependent on them.

Isabel Briggs Myers (1980) furthered Jungian study of personality type by enlarging upon Jung's somewhat esoteric presentation of personality. She suggested that "sensing types"

> Like an established way of doing things.
>
> Enjoy using skills already learned more than learning new ones.
>
> Work more steadily, with realistic ideas of how long it will take.
>
> Usually reach a conclusion step-by-step.
>
> Are patient with routine details.
>
> Are impatient when the details get complicated.
>
> Are not often inspired, and rarely trust inspiration.
>
> Seldom make errors of fact.
>
> Tend to be good at precise work.
>
> Like using experience and standard ways to solve problems.
>
> Prefer continuation of what is, with fine-tuning.

Murray and Murray (1988) developed a similar list of characteristics of people who are concrete and sensual: precise, observant, realistic, practical, tolerant of routine, doing things right, hard-working, and slowly changing. Thus, concrete people, or those who tend to prefer a concrete way of perceiving the world, are down-to-earth; perhaps simple and possibly simplistic; hard-working; solution oriented; and, of course, objective. Concrete people tend to be the doers of the world as compared to the dreamers of the world, and they tend to lack the ability to stand outside of themselves and view the ethical or social appropriateness of their perception or behavior because what counts is the ability to act pragmatically and successfully toward a "bottom-line" end in the concrete situation that they see.

Jung characterized the dreamers of the world as intuitive. Jung and his students suggested that intuitive people were at the other end of the continuum of perception, and hence subjective in what they perceived in the world. Jung (1959) said, "The intuitive function is represented in consciousness by an attitude of expectancy, by vision, and penetration. . . . The primary function of intuition . . . is simply to transmit images, or perceptions of relations between things" (366). Abstract intuitive people tend to ignore objects and objective reality because objectivity hinders what Jung calls a "clear, unbiased, and naïve perception." Such people have a subjective view of reality, and their distinct preference is to remain in the abstract because concretizing tends to diminish the power of their abstractions. Intuitive people try to apprehend the widest range of possibilities, and when possibilities are limited by concrete reality, such folks become bored, agitated, or even irritated because they are being forced to see limits: "Facts are acknowledged only if they open new possibilities of advancing beyond them and delivering the individual from their power" (368).

Myers (1980) identified intuitive persons as people who

Like solving new problems.

Dislike doing the same thing repeatedly.

Enjoy learning a new skill more than using it.

Work in bursts of energy powered by enthusiasm, with slack periods in between.

Reach a conclusion quickly.

Are impatient with routine details.

Are patient with complicated situations.

Follow their inspirations, good or bad.

Dislike taking time for precision.

Murray and Murray (1988) added that intuitive people are creative, are able to rely on hunches, explore new alternatives, love new and different ideas, use approximations, go beyond facts, and enjoy observing different things. In summary, people who are on the subjective end of the continuum of perception tend to be ideational; creative; imaginative; interested in change; problem oriented; and, of course, subjective.

The conception that people perceive the world differently is profound. When talking about perception, we are not referring to judgment, evaluation, or decision making. We are talking about what we actually perceive, whether with our five senses or with our so-called sixth sense. The profundity of this discovery by Kierkegaard, Jung, Myers, and others is in the basic nature of perception. We do not see the same things. Concrete/objective people see things as things. Abstract/subjective people see things as possibilities. The former group sees what is; the latter, what could be. Psychotherapists who are familiar with this dimension of personality often see relationship disturbances surrounding this dimension of personality in which, for instance, the wife sees the practical and the husband sees the theoretical, or the son sees the possibilities and the father sees the realities. Furthermore, in keeping with Jung's suggestion of the existence of archetypes, it appears likely that this objective/subjective dimension is present in many forms in society and is reflected also in cultural formation and maintenance. Some Western cultures, for instance, appear to be more concrete and practical, such as the British and the American, whereas others, such as the French and the Italians, appear to be more abstract and ideational. But certainly within every culture is a fair mixture of both subjective and objective individuals, and these individuals will tend to thrive in their specific cultures to the degree that their personalities are reflective of those cultures. There is distinctly less of a Left Bank in New York City than there is in Paris.

The Concrete Nature of Fundamentalism

The term *Fundamentalism* originated in the late nineteenth century, coming from a pamphlet that a number of conservative ministers created in reaction to the developing theology of the time perceived to be liberal or modernistic. Fundamentalism came to be associated with conservative Christianity, including a literal reading of the Scriptures as well as a concrete understanding of the biblical stories. The term has more recently been applied to extreme, and usually orthodox, wings of other religions, most recently, Islam and Judaism. Armstrong (2001) notes that the phenomenon is a relatively modern one, thus challenging the notion espoused by Fundamentalists that they are following the original teachings of their religions. Premodern peoples were less interested than we are in what actually happened but more concerned with the meaning of an event.

The power, and perhaps the attractiveness, of Fundamentalism is in its reference to a direct connection to God because those who think they literally follow God's instructions often believe they are above criticism because God is above criticism. This is a seductive syllogism because it assumes a God who is incapable of decreeing what the listener does not desire. Thus, in referring to God as their partner and leader, Fundamentalists can follow God's directions without admitting to any self-interest. In so doing Fundamentalists can make themselves quite powerful while espousing an appearance of submission to God and humility to humankind.

Kimball (2002) identifies several characteristics of Fundamentalists: (1) they make a distinction between the sacred and the profane, (2) they claim absolute truth, (3) they demand blind obedience, (4) they believe the ends justify the means, and (5) they believe in the idea of a holy war. The distinction between the sacred and profane is typified by statements that suggest that certain writings, acts, thoughts, or feelings are inherently godly, whereas others are distinctly not godly. Such is the case of the Taliban suggesting that the 9/11 attacks are godly whereas the U.S. retaliatory acts in Afghanistan are ungodly. Similarly, vigilant antiabortionists claim that abortion is ungodly, whereas their murder of persons who work at abortion clinics is godly. The claims of absolute truth are usually based on identifiable verses of sacred Scriptures, often interpreted out of context for specific political or personal purposes. Ends are seen to justify means when Fundamentalists engage in one kind of life taking to prevent another kind of life taking, claiming the former overrides the heinous character of the latter.

Armstrong (2001) provides an important look at Fundamentalism that has existed in one form or another for about 400 years, although Erasmus wanted to revitalize Christianity by returning to the fundamentals; *ad fonts*, to the wellsprings. All the Protestant Reformers, specifically the Wesleys, Zwingli, and Calvin, asked that Christians return to the "basic writings of the Scriptures." We hear their voices in the current wave of Evangelicalism in the United States. The earliest forms of modern Fundamentalism in Judaism came about with Isaac Luria, a Jew in sixteenth-century Palestine who came to believe that the Messiah would return to Israel. Interestingly, however, Luria was not specific about this return and was not associated with any kind of Zionism. About a century later Shabbetai Zevi "heard a heavenly voice" and came to believe that he was the Savior of Israel, thus developing a large messianic following until he was captured by the Ottomans and converted to Islam. Islamic forms of Fundamentalism came about after a millennium of relatively uninterrupted mythical understanding of Muhammad. Teaching Islam was largely left to *ulema*, the teachers and scholars of the various Arab cultures. But many reformers came into Islam over the next several centuries, among them Muhammad ibn Abd al-Wahab (1703–1792). Abd al-Wahab wanted Muslims to "return to the teachings of the Koran." His purposes were not significantly different from those of Osama bin Laden in Saudi Arabia in the 1990s or the Ayatollah Khomeini in Iran in the 1980s.

The Search for Concrete Religion

The dynamic between the objective and the subjective first discovered by Kierkegaard and more fully described by Jung and Myers is at the heart of the phenomenon of Fundamentalism. Kierkegaard best presented this dynamic in his suggestion that joy and sorrow exist at both ends of this spectrum, requiring each individual to understand the depth of this phenomenon in his or her life. The person favoring the objective, concrete, and sensual elements of life sees what exists, accepts what exists, and utilizes what exists. The person favoring the subjective, abstract, and intuitive elements of life sees what could exist, the necessity for constant change, and the ultimate emptiness of the absolute. These two means of perception are so profoundly different that most people are completely unaware that the mode of perception different from their own even exists, as is evidenced by their day-to-day speech, which is, itself, littered with evidence of their preference in perception. People who prefer the subjective value myths, symbols, and meaning and talk in abstractions and possibilities, disparaging what they see as the simplicity and triviality of objective reality. In comparison, objective people talk of what they perceive of visible reality as the only thing that matters in life and become easily bored with abstractions and irritated with possibilities.

It is understandable that the three predominant voices in discovering and elucidating this difference between the objective and the subjective, Kierkegaard, Jung, and Myers all distinctly favored the subjective over the objective. Similarly, developmental psychologist Piaget (1955) was probably unaware of his subjective nature in his suggestion that the "concrete operational" stage of cognitive development preceded the "formal operational stage" during which the person gains the ability to think abstractly. It would be unlikely that a person strongly favoring the objective and concrete would be able to see adequately the subjective side of life because such an understanding requires abstraction. The very nature of philosophy, as well as a developed theology, is abstract as philosophers attempt to move from issues of Aristotelian cause–effect thinking to issues of Platonic meaning–purpose thinking, from the concrete to the abstract in their understanding of how the world works and how the humans who inhabit the world survive in it.

More important for this discussion is that when a religion begins, it is almost always objective in original focus. While Jesus appears to have been a blend of the objective and the subjective, his followers became quite objective in their proselytizing and evangelizing. The first 400 years of Christianity saw distinct schools of thought regarding the essence of the faith develop along objective lines, culminating in the era of the Great Ecumenical Councils of the fourth and fifth centuries of the Common Era, from the Council of Nicea (325 C.E.) to that of Chalcedon (451 C.E.), with their strong preferences for the objective and the absolute. The towering personalities of psychologically obsessive, meticulous, concrete thinkers such as Tertullian of Carthage and Cyril of Alexandria dominated the developments of this era. Both Judaism and Islam had similar concrete beginnings and expressed purposes, the former out of a need to coalesce for the exilic Israel how God is in history in the face of the tragedy of "his people," and the latter to unify the fragmented tribes of Ishmael in monotheism.

Although the beginnings of these three religions were intrinsically concrete, the spokespersons and theologians for these religions became increasingly abstract as they sought to apply the concrete teachings of the founders of the faith to their increasingly diverse, educated, and sophisticated populations. In their abstractions religious leaders and theologians separate themselves from their constituents even as they think, discuss, and write in an attempt to make religion more meaningful. The Levites kept God behind the Holy of Holies. The Roman Catholic priests moved the sacraments away from parishioners and separated the priests from the laity with vows of celibacy and chastity. Islamic leaders moved God even farther from the masses by instituting requirements and traditions of Islamic believers that functionally separated them from God. The Protestant Reformers challenged the separation of priests and laypeople, but within a very few decades they fell into the same pattern of preferring abstractions and symbols to the concrete and practical. The pattern of all of these religions has been to produce a theological and ecclesiastical leadership increasingly separated from the populations to which they minister.

Fundamentalism in its various forms, and regardless of the ideology in which it is found, has routinely challenged the abstract nature of religious leaders. Fundamentalist leaders are usually very concrete, down-to-earth, and practical as compared to other ecclesiastical leaders. In that way, they are often more like the founders of the faith who often ministered to the physical needs of their followers, like Yahweh of the wandering Israelites feeding the masses manna from heaven, Jesus feeding the 5,000 fish and bread, or Muhammad meeting the needs of poverty and estrangement from tribal chiefs. Jim Jones, David Koresh, the leaders of Heaven's Gate in America, Asahara Shoko in Japan, Osama bin Laden in the Islamic world, and Shabbetai Zedi in sixteenth-century Palestine attracted followers, even longtime Christians, Buddhists, Muslims, and Jews, who had become functionally disenfranchised and disenchanted with a religion that had become esoteric, abstract, and impractical. Islamic Fundamentalist terrorism today surprises many of us who have known Islam as an abstracted theology of grace and peace. We should not be surprised. The contemporary Islamic terrorism is like that in all religious groups throughout history, occurring whenever concrete thinkers become dominant and powerful. Today the terror is more horrible to us and different in scope only because the tools for perpetrating the tragedies are so much more lethal. Religiously motivated terrorism is a psychological phenomenon to which Fundamentalisms, Orthodoxies, and concrete ideologies are always lethally susceptible. I am certain that the Eastern Christian inhabitants of Constantinople found the siege and destruction of their city by Western Roman Catholic Christians during the fourth crusade in 1204 C.E. infinitely more terrorizing even than the assault upon the World Trade Center towers in New York City on September 11, 2001.

Charismatic cultic leaders offer their constituencies clear, objective, practical, and absolute directives for their lives and answers for their theological questions. They are not satisfied with just asking questions and musing. They want answers. Those we have cited here provided answers. Some of these answers are clearly psychotic, as were the cases of David Koresh and Shabbetai Zedi, whereas others are satisfied with simply objectifying the truth of whatever gospel they preach, like Pat Robertson and Jerry Falwell of Christianity or bin Laden of Islam. Objectifying can be a very powerful tool in religion and even more powerful in political hands. The genocides in Nazi Germany, Bosnia, the Ottoman Empire, the Spanish Inquisition, Rwanda, and Native America are examples of a politic that threw out the confusion of the subjective equality of all humankind for the objective simplicity of defining certain peoples as evil. General Sheridan is said to have declared to his soldiers on the western plains, "The only good Indian is a dead Indian." Concrete to the terrifying uttermost. Life could be made very simple for his "Pony Soldiers" in the heat of the summer deserts or the wintry snows.

The Painful Integration of the Concrete and the Abstract

Kierkegaard had it right. He said that there is sin: faithlessness, despair, ultimate emptiness, whenever we fall solidly on the abstract or the concrete. Because the function of perception is so basic to personality, most of us perceive without realizing that our perceptions are, indeed, as Jung suggested, irrational. We perceive what we want to perceive, and we perceive what we are capable of perceiving. We can do no other. It seems as if we are doomed to be limited by what we perceive.

I know of two brothers who had very different preferences on the dimension of perception. The older of the two was very ideational, as well as deeply committed to the unknown, the abstract, and, in his words, "the unreal." The younger brother was very concrete, factual, and productive. Interestingly, the younger far surpassed the older in formal education and degrees, while the older brother was essentially self-taught and a voracious reader. The younger learned by experience, including many trials and failures, while the older learned by proxy and observation. Eventually, the older brother died quite young, and with his death a large amount of knowledge and understanding of the world died too, without ever contributing significantly to the body of knowledge in theology, psychology, and philosophy, his areas of expertise. The younger brother has made some minor contributions to these bodies as well, but only now, after 60 years, has he begun to make significant contributions.

Jung (1923/1971) suggested that psychological maturity was the development of one's shadow, or the elements of our personality construction that are in opposition to our natural talents or preferred style and values. Hence, maturity for introverts means learning the value of breadth and spontaneity in expression, which add to their basic nature: depth and internality. Similarly, extroverts need to learn the value of depth and quietude, which add to their breadth and externality. Of more concern to us in this discussion, however, is recognition of the essential need for one to develop one's shadow in the function of perception. This kind of maturity is very painful for most of us because it means admitting that we do not see everything. Even more painful is the fact that other people see things we do not see. Concrete people see the trees. Abstract people see the forest. But which is more important? If we are to believe the saying "You can't see the forest for the trees," we would suggest that it would be the abstractors. But is it really more important to see the forest than the trees? Tree-seeing people might be inclined to cut a few trees, build a fire, and get warm, whereas forest-seeing people are quite comfortable seeing the forest and wondering why they are still so cold.

Are we doomed to have the David Koreshes and Osama bin Ladens of the world continue to bring a message of objectivity to a population hungry for something hard that it can sink its teeth into? Is there some kind of solution for this dilemma of our limited perception, or are we forever doomed to see only half of God's world? Even in asking this question, we still have different perceptions. Objective people might charge right into the business of finding practical solutions to the problem, however, trivial, whereas subjective people would know that there are certainly no final answers to the problem except to muse about it. So with a tentative feeling, I suggest that we

1. Increase our awareness of our own styles and preference of perception.
2. Appreciate our own styles without reserve.

3. Begin to understand and appreciate that the other half of the world sees things we don't see.

4. Gather together in small and large bodies of students of life to more fully "see" what exists in the world.

5. Understand and disseminate the understanding of the necessity of both the abstract and the concrete so as to avoid disenfranchisement of any one element of humankind.

6. Add to our faculties of seminaries and schools of philosophy people who are atypically philosophical, for example, concrete and objective.

7. Understand that absolutes exist . . . but only for a time. And people need absolutes . . . for a time.

8. Understand that when absolutists begin to have an audience, we have failed in our need to practicalize our theories, specifically, the theories of theology that we have espoused.

9. Avoid challenging such absolutists, but rather, when they surface, seek ways to be even more practical and concrete in the expression of religion and philosophy.

10. Invite such absolutists into our seminaries and schools to discuss with others their opinions and discoveries.

Conclusion

Herein lies the (temporary) solution to this dreadfully important dilemma; we need each other just as Bonhoeffer suggested. This needing of each other is no simple listening to and enduring of one another's perceptions. We need to genuinely reach beyond our natural limitations to see more, and in so doing encounter the pain of personal growth. The alternative is the dogmatizing of our psychological preferences and their philosophical or worldview consequences. When we move to such dogmatizing, because we cannot perceive any functionality in the opposite perspective or tolerate the discomfort of its outlook, we feel the urgency to impose our "workable" system on the world around us. When this system is certified by religion and thus identified as God's ultimate truth, it breeds violence. This violence may range all the way from the violation of the emotions of the "different" others by simple slighting or insensitivity, to flying an airborne gasoline bomb into such national symbols as the World Trade Center towers. The entire spectrum is violation and violence, certified by sick religion.

References

Armstrong, K. (2001). *The battle for God: A history of fundamentalism.* New York: Random House.

Bonhoeffer, D. (1960). *The communion of saints.* New York: Harper and Row.

Costa, P. T., & McCrae, R. R. (1992). *Revised NEO Personality Inventory and NEO Five-Factor Inventory: Professional manual.* Odessa: Psychological Assessment Resources.

Jung, C. (1959). *The archetypes and the collective unconscious.* Princeton: Bollingen Press.

Jung, C. (1923/1971). *Psychological types.* Princeton: Bollingen Press.

Kierkegaard, S. (1843/1969). *Fear and trembling* and *The sickness unto death.* Princeton: Princeton University Press.

Kiersey, D., & Bates, M. (1978). *Please understand me.* Del Mar: Prometheus Nemesis.

Kimball, C. (2002). *When religion becomes evil.* San Francisco: Harper.

Murray, W., & Murray, R. R. (1988). *Reframing psychological types.* Gladwyne: Self-published.

Myers, I. B. (1980). *Introduction to type* (3rd ed.). Palo Alto: Consulting Psychologists Press.

Myers, I. B., & McCaulley, M. H. (1985). *Manual: A guide to the development and use of the Myers-Briggs Type Indicator.* Palo Alto: Consulting Psychologists Press.

Piaget, J. (1955). *The child's construction of reality.* London: Routledge.

CHAPTER 12

THE LASTING EFFECTS OF CHILDHOOD TRAUMA

Donald Capps

A Bundle of Weeds?

In one of his parables about the activity of God in the world, Jesus tells about a man who sowed good seed in his field, but while he was sleeping, his enemy came and sowed weeds among the wheat. When the plants began to spring up and bear grain, the weeds also began to appear. Noting the weeds, his servants came to him and pointed out what had happened. He immediately suspected his enemy of trying to sabotage his crop. When his servants asked if he wanted them to gather the weeds, he said no, lest in gathering the weeds they root up the wheat along with them: "Let both grow together until the harvest; and at harvest time I will tell the reapers, Gather the weeds first and bind them in bundles to be burned, but gather the wheat into my barn" (Matt. 13:30).

I am reminded of this parable when I hear the oft-repeated claim that Martin Luther viewed the letter of James as a bundle of straw, on the grounds that its author was confused about the relationship between faith and works. As he is quoted as saying of James in his *Table Talk* (1967):

> There's no order or method in the epistle. Now he discusses clothing and then he writes about wrath and is constantly shifting from one to the other. He presents a comparison: "As the body apart from the spirit is dead, so faith apart from works is dead." O Mary, mother of God!

> What a terrible comparison that is! James compares faith with the body
> when he should rather have compared faith with the soul! (424–425)

Obviously, Luther, whose profound reverence for the Bible is beyond
question, was nonetheless able to exhibit considerable intellectual
autonomy with respect to the letter of James. Luther, of course, was
especially sensitive to what he perceived to be the inferiority of this
particular letter to much of the rest of the Bible because it dealt with
his central theological issue: the relationship of faith and works. I,
too, have difficulties with the letter of James, because the author, in
making his case that faith without works is barren, cites Abraham's
threatened sacrifice of Isaac as an example of one whose faith was not
barren: "Was not Abraham our father justified by works, when he
offered his son Isaac upon the altar? You see that faith was active
along with his works, and faith was completed by works" (James
2:21–22). The analogy between body and faith and spirit and works
of which Luther is so critical follows this illustration (v. 26).

However, I am more concerned about the letter to the Hebrews
than that of James, for it provides a theological rationale for the abuse
of children. As Philip Greven (1991) points out:

> The key text in the New Testament cited in favor of harsh physical dis-
> cipline of children is Hebrews 12:5–11, which many Christians assume
> to have been written by the Apostle Paul, who converted to
> Christianity after Jesus had been crucified. Modern scholars, however,
> have concluded that Paul was not the author of this book, which thus
> remains anonymous. Although no one actually knows who wrote
> Hebrews, this unknown author has had, and continues to have, an incal-
> culable impact upon the lives of children. (52)

Greven notes that "the justifications of corporeal punishment by the
author of Hebrews . . . drew upon an ancient history filled with
instances of divine chastisements and pains, while he himself supplied
memories of the personal anguish that once felt 'grievous' to him and
to others" (53). Thus, in Hebrews 12:5–6, the author asks his readers:
"Have you forgotten the exhortation which addresses you as sons?"
and then proceeds to quote Proverbs 3:11–12: "My son, do not regard
lightly the discipline of the Lord, nor lose courage when you are punished by him. For the Lord disciplines him whom he loves, and chastises every son whom he receives."

The author next compares divine chastisement to the discipline
that sons receive from their earthly fathers: "It is for discipline that
you have to endure. God is treating you as sons; for what son is there

whom his father does not discipline? If you are left without discipline, in which all have participated, then you are illegitimate children and not sons" (12:7–8). In the light of recent arguments that Jesus may well have been illegitimate (Schaberg, 1987; Capps, 2000), this statement that the only children who are not adequately disciplined are the illegitimate ones is deeply ironic, especially because it occurs in the midst of the author's discussion of Jesus' death on the cross as the full and complete sacrifice for the sins of all humankind. He even alleges that Jesus' own attack on the sacrificial system in Jerusalem was not for the purpose of ending sacrifice, once and for all, but rather to abolish this system in order to establish another one, this one based on "the offering of the body of Jesus Christ once and for all" (10:5–10).

Having advanced his analogy between the discipline that he and other legitimate sons received from their fathers and the discipline that they, now adults, are enduring from God, he continues: "We have had earthly fathers to discipline us and we respected them. Shall we not much more be subject to the Father of spirits and live? For they disciplined us for a short time at their pleasure, but he disciplines us for our good, that we may share his holiness. For the moment all discipline seems painful rather than pleasant; later it yields the peaceful fruit of righteousness to those who have been trained by it" (12:9–11). Here, the author claims that God's discipline is "for your own good," and then distinguishes between earthly fathers who beat their sons for the pleasure it affords them and God who does so only so that we may become more like him.

Greven notes that nowhere in the letter to the Hebrews does the author "cite words spoken by Jesus to confirm his beliefs about the necessity for scourging sons. If any such text existed in his own time and place, the anonymous writer does not make use of it" (53). I would add that such a text would conflict with the Gospels, as they represent Jesus as an advocate of mercy toward errant sons (cf. the story of the prodigal son in Luke 15:11–32). But even more to the point is the fact that the Gospels have nothing to say about Jesus' death being a sacrifice. As René Girard points out in *Things Hidden since the Foundation of the World* (1987):

> It must be admitted that nothing in what the Gospels tell us directly about God justifies the inevitable conclusion of a sacrificial reading of the Epistle to the Hebrews. . . . If we keep to the passages [in the Gospels] that relate specifically to the Father of Jesus, we can easily see that they contain nothing which would justify attributing the least

amount of violence to the deity. On the contrary, we are confronted
with a God who is foreign to all forms of violence. The most important
of these passages in the synoptic Gospels formally repudiate the conception of a vengeful God, a conception of whose traces can be found
right up to the end of the Old Testament. Even if we discount all the
explicit and implicit identifications of God with love that we find in the
Gospel of John and in the Epistles attributed to the same author, we can
confidently assert that in respect of the rejection of violence, the
Gospels are fulfilling the work of the Old Testament. (182)

Girard then suggests that, in his opinion, the basic text that shows
us a God who is alien to all violence and who wishes to see humanity
abandon violence is Matthew 5:43–45: "You have heard that it was
said, 'You shall love your neighbor and hate your enemy.' But I say to
you, 'Love your enemies and pray for those who persecute you, so that
you may be [children] of your Father who is in heaven; for he makes
his sun rise on the evil and on the good, and sends rain on the just
and on the unjust.'" Girard adds, "Beside this text we can put all the
texts denying that God is responsible for the infirmities, illnesses and
catastrophes by which innocent victims perish—in particular, of
course, for conflict. No God can be blamed for this; the immemorial
and unconscious practice of making the deity responsible for all the
evils that can afflict humanity is thus explicitly repudiated" (183).
Then, against the contention that this seems to make God into a sort
of distant or indifferent deity, for, after all, at least the old Yahweh
was interested enough in humans to be roused to anger by their iniq-
uities, Girard counters:

> In fact, we do not meet an indifferent God in the Gospels. The God pre-
> sented there wishes to make himself known, and can only make himself
> known if he secures from men what Jesus offers them. This is the essen-
> tial theme, repeated time and time again, of Jesus' preaching: reconcili-
> ation with God can take place unreservedly and with no sacrificial
> intermediary through the rules of the kingdom. This reconciliation
> allows God to reveal himself as he is, for the first time in human his-
> tory. Thus mankind no longer has to base harmonious relationships on
> bloody sacrifices, ridiculous fables of a violent deity, and the whole
> range of mythological cultural formations. (183)

Also, against the argument that the Garden of Gethsemane story
implies that God the Father was making a sacrifice of his son, Jesus,
Girard argues that this is not the case at all. It *was* necessary for Jesus
to die, not, however, "to satisfy a deity's need to revenge his honor,
which has been tainted by the sins of humanity, and who therefore

The Gospel according to St. Matthew. Beginning with chapter 1, with vignette portrait of Matthew writing and of the star appearing to shepherds. Library of Congress.

requires a new victim, one who is very precious and dear to him, his very own son" (182). Rather,

> When Jesus says: "your will be done and not mine," it is really a question of dying. But it is not a question of showing obedience to an incomprehensible demand for sacrifice. Jesus has to die because continuing to live would mean a compromise with violence. I will be told that "it comes to the same thing." But it does not at all come to the same thing. In the usual writings on the subject, the death of Jesus derives, in the final analysis, from God and not from men—which is why the enemies of Christianity can use the argument that it belongs within the

same schema as all the other primitive religions. Here we have the difference between the religions that remain subordinated to the powers and [a religion that centers on] the act of destroying those powers through a form of transcendence that never acts by means of violence, is never responsible for any violence, and remains radically opposed to violence. (213–214)

The problem, then, is that the letter to the Hebrews introduces the logic of sacrifice, using it as a theological rationale for the punishment of children, even as it uses the punishment of children to support its view of God as requiring Jesus' death, as Girard puts it, "to revenge his honor, which has been tainted by the sins of humanity." In addition, the author of Hebrews links the love of God not to mercy, as the Gospel writers do, but rather to chastisement. Even with the sacrificial logic, he might have made a case for God's mercy on the grounds that God can now be merciful because Jesus' life has been sacrificed in our behalf, and therefore, there will be no more divine chastisements. But, according to the author of Hebrews, the sacrifice of Jesus does not put an end to all divine chastisements, for God now chastises because, through the sacrifice of Jesus, he views us through the eyes of love. The sign of God's love is not in his mercy, as Jesus taught, but in his chastisements.

The author also asserts that by means of these divine chastisements we become more like God (holy as God is holy). This means, in effect, that we become godlike in the degree to which we discipline our own children, and do so "for their own good" rather than for our own perverse pleasure. Of course, this distinction between beating for pleasure and beating for the good of the child may be totally lost on the child, for it hurts just the same. Chastisement "for the good of the child" is experienced as even more ruthless, since it is represented as an entirely rational act.

The author also warns that if we sin after receiving knowledge of the truth, then Jesus' sacrifice is no longer in effect, and we face "a fearful prospect of judgment, and a fury of fire which will consume the adversaries" of God (10:26–27). He continues:

A man who has violated the law of Moses dies without mercy at the testimony of two or three witnesses. How much worse punishment do you think will be deserved by the man who has spurned the Son of God, and profaned the blood of the covenant by which he was sanctified, and outraged the Spirit of grace? For we know him who said, "Vengeance is mine, I will repay." And again, "The Lord will judge his people." It is a fearful thing to fall into the hands of the living God. (Heb. 10:28–31)

Thus the letter to the Hebrews offers a view of God that is diametrically opposite to that affirmed by the Gospels, where God is presented as one whose mercy knows no bounds and as one who is
unalterably opposed to violence, including sacrificial violence, of any
kind. This view is already prefigured in the Hebrew prophets. Micah
says it well:

> With what shall I come before the LORD,
>   and bow myself before God on high?
> Shall I come before him with burnt offerings,
>   with calves a year old?
> Will the LORD be pleased with thousands of rams,
>   with ten thousands of rivers of oil?
> Shall I give my first-born for my transgression,
>   the fruit of my body for the sin of my soul?"
> He has showed you, O man, what is good;
>   and what does the LORD require of you
> but to do justice, and to love kindness,
>   and to walk humbly with your God?
> (MIC. 6:6–8)

The Letter to the Hebrews as Teaching Text

Does this mean that we should discard the letter to the Hebrews as
a bundle of weeds? In raising this possibility, I am reminded of
Thomas Jefferson's famous effort to pare down the Gospels to their
essentials, eliminating all "supernatural" elements, including the miracles and the resurrection narratives. As he wrote in a letter to John
Adams, the basic story and teachings of Jesus "are easily distinguished as diamonds in a dung-hill." But the parable of the wheat and
weeds gives me pause, and prompts me to ask if there is something
important for us to learn from the letter to the Hebrews, something
that the author surely did not intend for us to learn, but that we can
learn by reading his text in a way that he did not, could not, envision.

It is very significant that this is the one biblical text where the
author alludes to having been abused as a child. Alice Miller (1991,
ch. 8) suggests reading the book of Lamentations as though it were
the words of a mistreated child. But, by the author's own self-
attestation, the letter to the Hebrews *is* the work of an adult who was
the victim of child abuse (beaten by his father for his father's pleasure). We can learn a great deal from reading this text as the work of
a victim of child abuse, and, more specifically, as the work of an adult

who now identifies with those who inflicted abuse on him as a child. Thus, his text provides insight for us into the thought world of a person who remains trapped, emotionally and cognitively, in the abusive structure. To read the letter to the Hebrews is to allow oneself to experience the continuing effects of child abuse on the adult psyche, and to see how the abuse is transmitted to the next generation (i.e., as what Miller calls "poisonous pedagogy"). The letter to the Hebrews is a teaching text from which we can learn a great deal about the long-term effects of child abuse.

Greven points out that two of the most common long-term effects of child abuse are paranoia and dissociation. Paranoia "is a pervasive sense of being endangered. The anticipation of harm from outside is the core of paranoia. . . . Paranoia arises from the keen and persistent sense that the body, the will, and the self are at risk" (168–169). Dissociation takes many forms in later life, but a characteristic of all forms is the tendency toward self-splitting, in which one identifies with one's aggressor and surrenders one's will to him. Also, confused, disjointed, and disconnected thought sequences, especially involving the inability to connect the parts with the whole, are quite common (157–159).

It isn't difficult to discern in the letter to the Hebrews a similar paranoia, as the author is convinced that those to whom he is writing are in danger because they are provoking God's anger and wrath. Nor is it hard to perceive that his thought processes are often disjointed and disconnected, due mainly to the fact that he feels obliged to conform his own thoughts to those of the biblical authors whom he considers authoritative, and to whom he defers. In other words, the disconnectedness of his discourse (e.g., its irrationalities, its tendency to shift from one topic to another without appropriate transitions, its strained analogies) is caused not by any obvious cognitive deficiencies on the author's part, but by his need to relinquish his own intellectual autonomy. The letter reads like a student's term paper that is held together, more or less, by frequent quoting of sources, exhibiting a rather strained effort to make the quotations say what the author needs them to say. Moreover, the authoritative texts that he chooses are ones that support his paranoia, his pervasive sense of being endangered.

The warning that runs through the letter to the Hebrews is that those to whom the author is writing are in mortal danger, because they have provoked God through their rebellious attitude. Thus, in chapter 3, he cites the rebellion of the people of Israel in the wilderness and the psalmist's claim that God was greatly provoked with their generation and vowed that none of them would ever enter his rest (Ps. 95:7–11). He then cautions his readers: "Take care, brethren, lest there be in any of you an evil, unbelieving heart, leading you to fall away from the living God. But exhort one another every day, as long as it is called 'today,' that none of you may be hardened by the deceitfulness of sin" (3:12–13). Continuing, he asserts that a rebellious attitude is reflected in acts of disobedience, and disobedience is certain proof that one has an evil, unbelieving heart:

> Who were they that heard and yet were rebellious? Was it not all those who left Egypt under the leadership of Moses? And with whom was he provoked forty years? Was it not with those who sinned, whose bodies fell in the wilderness? And to whom did he swear that they should never enter his rest, but to those who were disobedient? So we see that they were unable to enter because of unbelief. (Heb. 3:16–19)

Thus rebellion, disobedience, and unbelief are intimately linked, and therefore the attitude of rebellion and the actions that flow from it are deserving of God's wrath.

In chapter 4, the writer begins, "Therefore, while the promise of entering his rest remains, let us fear lest any of you be judged to have failed to reach it" (4:1). Repeating his point that those who received the good news were unable to enter his rest because of disobedience (v. 6), he challenges his readers:

> Let us therefore strive to enter that rest, that no one fall by the same sort of disobedience. For the word of God is living and active, sharper than any two-edged sword, piercing to the division of soul and spirit, of joints and marrow, and discerning the thoughts and intentions of the heart. And before him no creature is hidden, but all are open and laid bare to the eyes of him with whom we have to do. (Heb. 4:11–13)

Thus, there is no point in trying to deceive God, for God sees all the way through us, and cannot be fooled. This capacity of the one who has absolute power over us to discern our inner thoughts, especially our hostile thoughts toward him, is what strikes the greatest terror in the heart of the child. Punishment for their inner thoughts ("I know what you are thinking and I don't like it") is typically more vicious than punishment for wrongful deeds precisely because inner thoughts are less subject to the abuser's control.

In chapter 5, the author introduces the idea that Jesus is our high priest, standing before God in our behalf, because he was obedient even unto death (5:1–10). He tells his readers that he will have more to say later about Jesus as the high priest whose obedience is counted as righteousness in our behalf, but admits that this idea

> is hard to explain, since you have become dull of hearing. For though by this time you ought to be teachers, you need someone to teach you again the first principles of God's word. You need milk, not solid food; for everyone who lives on milk is unskilled in the word of righteousness, for he is a child. But solid food is for the mature, for those who have their faculties trained by practice to distinguish good from evil. (Heb. 5:11–14)

Here the author's tone reflects his identification with the aggressor, as he puts down his readers because, in spiritual matters, they are like children when they should be more like adults. And what is the basic difference between children and adults? Well, children don't listen to their parents (they are "dull of hearing"?) whereas adults "have their faculties trained by practice to distinguish good from evil." The implication here is that children are unable to distinguish between the two, which is why they need to be punished, for otherwise, how will they learn? Also, we must physically punish them because they are dull of hearing, that is, they do not listen to their parents' and teachers' voices, so the only way to get through to them is by striking their bodies and inflicting physical pain.

In chapter 6, the author assures his readers that, while he has warned them about their immaturity, he is certain that God will not abandon them, "for God is not so unjust as to overlook your work and the love which you showed for his sake in serving the saints, as you still do" (6:10). He cites the example of Abraham, to whom God made a promise that he kept, and notes how Abraham, by "patiently enduring," obtained that promise (v. 15). Melchizedek, too, obtained the promise, not, however, because he had any descent to which he could appeal, "but by the power of an indestructible life" (7:16). In other words, we are not to ask why it is necessary to suffer, as the people of Israel did during their wanderings in the desert, but we are to endure patiently, proving by our endurance that we are indestructible. Thus, we need to be able to show that we can take it, that we can endure his chastisements without whimpering, whining, or complaining. In the passage that links the punishment of sons by their fathers to God's chastisement, there is the same emphasis on endurance, on taking one's punishment like a man, and not "shrinking back," for those who shrink back will be destroyed. The author's authority here is Habakkuk (Hab. 2:3–4), who speaks not, however, of "shrinking back" but simply of waiting patiently for the one who is coming, that is, endurance is demonstrated in the capacity to wait. Shrinking back has the further and more ominous connotation of seeking to avoid one's punishment by moving backward as one's abuser advances and eventually corners his victim.

There are numerous references in the letter to the Hebrews to those who suffered abuse, and, as a result, received the promise of God. In 10:32–33, there is a reference to the abuse that his own readers have suffered. In 11:26, Moses is cited as having "considered abuse suffered for the Christ greater wealth than the treasures of Egypt, for he looked to the reward." In the same chapter there is a list of judges and kings who "won strength out of weakness" and are judged by the author to be great men of faith. This list includes Jephthah, the harlot's son who was thrown out of the house by his brothers because his mother was not their father's wife. He subsequently sacrificed his virgin daughter to the Lord because he felt he could not renege on his intemperate, ill-considered vow (Judg. 11). That he murdered his innocent daughter has little if any influence on the judgment of the author of Hebrews that Jephthah was a great man of faith because he suffered at the hands of his military enemies and prevailed. In Hebrews 13:12–13, Jesus is described as having "suffered outside the gate in order to sanctify the people through his own blood," and "therefore let us go forth to him outside the camp, and bear the abuse he endured."

These references to abuse could be due to the possibility that those to whom the author is writing are under threat, subject to imprisonment and even martyrdom for their faith. The fact that he centers on the abuse suffered by Moses and others who died in their faith supports this conclusion: "They were stoned, they were sawn in two, they were killed with the sword; they went about in skins of sheep and goats, destitute, afflicted, ill-treated—of whom the world was not worthy—wandering over deserts and mountains, and in dens and caves of the earth" (11:37–38). But the author's basic theme throughout the letter is that his readers' sufferings are caused by their sinfulness. Even if there is some evidence that they have struggled against sin, they "have not yet resisted to the point of shedding [their] blood" (12:4). It is not as though they are innocent victims of whatever suffering they are being made to endure, but that they are being chastised for their sinfulness, and, even then, they have not yet been chastised to the point where they have actually shed blood. (Is he recalling those times when, as a child, he was beaten so badly that blood was shed?)

Another possible allusion to the punishment scenario in childhood is an image that recurs throughout the letter to the Hebrews, that of the voice of God, a voice that one ignores at one's peril. Chapter 1 begins with the observation that God spoke to our fathers in many and various ways, and chapter 2 begins with the admonition to "pay the closer attention to what we have heard, lest we drift away from it" (2:1). To ignore the voice of God is the most foolish thing one can do, for his voice can shake the very foundations of one's existence:

> See that you do not refuse him who is speaking. For if they did not escape when they refused him who warned them on earth, much less shall we escape if we reject him who warns from heaven. His voice then shook the earth; but now he has promised, "Yet once more I will shake not only the earth but also the heaven." This phrase, "Yet once more," indicates the removal of what is shaken, as of what has been made, in order that what cannot be shaken may remain. Therefore let us be grateful for receiving a kingdom that cannot be shaken, and thus let us offer to God acceptable worship, with reverence and awe; for our God is a consuming fire. (Heb. 12:25–29)

This image of the voice that strikes terror and fear is reminiscent of the childhood punishment scenario, in which the adult thunders at the child while the child shivers and quakes, and then dissociates from the scene by tuning out the voice of the parent and imagining being in some other place, far removed, a place of peace and quiet. Even the author's observation that Noah, Abraham, and Sarah could have returned to the land from which they had gone out but chose not to, for they desired a better home (11:13–16), may express the feelings of adults who have no desire to return to their childhood homes, where they were objects of parental abuse.

Thus far I have centered on the paranoid tone of the letter, as reflected in its anticipation of harm from outside, and its keen and persistent sense that the body, the will, and the self are at risk. I want also to comment on its dissociative features as reflected in its rhetorical style, which is so disconnected and disjointed that the reader is often confused and unclear about the point that the author is trying to make. One example will need to suffice, as it will alert the interested reader to similar instances throughout the text:

> For you have not come to what may be touched, a blazing fire, and darkness, and gloom, and tempest, and the sound of a trumpet, and a voice whose words made the hearers entreat that no further messages be spoken to them. For they could not endure the order that was given,

"If even a beast touches the mountain, it shall be stoned." Indeed, so terrifying was the sight that Moses said, "I tremble with fear." But you have come to Mount Zion and to the city of the living God, the heavenly Jerusalem, and to innumerable angels in festal gathering, and to the assembly of the firstborn who are enrolled in heaven, and to a judge who is God of all, and to the spirits of just men made perfect, and to Jesus, the mediator of a new covenant, and to the sprinkled blood that speaks more graciously than the blood of Abel. (Heb. 12:18–24)

The basic idea here is clear enough. The God with whom we have to do is more terrifying than anything we have ever experienced, and this God requires a sacrifice that is equally powerful. The blood of Jesus is such a sacrifice, as it is far more perfect than the blood of Abel, and because it is, it ushers in a new covenant. This is all logical enough. Yet the passage lurches along in run-on fashion, with the author making several connections at once: God's injunction to the people of Israel not to touch Mount Sinai on pain of death; the author's own theme of Jesus as mediator or high priest in our behalf; the story of Abel's death at the hands of Cain. The passage seems excessively compressed and, at the same time, oddly disjointed, as image is piled on image.

Because this passage begins by depicting a terrifying threat (God's order that no living thing touch the holy mountain or it will be instantly killed), and because it occurs shortly after reference to the author's own experience of being abused by his father, this simultaneous compression and disconnectedness is reminiscent of the terror the author experienced as a child. In the threatened child's world, the experience of being severely beaten produces a dissociative effect wherein the discrete elements of the event are compressed (i.e., there is not much recall of the separate features of the episode), and are disconnected from one another (i.e., following no discernible temporal sequence). This compression and disjointedness reveal the extent to which the child feels threatened and defenseless. These stylistic features of this particular passage are also true of the letter as a whole, as it gives the appearance of following a logical progression of thought (e.g., frequent use of the word "therefore" contributes to the impression that the author is developing an argument that moves from premise to conclusion). Yet its content is so filled with threatening, even violent imagery that the experience of reading the letter is not at all like reading a letter written by Paul, where a logical progression of thought may actually be far less apparent, yet communicates a far more settled and self-confident mind at work. From passage to passage, and page to page, the profound insecurity of the author of Hebrews is apparent to the reader, at least to the reader who is not under the thrall of the abusive structure itself. Even the author's claim that Christ's sacrifice puts an end to the need to propitiate God offers no real comfort or relief, because for those who persist in sinful behavior, not only is Christ's sacrifice of no avail, but the punishment will be even more severe than if Christ had made no sacrifice at all. That there is no final resolution is communicated both in the content and in the style of the letter. There is a pervasive sense of endangerment throughout, and the source and cause of such endangerment is God, the very one on whom one's hope for ultimate rest and peace depends.

A Plea for Intellectual Autonomy

What purpose is served by interpreting the letter to the Hebrews as the work of an adult who was abused as a child and who has not, in adulthood, repudiated this abuse? For one thing, it challenges the use that is made of this letter to justify and legitimate the beating of children. It does so by asking what else would we expect of an author who was abused as a child and now, as an adult, uses the abuse he suffered as a child to support the idea of God as one who similarly chastises us? For another, it establishes the intimate relationship between child abuse and intellectual heteronomy, for there is no other book in the New Testament that quotes other biblical sources to the extent that Hebrews does. The author does not believe that his ideas can stand on their own merits but instead quotes from other biblical sources so extensively, so copiously, that his own voice can barely be heard apart from theirs. Furthermore, he conforms his ideas to the quotations he uses, often getting distracted by a phrase in the quotation that has little relevance to his main point, the reason for selecting this quotation in the first place. Third, the interpretation of the letter offered here points up the need for us to have the courage to confront biblical literalism where it is responsible for the suffering of innocent victims. This is one way in which we can be what Alice Miller calls "enlightened witnesses." Rather than seeking to make sense of the letter to the Hebrews, and instead of deferring to it, on the supposition that if we do not "understand" it the problem must be with us, we need to have the courage to say that there is something fundamentally wrong with the way in which the author portrays God and understands the relationship of human selves to God.

While the letter to the Hebrews may have gained inclusion in the biblical canon because it represented itself as written by Paul (cf. all or parts of chapter 13), the best argument for its inclusion in the Bible today is that it witnesses to the fact that child abuse is a terrible thing, for consider what it did to the author of Hebrews. As Alice Miller (1990) writes in the concluding paragraph of her essay on Friedrich Nietzsche's struggle against the truth: "If Nietzsche had not been forced to learn as a child that one must master an 'unbearable fit of sobbing,' if he had simply been *allowed* to sob, then humanity would have been one philosopher poorer, but in return the life of a human being named Nietzsche would have been richer. And who knows what that *vital* Nietzsche would *then* have been able to give humanity?" (133). Similarly, if the author of Hebrews *had* been illegitimate, and not a "valued" son, then he would not have been beaten "for his own good," and he would not then have written words that justify the abuse of children, nor given us an image of God as an abuser too.

In his *Table Talk*, Luther contrasts his experience as a child who was beaten by his mother for stealing a nut (noting that the punishment was excessive for the crime committed) with a scene he had witnessed earlier that day where his children resolved a controversy between them without adult intervention. This, he told his listeners, is how it is with God, who encourages us to use our own skills at reconciliation to resolve our differences and conflicts. It is noteworthy that the children did not settle their argument by beating one another. Instead, they spoke to one another, face-to-face, and then returned to their common play. Here, the children themselves model a nonpunitive approach to conflict resolution. If the children can talk out their differences, why is it necessary for adults to inflict pain on children? If children can use language to overcome misunderstanding, why must adults use physical blandishments (235, 300)?

In another episode recounted in Luther's *Table Talk*, Luther was describing to the group assembled around the supper table his interpretive principle as he reads the Bible, that is, he distinguishes between biblical passages that make him experience condemnation versus those that confirm his sense of being enveloped by God's grace. He indicates that this insight that biblical passages could be so discriminated has had a profound influence on him, for he can now read the Bible without becoming demoralized and despairing. Whereupon John Bugenhagen, a friend who often frequented Luther's evening table, related a similar experience when it had occurred to him that the love of God was the central theme in the Bible, and he could therefore take hold of those passages in which the love of God was clearly expressed and was felt by him, and dispense with those passages in which God's love was compromised, obscured, or even obliterated (443). This conversation not only supports the idea that the Bible need not be read as a unitary whole and that some biblical texts ought to be privileged above others. It also encourages the intellectual autonomy of each individual reader, as it shows that these two men could experience the Bible as profoundly transformative when they no longer treated it with undue reverence.

References

Capps, D. (2000). *Jesus: A psychological biography.* St. Louis: Chalice Press.

Girard, R. (1987). *Things hidden since the foundation of the world* (S. Bann & M. Metter, Trans.). Stanford: Stanford University Press.

Greven, P. (1991). *Spare the child.* New York: Knopf.

Luther, M. (1967). *Table talk* (T. G. Tappert, Ed. & Trans.). Philadelphia: Fortress.

Miller, A. (1990). *The untouched key* (H. & H. Hannum, Trans.). New York: Doubleday.

Miller, A. (1991). *Breaking down the wall of silence* (S. Worrall, Trans.). New York: E. P. Dutton.

Schaberg, J. (1987). *The illegitimacy of Jesus: A feminist theological interpretation of the infancy narratives.* San Francisco: Harper & Row.

CHAPTER 13

REVENGE, JUSTICE, AND HOPE: LAURA BLUMENFELD'S JOURNEY

J. Harold Ellens

Introduction

Violence seems everywhere present in our world today. It has personally touched almost every one of us. At no time is the memory of it, the current experience of it, or the possibility of it very far from our conscious minds. It has afflicted some of us more massively than others, and more than is usual in this tragic human adventure of life, but none of us gets clean away from it. The worst of all the terrors of violence is the sudden close-in untimely, brutal, and unnecessary death of a beloved family member. A drunk driver kills a child. A brother is lost in war. A dear friend burns to death. A suicide bomber anonymously exterminates an innocent acquaintance. A lover is shot with careful calculation by an assassin who does not even know the man he is killing or why he kills him. All these are infinitely obscene; one human being to another!

One of the most poignant books published during the last year is Laura Blumenfeld's *Revenge*.[1] The cover quotes the author: "My father was shot by a terrorist. A decade later, I went looking for him. . . ." An Islamic Fundamentalist anonymously shot David Blumenfeld and set in motion Laura's aggressive pilgrimage. She insisted upon entering into the world of the assassin's community, family, life, and mind. She determined to discover the dynamics of terrorism and revenge. In the process she discovered herself, her own mind, life, family, and soul. The subtitle of her book surprises the reader. She styles it *A Story of Hope*. This final chapter of *The Destructive Power of Religion* is an attempt to summarize the narrative of that terrorist violence, and Laura's vision of our only hope for a usable future for humankind.

Exposition

In a recent survey of brutal international violence titled *Surviving Terror*, Erickson and Jones present the work of twenty-one colleagues from a dozen nations commenting on the relevance of politics, sociology, history, theology, and Christian reflection.[2] While the book is a rather scattered pattern of ideas, intended to be a fervent call to the church to act in this area in which it is virtually impotent, the work focuses two points in the mind of the American reader. First, it makes the fact unforgettably plain that our former American insulation from foreign horrors is now permanently gone. Second, the human potential for wreaking horrifying trauma on masses of other humans is infinitely enlarged by all the very benefits of technology, which we spent the last century devising so wonderfully and cleverly.

Those facts have, of course, run like a leitmotif throughout the four volumes of *The Destructive Power of Religion*. Most of all, we have analyzed in this work the way in which religions of all kinds, and the metaphors of meaning that they generate, have fed sick minds, psychologically prone to the Orthodoxies and heresies of the Fundamentalisms of this world. This religious dynamic has caused or facilitated unimaginable acts of human destruction. It is obviously true today, in cases of terrorist violence, that the old adage "the devil made me do it" is never true, and that, instead, "religion made me do it" is too often true! Religion, and the politics that it shaped, was the motivating force driving the Muslim Palestinian who shot Laura Blumenfeld's father.

Julian Bond attended a dialogue of religious leaders and politicians convened in Detroit in the late 1960s. He was then a rising political star in the African American community. He was brilliant, articulate, and admirable in every way. He gave us a sense of focus, energy, hope, and a usable future, in a chaotic time of internal American turbulence and violence. He made a point that I shall never forget. He said that justice is the only way in which institutions can love, can express love to human beings and communities. We were all for love. We were, after all, highly motivated Christian leaders. But we also had a sense

Julian Bond gestures during a speech at Harvard University, October 2, 1998. AP/Wide World Photos.

of helplessness and hopelessness as to how love worked in the traumatic ferment of the kind of irrepressible social unrest that plagued that decade. It sounded for a moment as though Julian Bond had given us an insight and a mechanism that made hope possible again, and a course of action open and plain.

To some extent that turned out to be true. However, in the end it was not justice that resolved the sociopolitical and spiritual impasse of the American revolution of the 1960s. What happened instead was that the movement just wore itself out. Some of its proponents lost themselves in the drug culture and became irrelevant. Most of the others grew up and found in the traditional values and patterns of American life an infinitely higher and more satisfying meaning for their lives and loves. The upshot of the essays in the Erickson and Jones volume, particularly those of Moltmann on the tortured Christ,

Burghardt on fear, and Scroggs on terror in the NT, is focused in the claim that, in the end, justice is not a possible solution to the trauma and loss inflicted by terrorism and violence, even the horrific violence of war.

Victory? Of course! That part is easy! I spent 37 years actively serving my country as a senior army officer. I know about victory. We can do that! No sweat! But there will never again be any victories, except Pyrrhic victories. Is that victory? Over what? For what? In any case, the notion that somehow at the center of such victory is some kind of justice simply evaporates as an irrelevant equation. Just war theory may be an elegant intellectual or even philosophical exercise, but it is an inherently obscene proposal. It works only in words, not in reality. The massive violence of war on either side is grossly subhuman. What difference does it make at that point if the evildoers are brought to justice? Who does that heal?

Can one ever balance the scales again after standing helplessly watching one's dearest little five-year-old friend burn to death in a remote and apparently God-forsaken rural wasteland? Is there ever again any possibility of a righteous world for a pubescent daughter whose father is murdered before her eyes? Can one's mind ever think again of a just world after 3,500 innocent people are incinerated in a thriving and exciting city like New York? Who knows what honor and decency mean after a hardworking African immigrant from Ethiopia is gunned down like a rat in a barrel by police officers who have forgotten that when you put on a uniform it means that you have given up your life for the citizen in risky situations, not the other way around?

To what sort of logic can one resort, to hold on by teeth and toenails to a convincing sense of hopefulness, for a world in which 40 percent of the human race is genetically borderline psychotic and one third of those are actively delusional, viciously dysfunctional, and lethally violent if given a precipitating event or opportunity?[3] How shall we transcend our helplessness if our very sources of spiritual vitality, our religions and their sacred scriptures, fuel the fires of the worst pathologies in those sick, sordid, and sadistic souls? Justice is important, psychotropic medicine is probably more important, but neither resolves the impasse we face, neither restores the soul. What restores the hopes and empowerments for a healthy soul?

Laura Blumenfeld wants to suggest an answer to those questions. She claims that her quest for revenge is a story of hope. Her father was a tourist in Israel, and he was shot by a member of a rebel faction of the PLO in 1986. This was not an uncommon event. This band of terrorists made it their business to attack tourists in the Old City of Jerusalem. Her father survived but Laura's familiar world did not. The shooting changed everything, as such violence and loss always does. Laura began a pilgrimage toward recovery of meaning that took her to Europe, the United States, and the Middle East, including Iran and Iraq as well as Israel. She went as a reporter and journalist, under the name of Laura Weiss. She was on a crusade to collect stories about the nature and the methods of those who wreak irrational violence and those who avenge that sadism. She interviewed the right-wing Jewish Fundamentalist assassin of Yitzhak Rabin. She took the story of members of the Albanian Blood Feud Committee, of the chief of the Iranian judiciary, of an Egyptian heroin smuggler, of senior officials in Israeli government and the IDF, of priests and prostitutes around the world.

It was a long story, a journey of stories, and the further she went in it, the nearer she came to home and her own inner story. Glenn Frankel said that this odyssey is a meditation on love and hate, a personal pilgrimage of self-revelation. She found that her father was just one of many tourist tragedies inflicted by PLO gunmen that month—Germans, British, Italians, but mostly and intentionally Americans, like her father. Laura wanted to know the inside story of the young man who could do that. She tracked down his name, then she ferreted out his address, then she went to find his home, and she introduced herself to his family as a journalist, interested in the PLO story. His family introduced her to him. They thought she had never heard the story before. She stayed incognito for more than two years as she explored the inner story and life of that family and of that very pleasant and sensitive young man. To her surprise she became increasingly emotionally bonded with him and his family. She found them to be humans, caught in their own quest for meaning in a meaningless and apparently irresolvable crisis of cultures and political conflict.

When Laura first visited the assassin's home thirteen years after the assault upon her father, the family welcomed her with typical warm Middle Eastern hospitality and pointed to a picture of the young man who had fired the gun. His name was Omar. He had been apprehended and was then in prison. They told her laughingly that he had tried to kill some Israeli, a Mossad agent. The shooter's father said, "He never talks about it, even now." They were all at ease and Laura laughed with them. They talked about what made him do it. He had done it willingly, returned home and ate a good meal, cautioning his family not to go into Jerusalem for a while because there had been a violent crisis there. They said he had done his duty, to secure justice for the Palestinians, in view of the Israeli theft of their homeland and cities. They fed Laura, touched her hand. When Laura probed for more of the story, they told her that Omar had never met the man he shot. There was nothing personal in it. It was not a vendetta. He did it so people would pay attention to the Palestinians. It was not an act of revenge.

Laura explored, enticed, probed, dialogued, visited, and revisited Omar and his family over a period of a year. She asked him to repeat the story of the shooting, to tell her how he felt, what he expected from it, how it affected his sense of himself and of his future. She had wondered often how she would feel when she actually finally met him, and now he seemed like a natural part of her life. She wrote poems about her encounter with him, wrote letters asking him for more details about the event and its effect upon him. He found it painful to recount it and to open himself to her about it. Little by little he revealed his perplexity, quest for honor, grief, desire for vindication. Piece by piece she put the picture together.

It was unclear to Laura when and how she would finally achieve the revenge she sought, unclear how and when she would reveal her real identity and the purpose of her quest. One day, while visiting the Wailing Wall at the temple mount in Jerusalem she wrote a brief prayer and stuffed it between the stones. She began to realize that what she longed for was Omar's acknowledgment of what he had done. She needed to hear his acceptance of moral responsibility for his deed. She began to wonder what was happening to her quest for revenge. Was she simply getting exhausted by this long journey? Was she getting too empathic? Psychologists are quick to suggest some strange reaction formation was going on. What need was this intimacy with her father's assassin filling in her?

Laura informed Omar that the man he shot had survived and that she knew of him. Omar wrote from prison and began to express an interest in the man, David Blumenfeld, not knowing, of course, that he was Laura's father. Laura steered the dialogue around to thoughts of how David had felt and how he had put his life back together after the injury. Omar felt a need, not only to acknowledge responsibility for what he had done, but also for David to understand what he had done and why he had done it. He wondered whether Laura could arrange a meeting between Omar and David. He hoped she would be present then.

Omar came up for a hearing and Laura was invited to attend as a friend of the family. Leah Zemel was his defense attorney. Laura revealed her identity to Leah. At the crucial moment of the trial Laura was invited to speak, despite protests about its being unconventional. Laura mentioned that the judges should take into account that Omar was now chronically ill. She said that she had come to know the family well and that Omar was genuinely sorry for his violent actions and had promised not to resort to them again. Her mother had encouraged him to follow Gandhi and Martin Luther King, Jr. She told the court that she knew well the man Omar had shot and that David wished Omar set free, in view of his illness and his thirteen years in prison. When the judges asked her who she was, to be speaking for David and his family, she revealed her true identity. "I am his daughter, Laura Blumenfeld."

The judges examined her aggressively, wondering why she would have done so strange a thing as she did. They were in disbelief over how she could conceal her identity for this yearlong odyssey. They asked her straight out, "Why did you do this?" She replied, "I wanted them to know me as an individual, and for me to know them. I didn't want them to think of me as a Jew, or as a victim. Just Laura. And I wanted to understand who they were, without them feeling defensive or accused. I wanted to see what we had in common." "Why did you do such a dangerous thing?" asked the judge. "You have to take a chance for peace," she said. "You have to believe it is possible."

When the rumble in the courtroom settled and the tears were flowing freely on all sides, Laura's mother stood in the rear of the courtroom and said aloud, "I forgive Omar for what he did!" Laura said she had an immediate emotional reaction to her mother's words. "*Forgive?* . . . This was not about forgiveness. Didn't she understand? This was my *revenge.*"

The judge broke in to say he thought it took a lot of guts for Laura to do what she did. She replied, "I did it for one reason, because I love my father very much, and I wanted them to know—he is a good man, with a good family. I wanted them to understand, this conflict is between human beings, and not disembodied Arabs and Jews. And we're people with families. And you can't just kill us."[4]

Laura's pilgrimage proved to be a redemptive journey. David and Omar were able to establish a genuine human friendship. The two families continue to think of each other as family. Laura's prayer at the Wall had been a one-word request: "Transformation!"

Conclusion

It is interesting that in the end what satisfies the heart of a healthy human is not justice. That is necessary. It does a lot for the head, but nothing for the heart. In the end, it is possible to balance the scales in some degree before the law, but there is nothing that can balance the scales of the soul. Revenge as vengeance is a long journey into night, not a way toward the sunrise of peace and joy. At the last there is something about forgiveness that is the only productive revenge, not so much revenge against the perpetrator of the evil deed, but revenge against the evil itself. The revenge of forgiveness as a way of turning the flank of the evil done. Forgiveness is the revenge that forbids the evil act from maintaining the ultimate control in shaping our lives. Forgiveness and reconciliation seem to offer the only chance we have at transformation.

Simon Wiesenthal once asked a number of ethical philosophers from various religious traditions if he did right by rejecting a lapsed Lutheran SS trooper who begged his forgiveness for atrocities he had perpetrated against Jews. He had been assigned to a unit that had burned ghetto tenements and shot the women and children as they fled. Some of the philosophers said they would have killed the young man in his bed where he lay dying of wounds. Others said that Simon could not forgive the soldier. Only God could forgive him. Still others said only the Jews he killed could forgive him, and his hope was lost because they were dead. Jacques Maritain said Simon should have forgiven him. God does and Simon was God's man on the spot. I liked Martin E. Marty's answer best. Yes, Maritain was right, said Marty, but the more urgent reason Simon should have forgiven the soldier who had done these dastardly deeds against Simon's kith and kin lay in two facts. First, Simon was getting too much mileage out of his guilt and quandary. Second, forgiveness frees the forgiver more than the forgiven.

I doubt that, finally, it is justice that satisfies us at the center. It is the revenge against the evil that forgiveness effects, freeing us from the baggage we must otherwise bear all our life long. Nothing else equals the weight of the evil done. Nothing else heals.

Of course, these four volumes have been about a deeper problem. Can one bring God to justice? Can one forgive God? When a beautiful, blond, blue-eyed girl, five years old, burns to death before the eyes of her helpless five-year-old friend, how can God be forgiven? A joyful, playful little girl, in a frilly, lacy dress, inadvertently inflamed at the kitchen stove while she fooled with the newfangled telephone in 1937! Justice for God? Forgiveness for God? It is the same question with 3,500 dead in New York.

I have figured out that the question is erroneous. It is not a question of justifying God or bringing God to justice. It is not a question of forgiving God or holding God accountable. It is a matter of recognizing the limitations of God. God is not in charge in this world. We are. We should have gotten that clue at a more profound level of awareness than we seem to have done, from Genesis 1:28, where the ancient Israelite narrative informs us that God assigned *us* the task of dominion in this world, to bring it to its potential fruitfulness. If we do not take care of beautiful blond and blue-eyed Esther, God cannot. If we do not find reconciliation with Omar, God cannot stop the masses of murders. If we do not reach beyond the alienations and transcend the terrors of the terrorists, God cannot save us.

Justice is a good *idea*. "Revenge" of the transforming and healing kind works. Forgiveness alone frees us from each other and ourselves. Laura's journey is our only hope. Because in the end our only chance is grace.[5]

Notes

1. Laura Blumenfeld, *Revenge, A Story of Hope* (New York: Simon and Schuster, 2002).

2. Victoria Lee Erickson and Michelle Lim Jones, *Surviving Terror, Hope and Justice in a World of Violence* (Grand Rapids: Baker/Brazos, 2002).

3. See J. Harold Ellens, "Sin or Sickness, the Problem of Human Dysfunction," in *Seeking Understanding, The Stob Lectures, 1986–1998* (Grand Rapids: Calvin College Alumni Press, 2001) 442–489.

4. Blumenfeld, 362–363.

5. Grace: The biblical word for unconditional forgiveness and acceptance of another person.

AFTERWORD

Chris E. Stout

Series Editor
Contemporary Psychology

Religion and politics. Lightning rods and powder kegs. Such are the thoughts and images that may be conjured up reviewing this dynamic collection of works. Few topics can stir more opinion, bring more varied viewpoints, stimulate more debate and contention, or spark more potentially volatile reactions than discussions of religion as a motivator for murder, terrorism, and even war. Dr. Ellens has successfully assembled some of the best and the brightest contemporary scholars to expound on this most controversial, yet classically delicate, relationship.

So it is fitting that this set of volumes launches the new Praeger Series in Contemporary Psychology. In this series of books, experts from various disciplines will peer through the lens of psychology to examine human behavior as this new millennium dawns. Including modern behaviors rooted back through history, the topics will include positive subjects like creativity and resilience, as well as examinations of humanity's current psychological ills, with abuse, suicide, murder, and terrorism among those. At all times, the goal of the series remains constant—to offer innovative ideas, provocative considerations, and useful beginnings to better understand human behavior.

Developing a collection of the size, substance, and quality shown in *The Destructive Power of Religion* is no easy task. Indeed, I first met Dr. Ellens when he contributed to my earlier, similar four-volume set,

The Psychology of Terrorism (Westport: Praeger, 2002). The goal was
to organize well-researched content and weave it into a fabric appealing to readers of differing backgrounds and interests. Certainly, this
goal was achieved in Dr. Ellens' volumes.

While no editor of such a work wishes for homogenization of the
content, it becomes a fine balance between maintaining thematic consistency among chapters with a healthy tension between differing
perspectives. Therein again, this collection succeeds.

The first time I had the honor and the pleasure of meeting Dr.
Ellens, he struck me as a virtual Roman candle of intellectual enthusiasm. Therefore, it comes as no surprise that he has been successful
in gathering some of the greatest thinkers on the topic from around
the world, including a Pulitzer Prize–winning author.

There is potential for these volumes to unleash a Niagara of discussion and debate.

Ideally, there is potential for these volumes to spark understanding
that will trigger solutions to the problem of destructive powers
unleashed in the name of religion.

This is to Dr. Ellens' credit, and it is to us readers' marked benefit.

INDEX

ABOUT THE SERIES

As this new millennium dawns, humankind has evolved—some would argue has devolved—exhibiting new and old behaviors that fascinate, infuriate, delight, or fully perplex those of us seeking answers to the question, "Why?" In this series, experts from various disciplines peer through the lens of psychology telling us answers they see for questions of human behavior. Their topics may range from humanity's psychological ills—addictions, abuse, suicide, murder, and terrorism among them—to works focused on positive subjects including intelligence, creativity, athleticism, and resilience. Regardless of the topic, the goal of this series remains constant—to offer innovative ideas, provocative considerations, and useful beginnings to better understand human behavior.

Chris E. Stout
Series Editor

About the Series Editor
and Advisory Board

CHRIS E. STOUT, Psy.D., MBA, holds a joint governmental and academic appointment in Northwestern University Medical School and serves as Illinois' first chief of psychological services. He served as an NGO special representative to the United Nations, was appointed by the U.S. Department of Commerce as a Baldridge examiner, and served as an adviser to the White House for both political parties. He was appointed to the World Economic Forum's Global Leaders of Tomorrow. He has published and presented more than 300 papers and 29 books. His works have been translated into six languages.

BRUCE E. BONECUTTER, Ph.D., is director of behavioral services at the Elgin Community Mental Health Center, the Illinois Department of Human Services state hospital, serving adults in greater Chicago. He is also a clinical assistant professor of psychology at the University of Illinois at Chicago. A clinical psychologist specializing in health, consulting, and forensic psychology, Bonecutter is also a longtime member of the American Psychological Association Taskforce on Children and the Family.

JOSEPH A. FLAHERTY, M.D., is chief of psychiatry at the University of Illinois Hospital, a professor of psychiatry at the University of Illinois College of Medicine, and a professor of community health science at the University of Illinois College of Public Health. He is a founding member of the Society for the Study of Culture and Psychiatry. Dr. Flaherty has been a consultant to the World Health Organization, to the National Institutes of Mental Health, and also to the Falk Institute in Jerusalem.

MICHAEL HOROWITZ, Ph.D., is president and professor of clinical psychology at the Chicago School of Professional Psychology, one of the nation's leading not-for-profit graduate schools of psychology. Earlier, he served as dean and professor of the Arizona School of Professional Psychology. A clinical psychologist practicing independently since 1987, his work has focused on psychoanalysis, intensive individual therapy, and couples therapy. He has provided disaster mental health services to the American Red Cross. Dr. Horowitz's special interests include the study of fatherhood.

SHELDON I. MILLER, M.D., is a professor of psychiatry at Northwestern University and director of the Stone Institute of Psychiatry at Northwestern Memorial Hospital. He is also director of the American Board of Psychiatry and Neurology, director of the American Board of Emergency Medicine, and director of the Accreditation Council for Graduate Medical Education. Dr. Miller is also an examiner for the American Board of Psychiatry and Neurology. He is founding editor of the *American Journal of Addictions* and founding chairman of the American Psychiatric Association's Committee on Alcoholism.

DENNIS P. MORRISON, Ph.D., is chief executive officer at the Center for Behavioral Health in Indiana, the first behavioral health company ever to win the JCAHO Codman Award for excellence in the use of outcomes management to achieve health care quality improvement. He is president of the board of directors for the Community Healthcare Foundation in Bloomington and has been a member of the board of directors for the American College of Sports Psychology. He has served as a consultant to agencies including the Ohio Department of Mental Health, Tennessee Association of Mental Health Organizations, Oklahoma Psychological Association, the North Carolina Council of Community Mental Health Centers, and the National Center for Health Promotion in Michigan.

WILLIAM H. REID, M.D., MPH, is a clinical and forensic psychiatrist and consultant to attorneys and courts throughout the United States. He is clinical professor of psychiatry at the University of Texas Health Science Center. Dr. Miller is also an adjunct professor of psychiatry at Texas A&M College of Medicine and Texas Tech

University School of Medicine, as well as a clinical faculty member at the Austin Psychiatry Residency Program. He is chairman of the Scientific Advisory Board and medical adviser to the Texas Depressive & Manic-Depressive Association, as well as an examiner for the American Board of Psychiatry and Neurology. He has served as president of the American Academy of Psychiatry and the Law, as chairman of the Research Section for an International Conference on the Psychiatric Aspects of Terrorism, and as medical director for the Texas Department of Mental Health and Mental Retardation.

About the Editor
and Advisers

J. HAROLD ELLENS is a Research Scholar at the University of Michigan, Department of Near Eastern Studies. He is a retired Presbyterian theologian and ordained minister, a retired U.S. Army Colonel, and a retired professor of philosophy, theology, and psychology. He has authored, coauthored, and/or edited 86 books and 165 professional journal articles. He served 15 years as Executive Director of the Christian Association for Psychological Studies and as founding editor and Editor-in-Chief of the *Journal of Psychology and Christianity*. He holds a Ph.D. from Wayne State University in the Psychology of Human Communication, a Ph.D.(Cand.) from the University of Michigan in biblical and Near Eastern studies, and master's degrees from Calvin Theological Seminary, Princeton Theological Seminary, and the University of Michigan. He was born in Michigan, grew up in a Dutch-German immigrant community, and determined at age seven to enter the Christian ministry as a means to help his people with the great amount of suffering he perceived all around him. His life's work has focused on the interface of psychology and religion. He is the founder and director of the New American Lyceum.

LeROY H. ADEN is Professor Emeritus of Pastoral Theology at the Lutheran Theological Seminary in Philadelphia, Pennsylvania. He taught full-time at the seminary from 1967 to 1994 and part-time from 1994 to 2001. He served as Visiting Lecturer at Princeton

Theological Seminary, Princeton, New Jersey on a regular basis. In 2002 he coauthored *Preaching God's Compassion: Comforting Those Who Suffer* with Robert G. Hughes. Previously, he edited four books in a Psychology and Christianity series with J. Harold Ellens and David G. Benner. He served on the Board of Directors of the Christian Association for Psychological Studies for six years.

ALFRED J. EPPENS was born and raised in Michigan. He attended Western Michigan University, studying history under Ernst A. Breisach, and receiving a B.A. (Summa cum Laude) and an M.A. He continued his studies at the University of Michigan, where he was awarded a J.D. in 1981. He is an Adjunct Professor at Oakland University and at Oakland Community College, as well as an active church musician and director. He is a director and officer of the Michigan Center for Early Christian Studies, as well as a founding member of the New American Lyceum.

EDMUND S. MELTZER was born in Brooklyn, New York. He attended the University of Chicago, where he received his B.A. in Near Eastern Languages and Civilizations. He pursued graduate studies at the University of Toronto, earning his M.A. and Ph.D. in Near Eastern Studies. He worked in Egypt as a member of the Akhenaten Temple Project/East Karnak Excavation and as a Fellow of the American Research Center. Returning to the United States, he taught at the University of North Carolina–Chapel Hill and at the Claremont Graduate School (now University), where he served as Associate Chair of the Department of Religion. Meltzer taught at Northeast Normal University in Changchun from 1990 to 1996. He has been teaching German and Spanish in the Wisconsin public school system and English as a Second Language in summer programs of the University of Wisconsin–Stevens Point. He has lectured extensively and published numerous articles and reviews in scholarly journals. He has contributed to and edited a number of books and has presented at many national and international conferences.

JACK MILES is the author of the 1995 Pulitzer Prize winner *God: A Biography*. After publishing *Christ: A Crisis in the Life of God* in 2001, Miles was named a MacArthur Fellow in 2002. Now Senior Adviser to the President at J. Paul Getty Trust, he earned a Ph.D. in Near Eastern languages from Harvard University in 1971 and has been a Regents Lecturer at the University of California, Director of the Humanities Center at Claremont Graduate University, and Visiting

Professor of Humanities at the California Institute of Technology. He has authored articles that have appeared in numerous national publications, including the *Atlantic Monthly*, the *New York Times*, the *Boston Globe*, the *Washington Post*, and the *Los Angeles Times*, where he served for 10 years as Literary Editor and as a member of the newspaper's editorial board.

WAYNE G. ROLLINS is Professor Emeritus of Biblical Studies at Assumption College, Worcester, Massachusetts, and Adjunct Professor of Scripture at Hartford Seminary, Hartford, Connecticut. His writings include *The Gospels: Portraits of Christ* (1964), *Jung and the Bible* (1983), and *Soul and Psyche: The Bible in Psychological Perspective* (1999). He received his Ph.D. in New Testament Studies from Yale University and is the founder and former chairman (1990–2000) of the Society of Biblical Literature Section on Psychology and Biblical Studies.

GRANT R. SHAFER was educated at Wayne State University, Harvard University, and the University of Michigan, where he received his doctorate in Early Christianity. A summary of his dissertation, "St. Stephen and the Samaritans," was published in the proceedings of the 1996 meeting of the *Societe d'Etudes Samaritaines*. He has taught at Washtenaw Community College, Siena Heights University, and Eastern Michigan University. He is presently a Visiting Scholar at the University of Michigan.

About the Contributors

LeROY H. ADEN is Professor Emeritus of Pastoral Theology at the Lutheran Theological Seminary in Philadelphia, Pennsylvania. He taught full-time at the seminary from 1967 to 1994 and part-time from 1994 to 2001. He served as Visiting Lecturer at Princeton Theological Seminary, Princeton, New Jersey, on a regular basis. In 2002 he coauthored *Preaching God's Compassion: Comforting Those Who Suffer* with Robert G. Hughes. Previously, he edited four books in a Psychology and Christianity series with J. Harold Ellens and David G. Benner. He served on the Board of Directors of the Christian Association for Psychological Studies for six years.

PAUL N. ANDERSON is Professor of Biblical and Quaker Studies and Chair of the Department of Religious Studies at George Fox University, where he has served since 1989 except for a year as a visiting professor at Yale Divinity School (1998–99). He is author of *The Christology of the Fourth Gospel: Its Unity and Disunity in the Light of John 6* and *Navigating the Living Waters of the Gospel of John: On Wading with Children and Swimming with Elephants*. In addition, he has written many essays on biblical and Quaker themes and is editor of *Quaker Religious Thought*. He serves on the steering committee of the Psychology and Biblical Studies Section of the Society of Biblical Literature and teaches the New Testament Interpretation course in the Psy.D. program of George Fox University. His Ph.D. in the New Testament is from Glasgow University (1989), his M.Div. is from the

Earlham School of Religion (1981), and his B.A. in psychology and B.A. in Christian ministries are from Malone College (1978).

DONALD CAPPS, Psychologist of Religion, is William Hart Felmeth Professor of Pastoral Theology at Princeton Theological Seminary. In 1989 he was awarded an honorary doctorate from the University of Uppsala, Sweden, in recognition of the importance of his publications. He served as president of the Society for the Scientific Study of Religion from 1990 to 1992. Among his many significant books are *Men, Religion, and Melancholia: James, Otto, Jung, Erikson and Freud; The Freudians on Religion: A Reader; Social Phobia: Alleviating Anxiety in an Age of Self-Promotion;* and *Jesus: A Psychological Biography.* He also authored *The Child's Song: The Religious Abuse of Children.*

RAFAEL CHODOS has been a practicing business litigation attorney in the Los Angeles area for nearly 25 years. He holds a B.A. in philosophy from UC–Berkeley (1964). He earned his way through college teaching Hebrew, Latin, and Greek, intending to become a rabbi. But after graduating from Berkeley he entered the then-fledgling computer software field, where he worked for 15 years. He founded his own software company, which developed expert systems and sold them to most of the Fortune 500 companies. He then returned to law school and received his J.D. from Boston University in 1977. He is the author of several articles on legal topics as well as topics relating to computers, software design, operations research, and artificial intelligence. He has authored two books: *The Jewish Attitude Toward Justice and Law* (1984) and *The Law of Fiduciary Duties* (2000).

JOHN J. COLLINS is Holmes Professor of Old Testament Criticism and Interpretation at Yale University. He previously taught at the University of Chicago and at Notre Dame. He received his Ph.D. from Harvard (1972). His more recent books include a commentary on *The Book of Daniel* (1993), *The Scepter and the Star: The Messiahs of the Dead Sea Scrolls* (1995), *Jewish Wisdom in the Hellenistic Age* (1997), *Apocalypticism in the Dead Sea Scrolls* (1997), *Seers, Sibyls, and Sages* (1997), *The Apocalyptic Imagination* (revised ed., 1998), and *Between Athens and Jerusalem: Jewish Identity in the Hellenistic Diaspora* (revised ed., 2000). He has served as editor of the *Journal of Biblical Literature*, as president of the Catholic Biblical Association (1997), and as president of the Society of Biblical Literature (2002).

CHARLES T. DAVIS III studied at Emory University with Dr. Norman Perrin, graduating with the B.D. and Ph.D. degrees after special study at the University of Heidelberg. Although specializing in New Testament Studies, he has also published articles and book reviews in the fields of American religion, computers and the humanities, philosophy, and Buddhist studies. He is the author of the book *Speaking of Jesus* and currently serves as Professor of Philosophy and Religion at Appalachian State University, where he teaches biblical literature, Islam, and seminars on symbols and healing.

SIMON JOHN DE VRIES, an ordained minister in the Presbyterian Church, was born in Denver. He served in the U.S. Marines during World War II as a First Lieutenant, pastored three churches, and received his Th.D. from Union Theological Seminary in New York in Old Testament Studies before beginning seminary teaching in 1962. He is the author of numerous scholarly articles and reviews in the field of Old Testament exegesis and theology in addition to nine books, the latest of which is *Shining White Knight, A Spiritual Memoir.*

J. HAROLD ELLENS is a Research Scholar at the University of Michigan, Department of Near Eastern Studies. He is a retired Presbyterian theologian and ordained minister, a retired U.S. Army Colonel, and a retired professor of philosophy, theology, and psychology. He has authored, coauthored, and/or edited 86 books and 165 professional journal articles. He served 15 years as Executive Director of the Christian Association for Psychological Studies and as founding editor and Editor-in-Chief of the *Journal of Psychology and Christianity*. He holds a Ph.D. from Wayne State University in the Psychology of Human Communication, a Ph.D.(Cand.) from the University of Michigan in biblical and Near Eastern studies, and master's degrees from Calvin Theological Seminary, Princeton Theological Seminary, and the University of Michigan. His publications include *God's Grace and Human Health* and *Psychotheology: Key Issues*, as well as chapters in *Moral Obligation and the Military, Baker Encyclopedia of Psychology, Abingdon Dictionary of Pastoral Care, Jesus as Son of Man, The Literary Character: A Progression of Images*, and *God's Word for Our World* (2 vols.).

MARK ADAM ELLIOTT holds M.Div. and Th.M. degrees from the University of Toronto and a Ph.D. in New Testament from the University of Aberdeen, U.K. His area of concentration is Christian origins in Judaism. His first major publication was *Survivors of Israel:*

A Reconsideration of the Theology of Pre-Christian Judaism (2000). He has served as pastor in both the United Church of Canada and Baptist Convention of Ontario and Quebec, and taught biblical studies in two Ontario universities. Presently, he is executive director of the *Institute for Restorationist and Revisionist Studies* (www.irrstudies.org) and carries out research at the University of Toronto.

ALFRED J. EPPENS was born and raised in Michigan. He attended Western Michigan University, studying history under Ernst A. Breisach, and receiving a B.A. (Summa cum Laude) and an M.A. He continued his studies at the University of Michigan, where he was awarded a J.D. in 1981. He is an Adjunct Professor at Oakland University and at Oakland Community College, as well as an active church musician and director. He is a director and officer of the Michigan Center for Early Christian Studies, as well as a founding member of the New American Lyceum.

JACK T. HANFORD is a Professor Emeritus of Biomedical Ethics at Ferris State University in Michigan. He is a member of the American Philosophical Association, the American Academy of Religion, the Christian Association for Psychological Studies, and the Association of Moral Education. He is also an associate of the Hastings Center, the foremost center for biomedical ethics, the American Society of Bioethics and Humanities, the Center for Bioethics and Human Dignity, and the Kennedy Institute of Ethics, as well as several other societies. He has published many professional articles, including those in *Religious Education,* the *Journal for the Scientific Study of Religion,* the *Journal of Psychology and Christianity,* and the *Journal of Pastoral Psychology, Ethics, and Medicine.* His highest degree is a Th.D.

RONALD B. JOHNSON has worked as a clinical psychologist in private practice for 30 years. His academic background includes a B.S. at the University of Wisconsin, M.Div. at Denver Seminary, and M.A. and Ph.D. in psychology from the University of Iowa. He is currently working on a Post-Doctorate in Neuropsychology. He holds licenses in several states and in Canada. His interests are in therapy with men and children, the psychology of men, psychological evaluations, and forensic psychology. He writes in the areas of "friendly diagnosis," which includes personality type, intelligences, gender differences, personal development, and theological-psychological integration.

D. ANDREW KILLE received his Ph.D. from the Graduate Theological Union in Berkeley in Psychological Biblical Criticism.

He is the author of *Psychological Biblical Criticism: Genesis 3 as a Test Case* (Fortress Press, 2001). A former pastor, Dr. Kille teaches psychology and spirituality in the San Francisco Bay area and is principal consultant for Revdak Consulting. He has served as cochair of the Psychology and Biblical Studies Section of the Society of Biblical Literature and on the steering committee of the Person, Culture, and Religion Group of the American Academy of Religion.

CASSANDRA M. KLYMAN is Assistant Clinical Professor at Wayne State University College of Medicine, where she teaches Ethics, and the Psychology of Women to residents in psychiatry and supervises their clinical cases. Klyman is also a lecturer at the Michigan Psychoanalytic Institute and chairperson of the Michigan Psychoanalytic Society's Committee on Psychoanalysis in Medicine. She is a Life-Fellow of the American Medical Association, the American Psychiatric Association, and the College of Forensic Examiners. She is also Past-President of the Michigan Psychiatric Society. She has published papers nationally and internationally in peer-reviewed journals. Most of her time is spent in the private practice of psychoanalysis and psychoanalytically informed psychotherapy. She earned her M.D. at Wayne State University.

EDSON T. LEWIS is an ordained minister (emeritus) of the Christian Reformed Church. During 47 years of active ministry, he served a suburban New York City congregation for 8 years, an inner-city parish in Hoboken, New Jersey, for 12 years, and the campus of the Ohio State University, Columbus, Ohio, for 17 years. He is a graduate of Calvin Theological Seminary (B.D.), New York Theological Seminary (STM), and Trinity Lutheran Seminary (D.Min). During the 1990s, he played a key role in the revitalization of the church's higher education ministries in the United States and Canada. His participation in antipoverty and peacemaking ministries has been extensive.

ZENON LOTUFO JR. is a Presbyterian minister (Independent Presbyterian Church of Brazil), a philosopher, and a psychotherapist, specializing in Transactional Analysis. He has lectured for undergraduate and graduate courses at universities in São Paulo, Brazil. He coordinates the course of specialization in Pastoral Psychology of the Christian Association of Psychologists and Psychiatrists of Brazil. He is the author of the books *Relações Humanas* (Human Relations) and *Disfunções no Comportamento Organizacional* (Dysfunctions in

Organizational Behavior), and coauthor of *O Potencial Humano* (Human Potential). He has also authored numerous journal articles.

CHARLES MABEE is Full Professor and Director of the Masters of Divinity Program at the Ecumenical Theological Seminary in Detroit, Michigan. He is also a Visiting Lecturer and United Ministries in Higher Education Ecumenical Campus Minister at Oakland University, where he founded two subsidiary institutions, the Institute for the Third Millennium and the Detroit Parliament for World Religions. He is a founding member of the Colloquium on Violence and Religion, chairman of the American Biblical Hermeneutics Section of the Society of Biblical Literature/American Academy of Religion, southeast region, and has been Chair of the Department of Religious Studies at Marshall University in West Virginia. Early in his career, he was a Research Associate for the Institute for Antiquity and Christianity at Claremont Graduate University.

J. CÁSSIO MARTINS is a Presbyterian minister (Presbyterian Church of Brazil) and a clinical psychologist. As a minister, he held pastorates in São Paulo and Rio de Janeiro. As a psychologist, he runs his own clinic in São Paulo. He holds a Master of Theology degree from Union Theological Seminary, Richmond, Virginia. He is one of the coordinators of the course of specialization in Pastoral Psychology of the Christian Association of Psychologists and Psychiatrists of Brazil. He has taught psychology at the Methodist University in São Paulo, as well as courses and seminars to pastors and psychologists throughout Brazil, leading the creation of and exercising the Office of Pastoral Support of his denomination until July 2002. He has written numerous articles on psychology and theology.

MARTIN E. MARTY is the Fairfax M. Cone Distinguished Professor Emeritus at the University of Chicago Divinity School, where he taught for 35 years and where the Martin Marty center has since been founded to promote "public religion" endeavors. An ordained minister in the Evangelical Lutheran Church of America, he is well known in the popular media and has been called the nation's "most influential interpretor of religion." He is the author of 50 books, including *The One and the Many: America's Search for a Common God*, as well as a 3-volume work entitled *Modern American Religion*. He has written more than 4,300 articles, essays, reviews and papers. Among his many honors and awards are the National Humanities Medal, the National Book Award, the Medal of the American

Academy of Arts and Sciences, and the Distinguished Service Medal of the Association of Theological Schools. He has served as president of the American Academy of Religion, the American Society of Church History and the American Catholic Historical Association. Marty has received 67 honorary doctorates.

CHERYL McGUIRE is a member of the Colloquium on Violence and Religion, and her work was presented at Purdue University during the colloquium in 2002. She is a graduate of the University of Michigan master's program in Ancient Civilizations and Biblical Studies and is now involved with postgraduate work at the University of Detroit.

EDMUND S. MELTZER was born in Brooklyn, New York, and attended Erasmus Hall High School. He developed a passion for the ancient world, especially Egypt, and attended the University of Chicago, where he received his B.A. in Near Eastern Languages and Civilizations. He pursued graduate studies at the University of Toronto, earning his M.A. and Ph.D. in Near Eastern Studies and working in Egypt as a member of the Akhenaten Temple Project/East Karnak Excavation. He also worked as a Fellow of the American Research Center in Egypt. After returning to the United States, he taught at the University of North Carolina–Chapel Hill and at the Claremont Graduate School (now University), where he served as Associate Chair of the Department of Religion. In 1990, Meltzer and his family traveled to China, where he taught at Northeast Normal University in Changchun for six years. Subsequently he has been teaching German and Spanish in the Wisconsin public school system and English as a Second Language in the summer programs of the University of Wisconsin–Stevens Point. He has lectured extensively and published numerous articles and reviews in scholarly journals. He has contributed to and edited a number of books and has presented at many national and international conferences.

JACK MILES is the author of the 1996 Pulitzer Prize winner, *God: A Biography*. After publishing *Christ: A Crisis in the Life of God* in 2001, Miles was named a MacArthur Fellow in 2002. Now Senior Adviser to the President at J. Paul Getty Trust, he earned a Ph.D. in Near Eastern languages from Harvard University in 1971 and has been a Regents Lecturer at the University of California, Director of the Humanities Center at Claremont Graduate University, and Visiting Professor of Humanities at the California Institute of Technology. He has authored articles that have appeared in numerous national publications, including the *Atlantic Monthly*, the *New York Times*, the *Boston Globe*, the *Washington Post*, and the *Los Angeles Times*, where he served for 10 years as Literary Editor and as a member of the newspaper's editorial board.

MICHAEL WILLETT NEWHEART is Associate Professor of New Testament Language and Literature at Howard University School of Divinity, where he has taught since 1991. He holds a Ph.D. from Southern Baptist Theological Seminary and is the author of *Wisdom Christology in the Fourth Gospel; Word and Soul: A Psychological, Literary, and Cultural Reading of the Fourth Gospel*, and numerous articles on the psychological and literary interpretation of the New Testament.

DIRK H. ODENDAAL is South African and was born in what is now called the Province of the Eastern Cape. He spent much of his youth in the Transkei in the town of Umtata, where his parents were teachers at a seminary. He trained as a minister at the Stellenbosch Seminary for the Dutch Reformed Church and was ordained in 1983 in the Dutch Reformed Church in Southern Africa. He transferred to East London in 1988 to minister to members of the United Reformed Church in Southern Africa in one of the huge suburbs for Xhosa-speaking people. He received his doctorate (D.Litt.) in 1992 at the University of Port Elizabeth in Semitic Languages. At present, he is enrolled in a Master's Degree course in Counseling Psychology at Rhodes University.

RICARDO J. QUINONES is Professor Emeritus of Comparative Literature at Claremont McKenna College. He is author of *Renaissance Discovery of Time* (1972), *Mapping Literary Modernism* (1985), *The Changes of Cain: Violence and the Lost Brother in Cain and Abel Literature* (1991), and several volumes on Dante, including *Foundation Sacrifice in Dante's Commedia* (1996). He is also Founding Director of the Gould Center for the Humanities.

ILONA N. RASHKOW is Professor of Judaic Studies, Women's Studies, and Comparative Literature at the State University of New York, Stony Brook. She has also been the visiting chair in Judaic Studies at the University of Alabama. Among her publications are *Upon the Dark Places: Sexism and Anti-Semitism in English Renaissance Bible Translation* (1990), *The Phallacy of Genesis* (1993), and *Taboo or Not Taboo?: Human Sexuality and the Hebrew Bible* (2000). Her areas of interest include psychoanalytic literary theory as applied to the Hebrew Bible and, more generally, as applied to Judaic studies, religious studies, feminist literary criticism, and women's studies.

WAYNE G. ROLLINS is Professor Emeritus of Biblical Studies at Assumption College, Worcester, Massachusetts, and Adjunct Professor of Scripture at Hartford Seminary, Hartford, Connecticut. His writings include *The Gospels: Portraits of Christ* (1964), *Jung and the Bible* (1983), and *Soul and Psyche: The Bible in Psychological Perspective* (1999). He received his Ph.D. in New Testament Studies from Yale University and is the founder and former chairman (1990–2000) of the Society of Biblical Literature Section on Psychology and Biblical Studies.

GRANT R. SHAFER was educated at Wayne State University, Harvard University, and the University of Michigan, where he received his doctorate in Early Christianity. A summary of his dissertation, "St. Stephen and the Samaritans," was published in the proceedings of the 1996 meeting of the *Societe d'Etudes Samaritaines*. He has taught at Washtenaw Community College, Siena Heights University, and Eastern Michigan University. He is presently a Visiting Scholar at the University of Michigan.

DONALD E. SLOAT, is licensed as a psychologist in Arizona, California, and Michigan. His training includes a B.A from Bethel College (Indiana), an M.A. from Michigan State University, and a Ph.D. from the University of Southern Mississippi. Since 1963, he has devoted his professional life to helping damaged people find healing for their pain. He has worked most often with people who have been trauma victims, including those with post-traumatic stress disorder (PTSD) and other effects of physical, emotional, verbal, sexual, and spiritual abuse. He has worked with Detroit's Youth for Christ, with outpatient drug-treatment programs, a community health center, psychiatric hospitals, and in his current private practice. He authored two books detailing spiritual abuse, *The Dangers of Growing Up in a Christian Home* and *Growing Up Holy and Wholly*. In addition, he has presented workshops on spiritual abuse and shame at national conferences. His professional affiliations include the American Psychological Association, American Association of Christian Counselors, Christian Association for Psychological Studies, and the International Society for the Study of Dissociation. He has served on the advisory board of the National Association for Christian Recovery. His private practice is in Michigan.

MACK C. STIRLING was born in 1952 in St. George, Utah. He was a Mormon missionary in Norway from 1971 to 1973 and graduated from Brigham Young University studies in chemistry in 1975. He received the M.D. degree from Johns Hopkins University in 1979 and thereafter underwent specialty training at the University of Michigan, where he was Assistant Professor of Thoracic Surgery from 1987 to 1990. Since 1990, he has been Director of Cardiothoracic Surgery at Munson Medical Center in Traverse City, Michigan.

ARCHBISHOP DESMOND TUTU is best known for his contribution to the cause of racial justice in South Africa, a contribution for which he was recognized with the Nobel Peace Prize in 1984. Archbishop Tutu has been an ordained priest since 1961. Among his many accomplishments are being named the first black General Secretary of the South African Council of Churches and serving as archbishop of Cape Town. Once a high school teacher in South Africa, he has also taught theology in college and holds honorary degrees from universities including Harvard, Oxford, Columbia, and Kent State. In addition to the Nobel Peace Prize, he has been awarded the Order for Meritorious Service presented by President Nelson Mandela, the Archbishop of Canterbury's Award for outstanding service to the Anglican community, the Family of Man Gold Medal Award, and the Martin Luther King Jr. Non-Violent Peace Award. The many publications Archbishop Tutu has authored, coauthored, or made contributions to include *No Future without Forgiveness* (2000), *Crying in the Wilderness* (1986), and *Rainbow People of God: The Making of a Peaceful Revolution* (1996).

JOHAN S. VOS is Associate Professor of New Testament, Faculty of Theology, Vrije Universiteit te Amsterdam, The Netherlands. He was born in Gouda, The Netherlands. He studied theology at the University of Utrecht, the University of Tübingen, and Union Theological Seminary in New York. He received his Th.D. from the University of Utrecht in 1973 and was Assistant Professor of New Testament Studies at the University of Leiden in 1974 and 1975. From 1975 to 1981, he worked as a social therapist at a psychiatric clinic for delinquents in Nijmegen. He has been Associate Professor at Vrije Universiteit since 1981 and has published many articles on New Testament subjects. He recently authored *Die Kunst der Argumentation bei Paulus* (The Art of Reasoning in the Letters of Paul), WUNT 149, 2002.

WALTER WINK is Professor of Biblical Interpretation at Auburn Theological Seminary in New York City. Previously, he was a parish minister and taught at Union Theological Seminary in New York City. In 1989 and 1990, he was a Peace Fellow at the United States Institute of Peace. His most recent book is *The Human Being: The Enigma of the Son of the Man* (2001). He is author of a trilogy, *The Powers: Naming the Powers: The Language of Power in the New Testament* (1984), *Unmasking the Powers: The Invisible Forces That Determine Human Existence* (1986), and *Engaging the Powers: Discernment and Resistance in a World of Domination* (1992). *Engaging the Powers* received three Religious Book of the Year awards for 1993, from Pax Christi, the Academy of Parish Clergy, and the Midwestern Independent Publishers Association. His other works include *Jesus and Nonviolence* (2003), *The Powers That Be* (1998), and *When the Powers Fall: Reconciliation in the Healing of Nations* (1998). He has published more than 250 journal articles.